W9-ANH-600

CITY OF
SOKRATES

CITY OF
SOKRATES

An introduction to Classical Athens

J. W. Roberts

WITHDRAWN

Routledge & Kegan Paul
LONDON, BOSTON, MELBOURNE AND HENLEY

(Burgess
DF
275
•R62
1984
copy 1

First published in 1984
by Routledge & Kegan Paul plc
39 Store Street, London WC1E 7DD, England
9 Park Street, Boston, Mass. 02108, USA
464 St Kilda Road,
Victoria 3004, Australia
Broadway House, Newtown Road,
Henley-on-Thames, Oxon RG9 1EN, England

Set in 10/12 Linotron Sabon by
Input Typesetting Limited,
and printed in Great Britain by
Robert Hartnoll Ltd, Bodmin, Cornwall

© J. W. Roberts 1984

No part of this book may be reproduced in
any form without permission from the publisher,
except for the quotation of brief
passages in criticism

Library of Congress Cataloguing in Publication Data

Roberts, J. W.
City of Sokrates

Bibliography: p.
Includes index.
1. Athens (Greece)—Social life and customs.
2. Athens (Greece)—Social conditions.
3. Greece—Civilization—To 146 B.C. I. Title.
DF275.R62 1984   938'.5   83–19142

ISBN 0–7100–9805–7

Contents

118459

84/10/05

Arg

Figures

Preface

The appearance of another book about Classical Athens may well be thought to need justification. The justification of this book must be that it attempts to give an *integrated* account of the Athens of Sokrates. It is towards the edges of obvious facets, such as democracy or drama or philosophy, that uncertainty increases. Nevertheless the attempt to interrelate the different facets should be made. Unless it is made, studies of this facet or that are unlikely to carry conviction. Unless, for example, the plays that were first performed in the theatre of Dionysos are related to their original audience – its composition, its size, its upbringing, its expectations and so on – it is hardly possible to interpret those plays. Again, the Athenians are of interest to us mainly because of their extraordinary creativity, but also because of their differences from us. If features of Athenian society that may strike a modern reader as odd, such as the seclusion of upper-class women or the prevalence of upper-class homosexuality or slavery, are treated in isolation, the Athenians may appear more different from us than in fact they were.

To attempt a short – mainly synchronic – study of a city as diverse as Athens involves many hazards. There are so many topics to be touched on that mistakes are not hard to make. About some of the better known topics there is much to say, and important points may be neglected. About some other, inescapable, topics there is little to say that is certain, but something has to be said, even at the cost of seeming to make bricks without straw. In the end it does, I hope, prove that a coherent, even convincing, picture can be built up.

Because the interrelations are so numerous, there is a stylistic hazard – that of repetition. To reduce the amount of repetition, the Index has been compiled with care, and the reader should be ready to use it. It is hardly possible to start describing some features of Athens without referring to others yet to be described, but I have tried not to presuppose information about Athens that cannot be found somewhere in the book. Chapter 2 is likely to prove the hardest going: after introducing the notions of citizenship and political rights, it treats of a variety of other basic matters – non-citizens, population 'figures', social structure, property and taxation – so that the remaining chapters can be largely devoted to the non-material life of the citizens of Athens: their politics and imperialism, their education and religion, their art and thought.

I have written with the readers of businesslike translations, such as the Penguin Classics, much in mind, and I have given in the text many references to the sources of knowledge (outlined in pages 6–7) and especially to the more accessible sources. I have tried to convey some idea of how my picture of Athens is built up. Conversely, I hope that the picture will assist the interpretation of particular authors or works.

There are obvious limits to what can be achieved by words written about plays that the reader has not seen or even read. There are equally obvious limits to what can be achieved by words written about topography, buildings or paintings that the reader has not seen. A mass of photographs would help him, but nothing could take the place of his seeing for himself. (Much the same applies to rowing in an Athenian warship, taking part in a blood-sacrifice and countless other features of life in Athens.) All the same, something can be achieved – something that should encourage the reader to see and read for himself some of what can still be seen and read.

All the places mentioned in the text that can be located on the ground are, I hope, located on one or other of the maps. All dates are BC unless given as AD.

The spelling of Greek proper names presents a difficulty. My own inclination is to transliterate from Greek as far as possible without discouraging the general reader. So, for example, I start more names with K than C and end more with -os than -us. As an aid to the pronunciation of proper names and transliterated general words, most long vowels are marked in the Index with a dash above them. Every e is sounded. Thus aretē rhymes not with 'beat' but with 'be' or, better, 'bay', and polītēs has three syllables.

My gratitude is due: to Mr James Howarth, Professor Peter Brunt, and Sir Moses Finley (begetter of JACT Ancient History) – for, amongst other things, convincing me that Greek History of the right sort still deserves our attention; to the scholarly authors of innumerable books and articles, and to colleagues and pupils – for information and ideas; to the Provost and Fellows of Oriel College, Oxford – for a term's hospitality; to Dr Simon Hornblower – for his invaluabe help; to my parents and my wife – for their patience and encouragement and everything else.

J.W.R.

Acknowledgments

Figures 5 and 6 are based on plates 4 and 5 in H. A. Thompson and R. E. Wycherley, *The Athenian Agora*, XIV, *The Agora of Athens* by courtesy of the American School of Classical Studies at Athens. Figure 7 is based, by permission, on the plan on page 90 of R. J. Hopper, *The Acropolis*, Weidenfeld & Nicolson.

Introduction

The culture of fifth-century Athens poses the question whether we have the evidence – literary, inscriptional, archaeological – to enable us to enter into the life of the people to whom we may be said to owe, amongst other things, democracy, tragedy, comedy, political history, ethics, mathematical astronomy, pictorial space and the Parthenon. Innovation in thought or art is never fully explained by reference to its cultural setting, but if we admire many of the products of a culture, it should be instructive to see how far we can penetrate that culture.

The main economic and political facts of fifth-century Athenian life are not too hard to recover, but it is more difficult to recover the outlines of the preceding centuries, because of the absence or scarcity of contemporary writing. With the extinction of Mycenaean civilisation came the Dark Age of Greece (roughly 1150–800), marked by a sharp drop in population and living standards, the disappearance of literacy and the loss of contact with the Near East. During the Archaic Age (roughly 800–480), the fires of civilisation, fed by a renewal of contact with the Near East, began to burn up again in south-east Greece. Athens and its surrounding territory, known as Attike, had been spared foreign occupation during the Dark Age, but had shared the drop in population and living standards. Athens itself had ceased to be a town: it was only a cluster of villages round the citadel or Akropolis. As early, however, as 1050 renewed contact with Cyprus had introduced iron-smelting to Athens, and at about the same time archaeology can detect the beginnings of an Athenian invention – the Geometric style of decorating pottery. Early in the Archaic Age the population began to rise steeply, and the villages round the Akropolis began to coalesce into a town. It was the large landowners who originally created the town, but throughout Attike a community or *polis* of land-owning Athenians, rich and poor, began to coalesce and focus on the new town. Athens became the political, judicial and religious centre of Attike. The first temple to the town's patron goddess, Athena, was built on the Akropolis perhaps as early as 700.

By the start of the sixth century, in the time of Solon, a predominantly agrarian society had begun moving, albeit erratically, towards democ-

racy, that is, towards the attainment by the farmer-soldiers of Attike –
and no doubt some craftsman-soldiers of Athens – of political rights
previously enjoyed by only the noble owners of large estates. (No women
enjoyed any political rights.) At the end of the sixth century, in 508,
Kleisthenes introduced a new Council of 500 members to prepare the
agenda for meetings of the Assembly of Athenians, which was growing
in power. The farmer-soldiers were not nearly as rich as the nobles, but
unlike the poorest Athenians, they could afford their own heavy armour.
Even the poorest Athenians guarded their independence fiercely and
Solon had indeed made it illegal to reduce any Athenian to slavery or
debt-bondage; so the noble owners of large estates, who were wanting
to acquire metals and luxury goods from the Near East, and who had
to pay for them with the surplus produce of their estates, needed a small
regular labour force of imported slaves, in addition to the seasonal
labour of the least fortunate of their fellow Athenians. At the same time,
with prosperity and demand for their products increasing, Athenian
craftsmen also needed a small regular force of such slaves. These agricultural and industrial slaves were brought to Athens and sold by slave-
traders.

The thin soil of Attike was better suited to growing olives, vines, figs
and even barley than it was to growing wheat, and as the population
increased, so did Athenian dependence on imported wheat. That wheat
was paid for with olive oil, and, more important, silver, mined in Laureion, in the south of Attike. Laureion silver also financed the construction
of the triremes or warships with three banks of oars that enabled Athens
to win the naval battle of Salamis in 480, ten years after she had
defeated the Persians on land at Marathon. Buoyed up by the victories of
Marathon and Salamis, the Athenians went on to lead an anti-Persian
naval alliance, which by slow degrees turned into a tribute-paying
empire. While the allies of Athens were turning into tribute-paying
subjects, the Athenians themselves moved further towards direct democracy, a process which was virtually completed by Ephialtes and Perikles
in 462.

Under direct democracy power lay with the Assembly, which consisted
of those few thousand Athenians, out of the total of those eligible to
attend, who were able and willing to attend its meetings – the proportion
of those ordinarily attending to those eligible to attend being about the
same as the proportion of those eligible to attend to the total population
(perhaps 1:8). This further move was helped by Athens' growing dependence upon imported slaves: without them not enough Athenians would
have been free for public service. The tribute of the allies helped too. It
not only paid the sailors of Athens (increasingly many of whom were
not Athenians), but it could also be used to help pay Athenians for
civilian service to the community – as jurors, councillors and, probably,

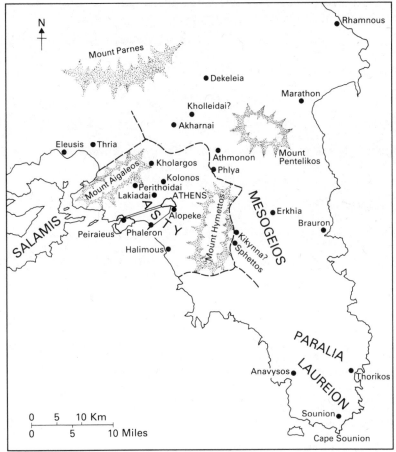

Figure 1 Attike

magistrates. Furthermore, the reserve of tribute, augmented by booty, made possible the building of the Parthenon and the other Periklean works. The introduction of direct democracy among the citizens of Athens depended both on the labour of imported slaves, who were usually not Greeks but 'barbarians', and on the tribute of subject allies, who were Greeks.

Although most Athenians had ancestral plots of land in Attike, there were also town-based craftsmen, both rich and poor, who had not. Since the time of Solon, who had encouraged Athenians to take up crafts (Plutarch, *Solon* 22.1), no Athenian countryman would voluntarily have left the land in order to become a town-based craftsman; so increasing demand for manufactures was met both by the importing of barbarian slaves and also by the immigration of Greek craftsmen. These immi-

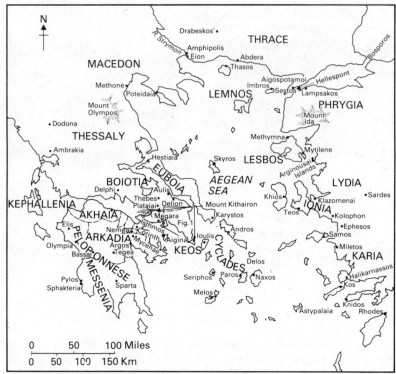

Figure 2   The Aegean

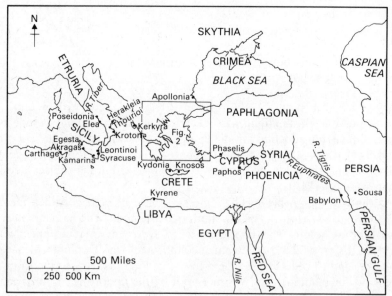

Figure 3   The Mediterranean and Near East

grants, commonly known as metics, formed the third main segment of
the population, enjoying a status between that of the native Athenians
and their slaves. The arrival of more and more slaves and metics shar-
pened the conception of the native Athenian as a full member of the
polis, a citizen or *polites*. In the course of time metics became increasingly
prominent in manufacture, and poorer metics rowed in the fleet.

The growth of Athens' imperial power was to alarm the Spartan
alliance and so precipitate the Peloponnesian War (431–404). Despite a
devastating plague, the death of Perikles and the revolt of the allied city
of Mytilene, Athens survived a number of Spartan invasions of her
territory. In 425 she captured Pylos from the Spartans, but the next year
she lost Amphipolis in the north. In 421 the first ten years of the war
were brought to an inconclusive end by the so-called Peace of Nikias.

Under the influence of Alkibiades, Athens was soon provoking a
renewal of hostilities. In 415 she sent a great expedition to Sicily. Mainly
through the failings of its commander, Nikias, the expedition was
destroyed two years later, by which time Sparta had established a permanent base in Attike. Persia now began to provide money for the Peloponnesian fleet. Athens' hold on her allies was shaken and her food supply
threatened. In 411 democracy was suspended but restored the next
year. Athens showed great resilience in adversity and won several naval
victories. She was, however, finally defeated at Aigospotamoi in 405 and
obliged to surrender the next year. With Spartan approval, democracy
was again suspended, but it was restored in 403.

Thanks to the historian Thucydides, we have a detailed and reliable
account of the first twenty years of the Peloponnesian War, but Thucydides was writing politico-military history for intelligent Greeks. Much
that we should like to be told he presupposed, and much else he regarded
as irrelevant to his purpose. It is the aim of this book to describe the
economic and social setting of fifth-century Athens' achievements in the
arts of peace, to describe those achievements themselves, and at the same
time to see how far we can enter into the thinking and feeling of the
Athenians. What sort of world did they think they were living in? What
sort of life did they think a man should lead, or try to lead, in such a
world? The Athenian about whom surviving literature tells us most is
Sokrates, but it is disputable how well we know even him. Nevertheless,
even if our knowledge of individual Athenians is as incomplete as our
knowledge of characters in Attic tragedy, it may still prove that we can
penetrate the mind of the community.

The Sources of Knowledge

The principal source of knowledge are contemporary writers who are (a) preserved in some bulk, (b) writing more or less directly about Athens, and (c) writing from a standpoint that we can discern. So the *History* of Thucydides and the comedies of Aristophanes are of prime importance. In Thucydides, the speeches given to Perikles, especially his Funeral Speech of the winter of 431/0 (2.35–46) and his Last Speech (2.60–64), deserve particular attention. We may claim to have a good understanding of Athens if we can translate the fine phrases and sentiments of the Funeral Speech into social and political realities. We may make the same claim if we can say what the Athenians laughed at and why.

Important, too are contemporary public inscriptions and the, admittedly short, work of the so-called Old Oligarch, who was certainly an oligarch but may not have been old at the time of writing. (I cite inscriptions by reference to *A Selection of Greek Historical Inscriptions* by R. Meiggs and D. Lewis, abbreviated in the text as 'ML'. Translations of the most important inscriptions and of the Old Oligarch may be found in the first part of *Greek Historical Documents: the Fifth Century B.C.* by N. Lewis.)

The surviving plays of Sophokles and Euripides take their plots from myth and make no explicit reference to contemporary events or persons, but they provide the best evidence we have for the emotional and intellectual concerns of most thoughtful Athenians at the time. Like the comic poets, the tragedians were competing for a prize and had to beware of affronting popular convictions. The *Histories* of Herodotos carry the story of the Persian War down to the spring of 478 and make few explicit references to later events, but they seem finally to have been published only a little earlier than 414, and they provide much evidence of contemporary Greek thought of a traditional kind. Whether Herodotos did in fact give readings from his *Histories* or not, they would have been suitable for the purpose.

The surviving speeches written by, or attributed to, Antiphon of Rhamnous, Lysias and Andokides – whether written to be delivered by themselves or others, or rewritten after delivery, or written as models for students (like the *Tetralogies* of Antiphon) – resemble the surviving plays in having been composed with a mass audience in mind, usually a jury several hundreds strong. It may sometimes be prudent to flatter a mass audience, but it is always prudent to respect its convictions.

The Sokratic writings of Plato and Xenophon resemble the pamphlet of the Old Oligarch and the *History* of Thucydides in having been composed with the private reader in mind. Whether we believe that Plato faithfully preserves the personality and thought of the historical Sokrates or not, he certainly gives us much incidental information about Athenian life. Xenophon's writing are of little philosophical value, but they too, especially his *Reminiscences*, give us much information about Athenian life.

In addition to more or less contemporary sources, it is necessary to consider other sources, both earlier and later. Because poetry was so prominent in Athenian education, poets from Homer and Hesiod to Aiskhylos did much to shape Athenian thinking, and because so few fifth-century speeches survive, we have to use fourth-century speeches, especially those of Isokrates, Isaios, Demosthenes and Aiskhines, to try to fill gaps in our knowledge of fifth-century law. Relevant too is the Aristotelian *Constitution of Athens*, the first part of which sketches the constitutional history of Athens down to the end of the fifth century, and the second part of which gives a more detailed account of the constitution as it was in the time of Aristotle.

Much later works may preserve valuable evidence. This is true of Plutarch's *Lives* – of Perikles, Nikias and Alkibiades – and also of such compilations as Diogenes Laertios' *Lives of Eminent Philosophers* and Athenaios' *Deipnosophists*. The account of the buildings of Athens in Pausanias' *Description of Greece* is a most valuable complement to the findings of archaeology.

· 1 ·

Country and Town

The community or *polis* of Athens comprised, strictly speaking, just the citizens (*politai*), a privileged minority of men within the total population. Whereas we might say 'Athens decided . . .', the Greek idiom was to say 'The Athenians decided . . .', and that meant that the citizens, rather than the entire adult population, had decided.

Geographically speaking, a Greek community normally comprised an urban settlement (*asty*) built around a defensible hill (*akropolis*), which was near, but not too near, the sea, together with its surrounding territory (*khora*), which was bounded by the sea or by mountains, beyond which lay the territory of some other community. And so it was with Athens, except that her frontier with Megara was not a mountain range.

The city of Athens developed round a citadel, the Akropolis. Its harbour, Peiraieus, was four miles distant. The surrounding territory, Attike, was roughly triangular in shape – the northern side of the triangle running from the south-eastern slopes of Mount Kithairon along the crest of Mount Parnes to a point on the coast north of Rhamnous, the eastern side running south from that point to Cape Sounion, and the third side running north-west to Kithairon. The total area of more than 800 square miles constituted a *khora* large by Greek standards, but no place in Attike, not even Sounion, was more than thirty miles from Athens or as much as fifteen from the sea.

No town or village in Attike was nearly as populous as Athens or, by the middle of the fifth century, Peiraieus. At the end of the sixth century, Kleisthenes had divided rural Attike into more than 100 administrative 'demes' or villages with their inhabitants. These rural demes were natural settlements, and varied greatly in size, the largest of them being Akharnai (Thucydides 2.19.2). (Kleisthenes also divided the urban area of Athens, Peiraieus and environs – between Mount Aigaleos and Mount Hymettos – into demes resembling our wards. For a fuller account of Kleisthenes' demes, see chapter 2.)

The natural resources of Attike were not very great. There were plains – round Athens, beyond Hymettos, beyond Aigaleos (the Thriasian plain), and beyond Mount Pentelikos (the plain of Marathon) – but the soil was light. Furthermore, the summers were very dry, and there were

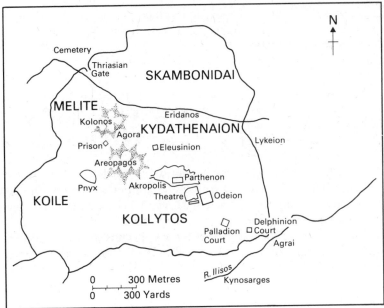

Figure 4   Athens *c.* 400 BC

no considerable rivers. One River Kephisos flowed by Athens, another by Eleusis, and a stream watered part at least of the plain of Marathon; but there was not enough water in any of them to permit extensive irrigation, or navigation. Thus there was little fodder suitable for cattle or horses. Donkeys were commonly used as beasts of burden. Sheep and goats, as well as providing wool and hair for textiles, also provided milk, from which cheese could be made. Many smallholders kept poultry and pigs. Only the biggest landowners could afford to keep horses (for sporting or military purposes) or more cattle than a yoke of oxen or cows as draught-animals.

Much of the arable land was devoted to growing cereals, but even so Attike produced only a third of the grain consumed by the population; the rest had to be imported by sea from the Russian steppe and else-where. Such grain as was grown was less commonly wheat than barley, which throve better on the light soil; so barley cakes and porridge were important parts of the national diet. There was also a good deal of market-gardening, especially around Athens. The mild winters permitted a long season. But for plentiful supplies of fish, the national diet would have been largely vegetarian. It was rare for most Athenians to eat meat except on the occasion of certain religious festivals, when the carcases of sacrificial beasts were distributed among the congregation.

By historical times the deforestation of Attike was far advanced.

Charcoal-burners were active on the southern slopes of Parnes; timber for ship-building had to be imported. The scrub on Hymettos supported many swarms of bees, and the honey they produced took the place of sugar today. Two fruit-trees that did flourish were the olive and the fig, and so did the vine. Olive oil was important in cookery and, when burnt in lamps, as a source of light. It was also used for anointing the body. Attike produced enough oil and wine to leave some for export, the oil being superior in quality to the wine.

Oil and wine were stored and transported in earthenware vessels, and there were plentiful supplies of potter's clay to be obtained from the beds of the Eridanos, Ilisos and Kephisos. The quarries on the western side of Pentelikos yielded inexhaustible quantities of marble. Of much greater economic importance were the lead and silver mines in Laureion. Like the quarries, they were the property of the community, and they contributed very greatly to its prosperity. Finally, Peiraieus afforded superb natural harbours, there being in addition to the main harbour of Kantharos the two smaller harbours of Zea and Mounykhia on the east.

When the Peloponnesian War, fought between Athens and the Spartan alliance, broke out in 431, most Athenians still lived in country villages, but the opening years of that war were to reveal, to all who cared to look, that Athens by then was more dependent on the sea than on her countryside. The pattern of rural life was the same as had in large part originally shaped the calendar of religious festivals, which provided the setting for so much of the cultural life of the city. Though there were gentlemen farmers living in Athens but owning large estates in the country, worked by slaves under the supervision of slave bailiffs, most farmers were smallholders owning at most a single slave. Primogeniture not being recognised in Athens, there was a tendency for ancestral lots of land to be progressively subdivided, with the result that some properties were hardly large enough to support a family.

For all who grew cereals (and most will have grown some cereals – very likely between their rows of olive trees), the working year began in October. Only with the coming of the autumnal rains was ploughing possible. There was then a busy period of two or three months, during which the ground had to be prepared and the seed sown in time for growth to begin before the coldest part of the winter. There was little to be done during January and February. Spring called for renewed activity, culminating in harvesting in May and threshing in June. There was again little to be done in July and August. Then it was time to gather the grapes and figs, and later the olives.

One of the recurrent motifs of history is tension between country and town, and Athens was not free from it. The failure of the farmers to improve their methods was a sign of a conservatism that was bound to disapprove of urban innovations. The Greek words for 'urban' and 'rustic' (*asteios* and *agroikos*) also mean 'witty' and 'boorish'. Our dependence on mechanical aids may lead us to exaggerate the distaste that an Athenian felt for a long walk. Andokides (1.38) mentions without comment a walk from Athens to Laureion, a distance of some twenty-six miles. It may therefore be that Athenian farmers were prepared to walk a long way to attend important meetings of the sovereign Assembly, provided that they did not fall at the busiest times of the year. On the other hand, because they did not live in the city, they were bound to be ignorant of the background of many of the matters debated in the Assembly. 'There's a lot that passes us by,' says the Chorus of Farmers in Aristophanes' *Peace* (618). We may assume that few farmers would dare to speak in the Assembly: their ignorance, their clothing and their unpolished speech would expose them to ridicule. Since very few farms were anything like self-sufficient, their owners had to buy and sell in the city from time to time. An Aristophanic farmer (*Assemblywomen* 817ff.) speaks of selling his grapes and going to the urban market-place or Agora for barley-groats. In the Agora farmers were liable to be cheated by the quicker-witted townsfolk.

The original town of Athens comprised the Akropolis and a settlement on its southern side. By the fifth century the centre of city life was the Agora, an area between the Areopagos and the Eridanos that appears to have been chosen as the main square early in the sixth century. It is possible to outline the course of public building in the Agora and elsewhere in the city from the sixth century, and to do so gives a clear insight into public concerns and priorities.

While the city remained small, the Agora, as well as being the formal and informal meeting-place of the citizens, and containing the principal administrative buildings, some temples, and many stalls for the sale of goods, also accommodated dramatic, musical, and athletic contests. On the west side, at the foot of Kolonos Agoraios, there stood from the middle of the sixth century the temple of Apollo Patroös, the Ancestral Apollo (Apollo was the father of Ion, the supposed ancestor of the Ionian Greeks, among whom the Athenians were included), with a temple of Zeus, the principal god, and the Stoa Basileios or Stoa of the Basileus (or King), one of the three principal magistrates, to the north of it, and administrative buildings to the south. (A stoa was essentially a rectangular building with columns taking the place of one long wall. It afforded shelter from rain or sun.) The Stoa Basileios was the earliest and also the smallest of the stoas round the Agora. The sons of the tyrant Peisistratos, who died in 527, built a large fountain-house, Enneakrounos, which may be the fountain-house found in the south-east of the Agora. (A Greek tyrant was a usurping ruler or a kinsman of one, who had succeeded to his rule.) The tyrants channelled water from the north-east of the city to fountain-houses in order to supplement privately owned

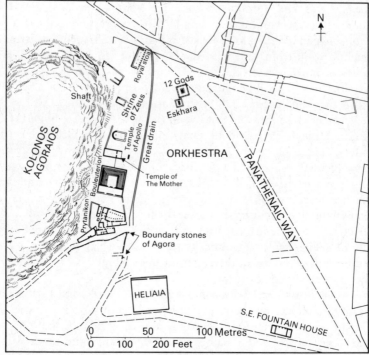

Figure 5   The Agora *c.* 500 BC

wells. In 522 or 521 the grandson and namesake of Peisistratos built the Altar of the Twelve Gods on the north side of the Agora. It was a place of asylum and the point from which distances were measured (Herodotos 2.7.1). The tyrants raised the status of the goddess Athena's main festival, the Panathenaia, to that of a great national festival, and many of its constituent events occurred in the Agora. In 510 the first statues to adorn the Agora, those of the Tyrant-killers, Harmodios and Aristogeiton, were set up near the Orkhestra, or dancing-place, in the middle of the Agora.

The adoption of the moderate democracy of Kleisthenes in 508 led to a spate of building at the beginning of the fifth century. South of the temple of Apollo was built a south-facing council house (Bouleuterion) for the new Council (Boule) of 500, and beside it was built a small temple for the Mother of the Gods, a goddess akin to Earth. An area enclosed by a stone wall on the south side of the Agora probably accommodated the original popular court, the Heliaia. It was open to the sky and could hold 1,500. A great stone drain was built to carry surface water northwards from the south-west corner of the Agora. And it was now that a quieter meeting-place was found for the Assembly –

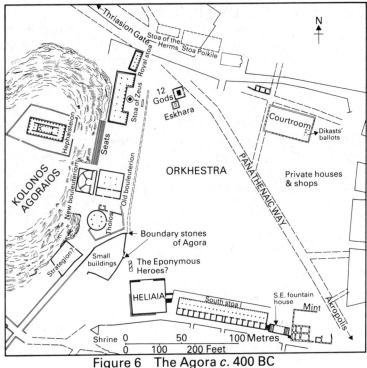

Figure 6   The Agora *c.* 400 BC

on the Pnyx, a hill some ten minutes' walk to the south-west, but visible from the Agora. The new site was not more spacious than the old, but it did provide a more steeply sloping auditorium. Only if an ostracism was to be held, to determine whether a prominent citizen should be exiled for ten years, did the citizens now gather in the Agora for a political purpose.

In 480 all buildings were severely damaged by the Persian invaders, but – unlike the temples of Zeus, Apollo, and the Mother – the Stoa Basileios, the council house and the Heliaia were soon rebuilt. In 477 new statues of the Tyrant-killers, the work of Kritios and Nesiotes, were set up to replace the earlier pair, which Xerxes had taken away to Persia. In about 465 or perhaps 460 were built the round-house (Tholos) for the standing committee of the Council and also the Painted Stoa (Stoa Poikile). A kinsman of a distinguished general, Kimon, was responsible for the building of the Painted Stoa. It stood on the north side of the Agora, facing south. What remains of its western end has now been excavated. Kimon himself, after wresting Eion-on-Strymon from the Persians in 476, was allowed to set up three statues of Hermes on the north side of the Agora, which then or later were housed in another stoa, the Stoa of the Herms, between the Painted Stoa and the Stoa Basileios. (Hermes was the god of travellers and lucky finds, and images of him could be seen all over Athens and Attike. The head and phallos were rendered realistically, projecting from a rectangular shaft. The arms were mere stumps and the legs were not indicated.) Kimon also planted plane trees in the Agora, More importantly, he brought back for burial from Skyros the supposed bones of the Athenian hero Theseus, but the Theseion which housed them has not yet been identified.

Soon after the conclusion of peace with Persia in 449, the Periklean building-programme got under way. This programme was primarily concerned with embellishing the Akropolis, and work already begun on the temple of the divine smith Hephaistos (the Hephaisteion) on Kolonos Agoraios was interrupted. There was, however, one new building completed, to the south-west of the Agora, and this is thought to have been the headquarters of the board of ten generals, now the most important magistrates. In the last thirty years of the century there was a fresh spate of building in the Agora. In the north-west corner, on the site of the old temple of Zeus, was built one new stoa – the elaborate Stoa of Zeus the Liberator (Eleutherios). Another, less impressive, new stoa was built on the south side of the Agora. It contained fifteen rooms, each of them containing seven dining-couches, and was probably used by the various boards of magistrates. West of the old council house was built a new council house, and the old council house became available for housing archives. Somewhere in the south-west corner of the Agora was built the first monument to the Eponymous Heroes, who had given their names to the ten tribes into which Kleisthenes had divided the citizen body. A new building in the south-east corner was probably the mint. In the north-east corner was built a courtroom.

Such, in outline, was the development of the Agora down to the end of the fifth century. There, as elsewhere in Athens, our distinction between sacred and secular is inapplicable. The open space in the centre was sacred to the life of the community. It was defined by boundary stones at the beginning of the fifth century, and those accused of homicide or convicted of various other heinous crimes were excluded from it by law. In a wider sense, the Agora was not only the defined square but also the whole commercial area, including much of the Kerameikos to the north-west.

There were also many important public buildings outside the Agora. To the south-east, above the south-east fountain-house and the mint but to the east of the Panathenaic Way, lay the Eleusinion, the precinct of Demeter and Kore, the goddesses whose Mysteries were celebrated at Eleusis. Beyond it, close under the Akropolis, lay the town hall (Prytaneion), in which burnt a fire that was never allowed to go out, because it symbolised the continuing life of the community, and which contained a dining-room where benefactors or guests of the community could be entertained. Nearby lay the shrine of Aglauros, one of the daughters of the legendary King Kekrops, and the Anakeion, the shrine of the Anakes or Dioskouroi – Kastor and Polydeukes.

We have already noted the circumstances in which the Pnyx became the regular meeting-place of the Assembly. For most of the fifth century the slope of the hill was exploited to make an almost natural theatre, with the speaker's platform at the bottom facing the sea, and the citizens facing the Akropolis. There was sitting room (Aristophanes, *Wasps* 32, 43) for about 6,000. At the end of the century a huge embankment was raised inside a curved retaining wall and the natural arrangement reversed. Thereafter the assembled citizens were better sheltered from the north-east wind.

Until the middle of the fifth century dramatic contests were probably held in the Orkhestra in the Agora. When the wooden stands from which the spectators used to watch collapsed, it was decided to establish a permanent theatre in a more sheltered spot than the slope of the Pnyx, which faced north-east. The spot chosen lay on the southern slope of the Akropolis, above the small temple containing the wooden image of the wine god Dionysos Eleuthereus. Here, on a level terrace behind a curved retaining wall, the god had been honoured with singing and dancing since the introduction of his cult, by Peisistratos or his sons, from Eleutherai, a village on the northern frontier with Boiotia. Only a few blocks of the fifth-century theatre survive. It must have been a simple affair with rows of wooden or stone benches overlooking the semi-circular terrace, which accommodated a round dancing-area (*orkhestra*) for the chorus, a low stage for the actors and behind it a wooden stage-building (*skene*). To the east of the theatre was built or rebuilt, at about the same time, the Odeion – the first roofed building in Athens – for concerts and musical contests. Its pyramidal roof rested on a nine-by-ten rectangle of ninety columns.

The main works in the Periklean building-programme were the new temple of Athena the Virgin (Parthenos) on the Akropolis, which we call the Parthenon, and the grand entrance to the Akropolis, the Propylaia. Work on the Parthenon, a Doric temple, all in Pentelic marble, began in 447. The structure of the Parthenon was completed in 438, when the cult image, Pheidias' colossal gold and ivory statue of Athena, was installed. The next year work began on the Propylaia, also all in marble, but was broken off after 432, because of the Peloponnesian War. The small temple of Athene Nike on the south-west bastion of the Akropolis was projected in the 440s but not built until the 420s. Work on the third great Akropolis building, the composite temple that we call the Erekhtheion, lasted from 421 to about 406. (Erekhtheus or Erikhthonios, a legendary king of Athens, was a son of Earth, reared

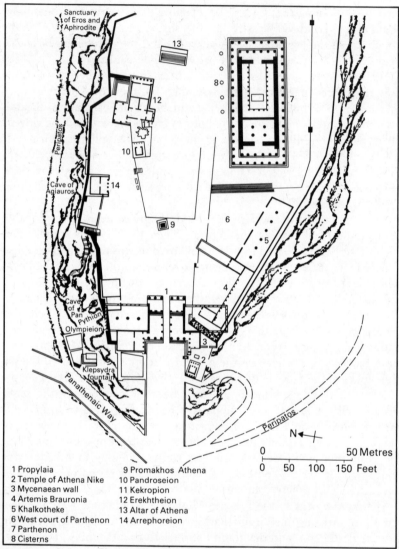

Figure 7   The Akropolis *c.* 400 BC

1 Propylaia
2 Temple of Athena Nike
3 Mycenaean wall
4 Artemis Brauronia
5 Khalkotheke
6 West court of Parthenon
7 Parthenon
8 Cisterns

9 Promakhos Athena
10 Pandroseion
11 Kekropion
12 Erekhtheion
13 Altar of Athena
14 Arrephoreion

by Athena. What was taken for his tomb was contained within the Erekhtheion.) The holiest object in Athens (Pausanias 1.26.6) was a primitive olive-wood statue of Athena the guardian of the *polis* (Polias). In 480 it had been removed from Athens to save it from the Persians, who duly burnt all the buildings on the Akropolis. When the Athenians returned in 479, they brought the olive-wood statue back, but where did they put it? Apparently they repaired the old temple of Athena

Polias, the earliest clear sign of the formation of the Athenian *polis*, that had stood on the site of the former Mycenaean palace, between the later Parthenon and Erekhtheion, in order to accommodate it. And then once more, at the quadrennial festival of the Great Panathenaia, the grand procession portrayed in the frieze that ran round the outside of the walls of the Parthenon could be held in honour of the goddess and her new robe could be presented. When the Erekhtheion was built, the statue was installed in it, probably in the western part. Apparently, the western end of the old temple was preserved as the state treasury.

The Panathenaic procession followed the Panathenaic Way which ran from the Thriasian Gate, on the north-west side of the city, through the Kerameikos, between the Stoa Basileios and the Stoa of the Herms, past the Altar of the Twelve Gods on the right, across the Agora and past the Eleusinion. The straight stretch of the Panathenaic Way from the Altar of the Twelve Gods to the Eleusinion was known as the *dromos* or course, because it was used as the track for equestrian events that formed part of the Panathenaic Games, founded in the 560s.

In describing the Agora, it was necessary to mention various kinds of construction that were not peculiar to the Agora: temples, statues, law-courts, fountains and shops. But to shops in general, and to shops selling a particular commodity, the Greek equivalent of our proverb 'Birds of a feather flock together' did largely apply. Xenophon goes so far as to say (*Oikonomikos* 8.22): 'You may order any sort of slave to buy you something in the Agora and bring it home, and he will have no difficulty. He will certainly know where to go to get each article, the reason being that each article is kept in its appointed place.' This is exaggerated, but shops were concentrated round the Agora, different areas tending to be reserved for shops selling different commodities. In many cases there was no distinction between house, workshop and shop. The Greek word *ergasterion* is sometimes to be translated 'workshop' and sometimes 'shop'. In other cases, goods were sold from movable booths, as at a fair. Bankers worked at tables (*trapezai*), hence their name (*trapezitai*). The area from the Agora to the cemeteries outside the Sacred and Thriasian Gates was called the Kerameikos because of the high concentration of potters (*kerameis*) living there. The smiths and sculptors in marble were concentrated near the temple of Hephaistos.

Most of the area within the city wall, apart from the Agora and the two main hills – the Akropolis and the Areopagos – was covered by housing, the most densely populated district being Koile, south-west of the Pnyx. In the better kind of house, irregularly shaped rooms opened off a court. Only the lower part of the walls was of stone; the upper part was of sun-dried brick. Floors were of clay except that the floor of the men's dining-room (*andron*) might be paved with pebbles or mosaics. Some houses were two storeys high. Roofs were wooden, with rain-

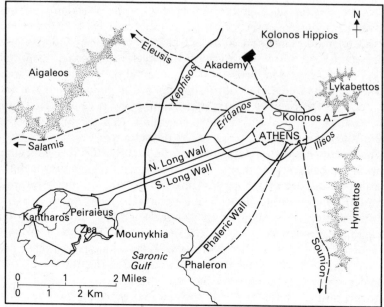

Figure 8   Athens and Peiraieus

proof terra cotta tiling. Sanitation was mostly a matter of cesspools.
Streets were narrow and crooked. By our standards, private squalor
contrasted strangely with public affluence.

Beyond the housing lay the four-mile-long city wall. Advised by
Themistokles, the whole people of Athens had raised it hastily after the
departure of the Persians. The wall consisted of several courses of large
well-shaped blocks of stone on either face of a core of rougher stone.
Above the stone courses brickwork rose to an unknown height. To build
the wall the Athenians used any available stone, including blocks from
buildings demolished by the Persians and even gravestones. It was on
this wall rather than on the frontier forts or the fortifications of the
Akropolis that the safety of the community depended. At the same time
Themistokles persuaded the Athenians to complete the fortifications of
Peiraieus. In the early 450s the city wall was extended to the sea by two
Long Walls, the northern one running to the northern side of the
Peiraieus wall, and the southern one to Phaleron. Later, perhaps when
Phaleron Bay was no longer used as a harbour, a third wall was built
between the two, running parallel with, and 183 yards from, the
northern wall. The lifeline between Athens and Peiraieus was now
completely enclosed.

In the city wall there were some fifteen gates, of which the Thriasian
(later called the Dipylon) was the most imposing. Outside a number of

gates the community built round bath-houses for travellers. On either side of the roads leading from the gates lay the cemeteries. The greatest concentration of cemeteries lay to the north-west of the city – outside the Sacred, Thriasian and Erian Gates. (The Sacred Gate was so called because through it ran the Sacred Way to Eleusis.)

Further out than the cemeteries lay the gymnasia, places where males stripped for exercise. The primary requirement was space – for running, for throwing the javelin and discus, and for riding. Other requirements were water for washing and trees for shade. The purposes originally served were perhaps military as well as athletic. Service in the hoplite phalanx – the heavy infantry *en masse* – necessitated both some special training in the use of the suit of armour or panoply and also general fitness. From their foundation early in the sixth century, gymnasia must have included a running-track (*dromos*). Though it is not always easy to distinguish gymnasia from *palaistrai* or wrestling schools, which were normally small, privately owned and located within or near the city walls, the three original gymnasia of Athens – the Akademy, Lykeion and Kynosarges – were large, publicly owned and located outside the walls.

The Akademy lay three-quarters of a mile beyond the Thriasian Gate, south of the Kephisos. It took its name from an obscure local hero, Hekademos, but Athena also was worshipped there, and Aristophanes mentions (*Clouds* 1005) her sacred olive trees (*moriai*). From the *moriai*, found all over Attike, came the oil that filled the jars awarded to the winners in the Panathenaic Games. The torch-races in honour of Prometheus, the Titan who restored fire to mankind, and Hephaistos started from the Akademy (Pausanias 1.30.2). The Lykeion, consecrated to Apollo Lykeios, lay just beyond the eastern wall of the city, by the source of the Eridanos. Like the Akademy, it was big enough to be used for cavalry displays, and for mustering troops. The etymology of the name 'Kynosarges' was obscure even to the ancients. The gymnasium lay to the south, beyond the Ilisos, and the principal deity there was Herakles. Kynosarges lacked the standing of the other two gymnasia. In the course of time, the gymnasia became social centres like the Agora with its stoas.

Four miles south-west of Athens lay the promontory of Peiraieus, with its three natural harbours: Zea and Mounykhia on the east, and Kantharos, the biggest, on the west. Each harbour contained shipsheds, but Zea was the main naval base. The town was laid out on a rectangular plan by Hippodamos of Miletos in about 460. The *agora* to the west of the hill of Mounykhia bore his name, Hippodameia. There was another, commercial, *agora* on the eastern side of Kantharos, and there stood the Periklean corn-market, the Alphitopolis or Long Stoa. Though it had its distinctive features, Peiraieus was in many ways a duplicate of the upper city, with its fortifications, its two *agorai*, its theatre (Thucydides 8.93.1), and its cults, shrines and temples.

· 2 ·

Population, Property, Taxation

The citizens of Athens, together with their womenfolk and children, constituted only about half the population of Attike. All other permanent inhabitants were either metics (free immigrants) or slaves (Thucydides 6.27.2).

Of these three elements most is, of course, known about the citizens. With them we start and to them we shall return, after some consideration of their womenfolk, the metics and the slaves.

The citizens (*politai, astoi*) of Athens were, very largely, those freeborn males who had been accepted by the members of their father's deme as satisfying both the following conditions:

(a) Both their parents were citizens – in so far as mothers could be citizens. This condition had been imposed by a decree moved by Perikles in 451/0. (The Greek year ran from, approximately, midsummer to midsummer, and we often do not know in which half of a Greek year a particular event occurred: hence this notation.) It is not known what lay behind the decree, which was presumably not retroactive, or at least did not disfranchise already existing children of mixed marriages; for otherwise Kimon could not have remained a general. It is possible that the citizens had become more concerned to secure husbands for their unmarried daughters, for Athenian casualties had not been light in the 450s, and spinsterhood was abhorred; but it seems more likely that the decree was intended to preserve racial purity, perhaps in the face of the increasing size and racial variety of the metic population. It is not hard to believe that mutually advantageous marriages between poor citizens and the daughters of rich metics were becoming more frequent.

(b) They had completed their seventeenth year. Since birth certificates were not kept, ages might be disputed. The boys Lysis and Menexenos were about the same age, but they did not know which of them was the elder (Plato, *Lysis* 207c).

If the deme agreed that they satisfied both conditions, it remained only for the young men to convince the Council too that they satisfied the

21

second condition. The names of those accepted by both deme and Council were recorded in the deme register.

Citizenship conferred rights and imposed duties, but Athenians, and Greeks generally, did not draw the line between rights and duties quite where we do. In the Archaic Age citizenship and membership of the hoplite phalanx had been closely linked. We regard jury service as a duty, but in Classical Athens it was seen as a right, originally because it conferred power and later because it also conferred pay. Whether regarded as rights or duties, the following activities were reserved for citizens: attending or addressing the Assembly (other than by special invitation), voting in the Assembly, standing for public office or jury-service, and undertaking most of the financial burdens known as liturgies, including the trierarchy – commanding a trireme or warship for a year. Furthermore, there was an immemorial link between citizenship and land-tenure: only citizens could own land or houses, and most of them derived most of their income from land. Finally, only citizens qualified for occasional distributions of free corn, such as that made possible in 445/4 by the gift of the Libyan prince Psammetikhos (Plutarch, *Perikles* 37.3f.) or that made by the state in 423/2 (Aristophanes, *Wasps* 717).

Even freeborn native females who could satisfy the two conditions of parentage and age were not citizens in the full sense: they were *politides* not *politai*, and they could do none of the things listed in the last paragraph. Nor did respectable married women (by 'respectable' may be understood 'upper- and middle-class', but in so far as lower-class wives or widows went out to work, they did so from economic necessity) enjoy their husbands' freedom of movement. They attended some festivals, including their own three-day autumn festival, the Thesmophoria. (In Sophokles' *Elektra* 911f., Aigisthos will not allow his step-daughter to leave the house 'even for worship'.) They may sometimes have attended the theatre, though not usually (Aristophanes, *Women at the Thesmophoria* 395 ff.). They certainly attended the funerals of close relatives. They did their personal shopping, accompanied by a maid, but they did not do the household shopping. That task fell to a slave, male or female (Lysias 1.8, 16), or to the husband. In general, it was rare for such a woman to leave the house without some excuse. (Their daughters rarely left the women's apartments.) 'Why', asks the Chorus of *Women at the Thesmophoria* (789ff.), 'if we are really a curse, don't you let us go out or even get caught peeping out, and instead prefer to guard your curse so zealously?'

Respectable married woman stayed at home partly because the streets of Athens were not policed (their sons went to school escorted by slaves called *paidagogoi*), and partly because they had plenty to do. There being no higher civil service, those husbands who did not have to earn their own living were very commonly involved in the extensive business of the community, and were obliged to make over to their wives the management of the house, which included a small workshop. Clothes had to be made from raw wool, bread had to be made from wheat, provisions had to be laid in against the winter. And, of course, a wife had to attend to the immediate needs of her children and her husband (Aristophanes, *Lysistrate* 16ff.). But the fundamental reason for the seclusion of women was a determination to preserve the integrity of the household or *oikos* by making adultery very difficult for the wife. The objections to adultery that involved a citizen's wife are listed in a speech of Lysias (1.33) and culminate in the consequent uncertainty about the children's paternity.

Unmarried girls were even more rigorously secluded than their mothers, in order to preserve their virginity. This was part of the reason why fathers married off their daughters so young, usually between fourteen and eighteen. Another part is given by Aristophanes' Lysistrate (596): 'A woman's opportunity is brief, and if she does not seize it, no one will marry her.' The words 'if she does not seize it' must not, however, be taken to imply that an Athenian bride chose her own husband. At least in the case of her first husband, the choice was not hers at all. All her life, from her admission to the *oikos* through her marriage to her death, an Athenian girl would be subject to the mastery (*kyrieia*) of her father or her husband or some other male kinsman. An Athenian marriage was essentially a solemn betrothal agreement (*engye*) between two *oikoi*, followed by the handing over of the bride to the groom by her *kyrios*, normally her father.

The seclusion of women in the house and their exclusion from political life did not mean that husbands despised their wives. The evidence of vase-paintings and of reliefs on gravestones shows that conjugal respect and affection were common enough. The ideal *oikos* is movingly depicted in Euripides' *Alkestis*. Nevertheless, it is accurate to describe Athenian women as 'second-class citizens'. Euripides (*Medeia* 232ff.) lets Medeia sum up what was in fact the position of respectable women in Athens (though hardly of herself in Corinth) thus:

First, we have to buy a husband for a huge sum, and gain a master of our persons, the second evil being yet more painful than the first. And there is the supreme hazard: whether one gets a good man or a bad. Separation is not respectable for women and it is impossible for us to refuse our husbands' demands. Thus landed among novel habits and customs, she must divine, what she cannot have learned at home, how best to manage her mate. If we accomplish this successfully, and our husband continues to live with us, not resenting the marriage-bond, enviable is our life; if not, better death.

When a husband grows tired of his family, he goes out and refreshes his heart. But we are compelled to look to one person. And people say that we lead a safe life at home, whereas men have to fight. Fools! I would much rather stand in the phalanx three times than bear one child.

There are several points to note. First, custom dictated that a bride should be provided with a dowry corresponding to her father's economic status. This dowry, which did not pass irrevocably into her husband's control, was her share of her father's estate, to be used for her maintenance. Its size might, however, be as interesting to the groom as her virtues. Second, while the marriage lasted, the husband was the wife's master (*kyrios*): no woman could enter into an important contract or plead her own case in court, and a wife could so act only through her husband. It was for her husband to decide, within ten days of its birth, whether a new-born child should be admitted to the *oikos* or exposed. In some respects, a wife stood to her husband as a slave to his owner. Third, though a wife could, with the help of her family, divorce her husband if she laid a written deposition before the appropriate magistrate, the Arkhon, it is likely enough that society disapproved of wives divorcing husbands. Only one fifth-century case is known: the attempt of Hipparete to divorce Alkibiades (Plutarch, *Alkibiades* 8.5). Fourth, unlike her husband, a respectable wife rarely left the house, and when her husband gave dinner-parties or drinking-parties at home, they were all-male affairs, apart from any dancing-girls or *aulos*-girls (an *aulos* was a musical instrument resembling an oboe or clarinet) that he hired to entertain his guests; she thus saw few eligible men other than her husband. (Drinking-parties often ended in drunken and disorderly behaviour that she would not have cared for.) Fifth, if a wife did commit adultery and was detected, the law, for reasons already given, took a very grave view of the matter, requiring the husband to divorce her, where it allowed the husband absolute freedom vis-à-vis both his own female slaves and the prostitutes, superior (*hetairai*, like Theodote in Xenophon's *Reminiscences* (3.11)) or inferior (*pornai*), that he could find elsewhere. (It did not, of course, allow him such freedom vis-à-vis the womenfolk of another citizen.) Sixth, the ultimate 'justification' of women's depressed status is suggested by Medeia's final words: since war was never far away and the possible consequences of losing (death or enslavement) were so frightful, the warrior was the most valuable member of society and entitled to the fullest privileges.

Much diverse evidence – literary, legal, archaeological, mythological – bears on the position of women in Athens. The first thing to be said about the literary evidence is that it was written by upper-class men for men. In the second place, the literary evidence of the late fifth century is primarily dramatic, and both comedy and tragedy have to be considered. The surviving comedies of Aristophanes were obviously grounded in contemporary life, but the tragedies of Sophokles and Euripides, though seemingly set in a bygone age, also to some extent reflected contemporary life. Medeia's speech, just quoted, related far more closely to Classical Athens than to Mycenaean Corinth.

Older than tragedy and comedy was a misogynistic tradition in Greek literature, reaching back at least as far as Hesiod (*Works and Days* 375). It would, however, be a mistake to suppose that all subsequent writing in that tradition represented its author's considered opinion. Two of Euripides' heroic characters, Jason and Hippolytos, express the view that it would be better if men could beget children without the aid of women, although ordinary thinking was perhaps closer to that of the Chorus-leader in his *Cyclops* (186f.): 'There should never have been a race of women – except for my benefit.' In both Aiskhylos (*Eumenides* 657ff.) and Euripides (*Orestes* 552ff.) we find a standard view: that the mother does no more than receive and foster the father's seed.

The main areas of achievement open to a respectable Athenian girl were three – marriage, management of her husband's *oikos*, and motherhood. A few would become priestesses of goddesses or gods: there were forty or more priestesses at any one time. At the end of his Funeral Speech of 431/0 (Thucydides 2.45.2) Perikles, who had divorced his wife and was living with the most notorious woman in Athens, the *hetaira* Aspasia of Miletos, briefly and paradoxically assured the newly widowed women of Athens that greatest would be the glory of her who was least talked about, for good or ill, among men. Even a respectable girl probably had little education, and when she married, she might be only about half her husband's age. As a married woman, she would spend her days in the company of her infant sons, her young daughters and her slaves. (Dead women are often portrayed with slave-girls in grave-reliefs.) If her husband owned few slaves, she herself would have to do 'slavish' work. Her husband valued what she did as manager and mother. He needed a secure economic base, and to preserve his *oikos* he needed one or perhaps two sons (one might so easily die or be killed in action) and he might feel that he owed it to the community to have at least one daughter. (Unless he were rich, he would not want more children than that.) The customary formula for giving in marriage ran: 'I give you this my daughter for the procreation [literally, "ploughing"] of legitimate children.' All the same, out of sight, out of mind. For men who did not have to earn their own living, the principal activities, in time of peace, were political, in the wide sense of 'pertaining to the *polis*'. Except in the sphere of public religion, women took no part in these activities, knew little about them and could say little about them. They were almost bound to seem stupid.

According to Xenophon (*Spartan Constitution* 1.3):

Elsewhere in Greece [than Sparta], the girls who are to become mothers, and are brought up in the approved fashion, are raised on the plainest fare, with the minimum of delicacies; they either drink no wine at all, or drink it diluted with water. Girls are expected to imitate the usually sedentary life of craftsmen, and to work their wool sitting quietly.

Respectable girls and women in Athens were virtually confined to houses that were small, dark and insanitary. No wonder if they were pale (the black-figure and white-ground painted pottery that gave women white skins was not far wrong), weak, timid and emotional. By our standards they were undereducated, underfed and underexercised. The system made them what it required them to be – in every respect but one.

Greek men's conviction that women derived much more pleasure from sexual intercourse than men did was as old as the Hesiodic corpus (fragment 275). According to Euripides' Jason (*Medeia* 569f.), women think that when their sex lives prosper they have everything. Athenian men judged women deficient in the cardinal virtue of self-control (*sophrosyne*), the opposite of wantonness (*hybris*). Their supposedly voracious sexual appetite made them dangerous. They had to be secluded.

The seclusion of respectable girls and women, combined with the prominence of *palaistra* and gymnasium in the lives of upper-class boys and young men, helped to make upper-class male homosexuality a phenomenon conspicuous by modern, though not by Greek, standards.

The practice enjoyed less recognition in Athens than it did in Sparta (*pace* Xenophon, *Spartan Constitution* 2.12–14), Elis or Boiotia, where its educational-cum-military role was highly valued. In Athens it was a distinguishing characteristic of the upper class, and this was one reason why it was much discussed, but the most discussed features of a community are often among the less important.

In the dialogue that he named after the Athenian general Lakhes, Plato makes him say that the city's public men were so busy that they neglected their own concerns, including the upbringing of their sons. As we shall see, it appears that between the ages of about fourteen and eighteen, when their sisters were getting married, upper-class Athenian young men (*meirakia, neaniskoi*) had little to do beyond attending *palaistra* and gymnasium. They had already attended the *palaistra* as boys (*paides*), from about seven to fourteen, but under the supervision of their *paidagogoi*, and normally segregated from the older boys (Plato, *Lysis* 206d). The latter, during the most impressionable years of their lives, were denied the company of girls, had outgrown the supervision of their *paidagogoi* and were neglected by their fathers. In these circumstances they might turn their attention to *paides*, but they also needed to associate with some adult male. At the age when they were considered to be most attractive, Athenian boys were unconsciously looking for men on whom they could model themselves – for surrogate fathers in fact. Equally, men between the ages of eighteen and about thirty, if they happened to be married, could not obtain much intellectual companionship from their wives, and if they were not, were denied any female company of their own class. Furthermore, as we shall see, the spirit of Athens was competitive, and it was not easy for men, especially prominent men, to form friendships with men of their own age and class. It was, therefore, natural that they should seek the admiration of adolescent boys of their own class. (The admiration of slave boys, for example, would not have sufficed.)

Thus was forged, in the fervid atmosphere of *palaistra* or gymnasium, the bond between lover (*erastes*) and beloved (*eromenos*). Such a bond might unite young man and boy, but more easily and more commonly would unite man and young man. As in some more thoroughly heterosexual societies, the lover was not condemned for pursuing, but the beloved was expected not to surrender, and still less to invite pursuit. The young man would soon be a citizen and a soldier. He might, however, model himself on a successful man, and the successful man would try to go on excelling in his eyes. Clearly there were educational possibilities in such a relationship. But since in time boys grew beards and became heads of households (*kyrioi*), such relationships tended to be transitory. It was normal for a good-looking upper-class boy to pass through the stages of being first an *eromenos* and then an *erastes* and finally to become a husband. It was abnormal and contemptible to get stuck at the first stage, though traces of the second might well persist, as they did in Sophokles. In Aristophanes' *Frogs* (52ff.) Dionysos confesses to having been smitten by a passion. 'For a woman?' asks Herakles. 'No!' 'Well, for a boy?' 'No!' 'Well, for a man?' 'Heaven help me!' 'You've been keeping company with Kleisthenes.' (Kleisthenes was notoriously epicene.)

This was a rational order of enquiry. A woman, even if not Dionysos' own wife – and of the Olympian gods only Zeus was at all effectively married, and Hera was much more a wife than he was a husband – was the most probable suggestion. Herakles' second suggestion was funny – not fantastic, but still improbable. Aristophanes asserted in *Wasps* (1023ff.) and again in *Peace* (762f.) that despite his success in comedy he had not toured the *palaistrai* making advances to boys.

Endlessly visible in *palaistra* and gymnasium was the naked male body, and this body was idealised in sculpture. The female body was sculpted often enough, but until the middle of the fifth century almost always fully clothed and almost always with stronger shoulders and

narrower hips than could be found in nature. Truly feminine figures do
not perhaps antedate 'Dione and Aphrodite' from the east gable of the
Parthenon, now in the British Museum. It was no surprise that the
person declared to be beautiful (*kalos*) in graffiti and in the inscriptions
painted on hundreds of fine pots before firing was much more commonly
male than female: good-looking young men were much more prominent
in Athenian life and thought than good-looking girls. But though the
young male athlete may have been the community ideal as the female
film star is in our own society, heterosexual behaviour was normal in
men. It does not, of course, follow that conjugal fidelity was normal. As
Medeia said, the husband could always go out when he was tired of
living with those at home. In Aristophanes' *Lysistrate* the sexual strike
by wives against husbands is more successful than it would have been
in reality.

   If it is hard for us to define the position of citizens' daughters in
Athens, it is hard to define the position of metics too. It was perhaps in
the time of Kleisthenes that the status of metics (*metoikoi*, people who
have changed their homes, immigrants) was first defined in Athenian
law. By the end of the fifth century foreigners (*xenoi*) staying in Athens
for more than a month or so may have been required to become metics
by paying the *metoikion*, a poll-tax levied at the rate of 1 *drakhme* (see
Appendix 1, page 250) a month for a man, and ½ *drakhme* for a
woman not in the *oikos* of husband or son. (If there were 10,000 metic
men, the tax would have brought in 20 talents a year from them.) In
the fourth century Xenophon (*Ways and Means* 2.1) summed up the
position of metics vis-à-vis citizens thus: 'So far from drawing pay for
their many services to the Greek communities, they contribute
metoikion.' Certainly, a metic had to be registered with the deme in
which he resided, though he could own neither land nor house. His
official designation was 'So-and-so, resident in such-and-such a deme'.
Certainly, too, a metic needed a citizen patron or *prostates*, since he
would otherwise be liable to prosecution (*graphe aprostasiou*), with
enslavement as the penalty, but the role of the *prostates* in relation to
registration with a deme and appearance in court is obscure. Finally, no
metic could trade in the Agora without paying a tax (Aristophanes,
Akharnians 896; Demosthenes 57.34).

   The chief benefit conferred on a metic by his status was his access to
Athenian courts. It was the business of the magistrate chiefly concerned
with metics, the Polemarch, himself to preside over the court that heard
some cases involving metics, such as *graphai aprostasiou* and cases
concerning estates and inheritance, and to pass on others to the appropriate court. If a metic was killed, his nearest male relative was expected
to bring the appropriate action before the Basileus and it was heard by
the Palladion, the court which tried the unpremeditated killing of citi-

zens. It seems that, though the premeditated murder of a citizen carried the penalty of death, the premeditated murder of a metic was classed with the unpremeditated killing of a citizen, and could incur no more than the penalty of exile. In this respect the metic was no better off than other *xenoi* in Athens or even slaves.

Metics were free to worship their own gods, and the worship of the Thracian goddess Bendis was actually made part of the religion of the community. Metics, male and female, took part in the Panathenaic procession, but not, it seems, in the sacrifice. They had some part in the festival of Hephaistos, the Hephaistia. If they were rich enough, metics could, under the system of 'liturgies', help to pay for some festivals by, for example, serving as impresarios or *khoregoi* at the festival of Dionysos called the Lenaia. They could also dance in Lenaian choruses. Rich metics were liable for the extraordinary taxes called *eisphorai*. Though they were not called on to serve as trierarchs (commanders of warships) or in the cavalry, metics who were rich enough were called on to serve in the infantry, usually in defence. Poorer metics could row in the fleet. 'The community needs metics,' says the Old Oligarch (1.12), 'because of the multiplicity of skills and because of the fleet,' though he also says (1.2) that it is the common people of Athens who pull the oars. Thucydides (1.143.1) has Perikles tell the Athenians that it would be a frightful thing for them if the enemy tried to seduce their allied oarsmen by offering higher pay, 'were we ourselves and our metics not a match for them at sea' ('allied', 'allies' and 'alliance' refer to the Athenian alliance, sometimes called the Delian League, see chapter 4). Very little is known about the recruiting and training of the oarsmen of Athens.

Most metics were Greeks from nearby communities, but Thracians, Phrygians, Lydians, Syrians and other *barbaroi* were not unknown. What brought them all to Athens? Some were exiles, victims of political necessity, but most came voluntarily, to share in the economic advantages of a populous city and a thriving port. Doubtless some who came merely to see remained to settle. All were free to go when they pleased.

The metics, ranging as they did from intellectuals to oarsmen, had a diversity of products and services to offer. Above all, however, they were associated with crafts and commerce. Most of them made or sold something material, from which it does not follow that only a handful of citizens did such things.

Metics were, it seems, dominant in large-scale manufacture, foreign trade and banking. They could own slaves, but their inability to own land or houses may have inhibited their business operations, since they could neither borrow nor lend on the security of land. Business success in one generation might lead to a good education and professional success in the next. Kephalos, a rich Syracusan, was induced by Perikles to emigrate to Athens (Lysias 12.4). His shield factory in Peiraieus, which eventually employed nearly 120 slaves (12.19), made him perhaps the richest metic of all. One of his three sons, Lysias, on his return to Athens from her colony Thourioi became a successful speech-writer (*logographos*) – more of an achievement, it must be admitted, for a metic than for a citizen. It is clear from the opening pages of Plato's *Republic* that at least this family of metics moved in the highest intellectual circles in Athens. On the other hand, despite his great services to democracy in 403, a decree conferring citizenship on Lysias and other metics was blocked on a technicality (Aristotelian *Constitution of Athens* 40.2). According to the Old Oligarch (1.12), metics were allowed freedom of speech, but it was also understood that when in Athens one should do as Athens did. In the speech already quoted from, Euripides (*Medeia* 222) has Medeia say: 'The *xenos* must comply fully with the community.'

What did Athenians think about the institution of the *metoikia*? Thucydides, the Old Oligarch and Xenophon recognised the usefulness of metics. Aristophanes was friendly towards them: as flour and bran were both necessary for making good bread, so Athens needed both citizens and metics (*Akharnians* 507f.). Despite his law of 451/0, Perikles could claim with truth (Thucydides 2.39.1) that Athens never had recourse to the Spartan practice of expelling immigrants.

It was, however, possible to recognise the usefulness of metics and yet to despise them, as the Old Oligarch (1.10) shows. Athenians who claimed to be autochthonous or sprung from the soil were bound to despise landless immigrants and especially those who came from foreign parts that supplied them with slaves.

The non-Greek proportion of the metic population was increased by the freeing, or manumission, of slaves. Freedmen became metics. A slave freed in his master's lifetime, very likely on terms, had to have him for his *prostates* or risk prosecution by him (*dike apostasiou*). It was common enough for a slave 'living apart' to buy his freedom out of his accumulated earnings. Very occasionally the community might free, and even enfranchise, a group of slaves, such as those who fought in the sea-battle at Arginousai in 406, it being thought incongruous that those who had rendered the supreme service should remain socially inferior (Xenophon, *Greek History* 1.6.24; Aristophanes, *Frogs* 33, 191, 693f.). Slaves could also earn their freedom by denouncing certain heinous crimes, such as treason or sacrilege.

In Athenian thinking, metic status was associated with barbarian, if not servile, origins. It was more closely associated with *banausia*, which was, roughly, having to earn a living by practising a craft, as opposed, pre-eminently, to being a gentleman farmer.

Strictly speaking a metic was a *xenos*. The word '*xenos*' had a wide range of meaning – 'Greek foreigner', 'metic', 'personal guest-friend', 'ally'. Ignoring the second and third senses for the moment, we have to recognise the presence in Athens of foreigners who were there for too short a time to become metics – merchants, craftsmen, tourists, intellectuals and the like – and of allied oarsmen, who rowed with the fleet but wintered at home. It seems that a typical Athenian crew was composed of poor citizens, poor metics and allies, but in what proportions we cannot say. Before the Congress of Allies of Sparta in 432 the Corinthian delegation declared, according to Thucydides (1.121.3): 'The power of Athens is more mercenary than native.' If this was true, and other evidence in Thucydides (7.63.3) suggests that it may have been, it might be thought to follow that more than half of the 60,000 men who would have been needed fully to man the 300 seaworthy warships that Athens possessed in 431 (Thucydides 2.13.8) were *xenoi*, in the sense of allies; but Athens would never have had all 300 triremes at sea simultaneously. We may perhaps assume that during the first ten years of the Peloponnesian War, from the start of the sailing and campaigning season, there arrived up to 10,000 *xenoi*, mostly allies lodging in Peiraieus and hoping to be taken on as oarsmen in the fleet. Not surprisingly, Athenian literature has little to say about them, but one of the qualifications of the dead but blessed Initiates in Aristophanes' *Frogs* (456ff.) was that on earth they had been respectful towards strangers. Allies involved in legal disputes with Athenians in Athens will have been covered by agreements on procedure (*symbola*) between Athens and the allied cities, but any other *xenoi* will have had no standing in Athenian law.

Metics occupied a position in society between the citizens and their slaves. Most slaves belonged to citizen or metic *oikoi*, but some were temple slaves, and some belonged to the community. Some slaves were home-bred, but most were imported. They were of various provenances, including Thessaly, Thrace, Skythia, Phrygia, Karia and Paphlagonia. Into the hands of the slave-trader fell victims of war, piracy, kidnapping or parental greed or poverty (Herodotos 5.6.1). On arrival, at least, most of them were unable to speak Greek (*barbaroi*). Since the legislation of Solon (Arkhon in 594), it had been illegal for a citizen to be reduced to slavery, a fate little better than death. But such a fate could overtake a metic who was discovered to have no *prostates*, or who failed to pay his *metoikion*, or any *xenos* who was detected posing as a citizen.

Something is known about the price of slaves in 414, when the confiscated possessions of men convicted of parodying the Eleusinian Mysteries or mutilating the Herms of Athens were sold. The particulars were given in a long inscription on ten slabs or *stelai* set up in the Eleusinion and sometimes known as the Attic Stelai. Kephisodoros, a metic resident in Peiraieus, had had at least sixteen slaves, and fifteen of the prices are preserved. Two Syrian men fetched the highest prices: 301 and 240 *drakhmai*. Three Thracian women fetched 220, 165 and

135 *drakhmai*. A young Karian boy (*paidion* is probably literal) fetched only 72 *drakhmai*. Clearly, men who earned less than a *drakhme* a working day were not in a position to buy such slaves.

According to the Old Oligarch (1.10) it was hard to tell a slave (or a metic or freedman) from a middle- or lower-class citizen either by his dress or by his looks. The similarity of dress is not surprising in view of the known overlap of occupation: citizen and slave artisans worked at the same tasks for the same wages, as we can see from the Erekhtheion building accounts. Nor need the similarity of looks be wholly fanciful: there is a connection between good looks and membership of the upper class – a connection which may owe something to more favourable living conditions and diet.

Slaves could take part in the Pithoigia, the first day of the spring festival of Dionysos (compare Euripides, *Bakkhai* 421ff.), and, if Greek, could be initiated into the Eleusinian Mysteries. They could not, however, use the three gymnasia of Athens (Aiskhines 1.138): it would have been incongruous to allow supposedly inferior beings to enjoy the physical and moral benefits conferred by athletic activity. Home-born slaves were unlikely to receive much education. In law slaves were little more than chattels. In the passage just referred to, the Old Oligarch records ruefully that it was illegal to strike another man's slave. Such an act might result in a prosecution for wanton assault. Still less was it legal to kill another man's slave. Nor was a master allowed to kill his own slave, and, if he did so, he had at least to undergo purification (Antiphon 6.4): the murder of *any* human being was offensive to the gods. Against lesser injury by his master a slave had no redress, beyond seeking asylum at the Theseion or at the altar of the Furies or Eumenides on the Areopagos (Aristophanes, *Knights* 1312), where he could beg a third party to buy him from his master. A runaway slave who was recaptured could expect to be branded. A slave could not, of course, plead in court, and his evidence was normally admitted only after torture, the theory apparently being that it was necessary to make him more afraid of the community than of his master.

The social position of the public slaves seems to have approximated to that of metics. They were petty civil servants: the public clerk who worked for the Council and helped the sellers and receivers (two boards of magistrates) and other such clerks, the public executioner, workers in the mint and the 300 Skythian archers, first imported in about 450 to keep order in the Assembly, the Council and the courts, who were stationed on the Areopagos.

The bulk of privately owned slaves were engaged in domestic service. In large *oikoi* male slaves would serve as porters, stewards, cooks and *paidagogoi*. Female slaves had to clean the house, fetch water from well or public fountain, grind corn, knead and bake, spin and weave. Either male or female slaves might do the household shopping or serve at meals. Male slaves would attend their masters in the streets and female slaves their mistresses. If his master were returning from a drinking-party (symposion), the slave would have to carry a lamp or torch, there being no street-lighting. On longer trips, including military expeditions, there would be baggage to carry, perhaps slung from each end of a pole. In oikoi employing both male and female slaves, sexual intercourse between them was controlled, permission to have children being used as a reward for good slaves (Xenophon, Oikonomikos 9.5).

A smallish class of mainly female slaves provided private entertainment: dancing girls and aulos-girls (who could be hired for the evening from their owner to provide cabaret) and, not wholly distinguishable from them, prostitutes.

As we have seen, estates tended to fragment. Many smallholdings in Attike were therefore too small to support a slave all the year round; instead, recourse might be had at specially busy times to hired labour, servile or free. No doubt, however, all those smallholders (autourgoi) who could possibly afford either a maid or an extra male hand did so. The bulk of agricultural slaves must have been concentrated in a fairly small number of large estates – few of them bigger than 70 acres – run for their owners by slave stewards.

In addition to slaves engaged in clerical work for the community, there was a small class of educated slaves similarly engaged in banks and business houses.

Many slave artisans worked in workshops. The largest such establishment known to us is the shield-factory left by their father to the metic brothers Lysias and Polemarkhos. Their slave labour force numbered nearly 120: the Peloponnesian War had ensured a constant heavy demand for their product. Nearly all industrial establishments were very much smaller – mere workshops hardly distinguishable from the house to which they were attached – if they were not actually part of it. Xenophon (Reminiscences 2.3.3) makes Sokrates say that those who can afford to do so buy slaves to help them with their work. Presumably, self-employed craftsmen would hope to make enough to buy a slave whom they could train as a fellow-worker, and on whose earnings they would eventually be able to live in retirement. 'I cannot yet', says a crippled tradesmen for whom Lysias (24.6) wrote a speech, 'afford to buy a slave to take over my trade.' There is no evidence of workshops that employed many slaves trying to undercut their smaller rivals.

Sometimes slave artisans went out to work alongside their masters, as his five slaves worked alongside the mason Simias on the Erekhtheion. All six earned the same wage, but all the wages belonged to Simias. Other slave artisans, living apart from the oikos in places perhaps of their own choosing, paid their owners a fixed return (apophora) each day, but were allowed to keep any additional money they could make, and might hope in due course to purchase their freedom out of their accumulated earnings. A fair price would have been the cost of their own replacement. There was little danger of their undercutting their free rivals, because of the *apophora* that they had to pay to their owners. Xenophon (*Reminiscences* 3.11.4) makes Sokrates class slave artisans with land and housing as sources of income.

Another way of investing in slaves was to buy some with a view to hiring them out to entrepreneurs at a fixed rate. Nikias is said (Xenophon, *Ways and Means* 4.14) to have owned 1,000 slaves, whom he leased to a mining entrepreneur for 1 obol (one-sixth of a *drakhme*) a day, the lessee feeding and clothing them and replacing casualties. If so high a figure as 1,000 may be believed, and Xenophon clearly expected his readers to believe it, it was no doubt the highest known. This was a profitable form of investment, since unskilled slaves cost no more than 140 *drakhmai* to purchase initially, and no more to replace when they grew too old to work. But an entrepreneur might well have been glad not to have to buy slaves outright. There is again no sign of slave-owners undercutting free hired labourers (*misthotoi*) except where employment was continuous, as in the mines, where *misthotoi* are never heard of. Normal economic relations between slave and *misthotos* are illustrated in Aristophanes' *Frogs* (167ff.), where the Corpse is willing to relieve the slave Xanthias of the burden of Dionysos' luggage, but only if Dionysos is willing to pay him the exhorbitant sum of 2 *drakhmai*. In other words, the *misthotos* will do a piece of slavish work, when he is satisfied with the reward offered.

Many thousands of slaves worked in the silver mines in Laureion. The community owned the mines and leased concessions. To work a concession of any size, the lessee would need the help of slaves, either owned by himself or hired from a big owner like Nikias. (Conditions in Laureion were frightful, though certainly not more so than in other ancient mines. The miners worked with primitive tools in narrow, stifling, murky galleries. At the surface fumes from the smelting works destroyed the surrounding vegetation, and the solace of female company was unknown.)

Finally, we may be sure that there was a servile class of seamen, dockers and carriers, but detailed information is lacking.

Such in outline was Athenian slavery. At least four questions arise.

First, how dependent on slavery was Athens? One reason why we hear nothing of slave revolts is that the slaves did not outnumber free people, though they may have outnumbered free men. Plato (*Republic* 578de) considers the perilous plight of a rich man and his family isolated somewhere with their fifty or more slaves, but lower-class Athenians had no slaves, and lower-middle-class Athenians only one or two.

Slavery was more widespread in fantasy than in reality. The dream of living on slaves resembled the dream of winning a huge prize in a lottery in being more widely entertained than fulfilled. All the same, it is evident that, deprived of slaves, the community would have lost much of the revenue that it had previously derived from the leasing of concessions in Laureion and that all its richest members, not to mention their wives, would have faced an enormous drop in their standard of living. Radical democracy (chapter 3) could not have survived: either the rich, who had previously been free to devote most of their time to the affairs of the community, would have had to concentrate on the affairs of their *oikoi*, or the poor, who had previously been full citizens, would have had to sink to a condition closer to slavery.

Second, how did the Athenians treat their slaves? Despite the opinion of the Old Oligarch (1.10) that in Athens there was the utmost licence among slaves, and despite Plato's description (*Republic* 563b), composed no doubt with one eye on his native city, of a democracy so extreme that purchased slaves, male and female, were every bit as free as their purchasers, we can hardly doubt that the tendency of power to corrupt operated in Athens as elsewhere. Nor should much be made of the fact that no one seems to have feared that the slaves of Athens might revolt. One reason has just been given: there were many fewer slaves than free people. And the situation of the slaves of Athens was quite different from that of the Helots of Sparta, who may have outnumbered the free population, in another respect too. Greek-speaking slaves born in Attike were a small minority. People torn from their families and traditions and speaking a babel of languages do not readily combine for revolt.

They may, however, desert. One justification given by Athens for her decree of 433/2 excluding the citizens of Megara from the Agora of Athens and from the harbours of the empire was that Megara had given refuge to runaway slaves (Thucydides 1.139.2). In Aristophanes' *Clouds* (6f.) Strepsiades says, with the annual Peloponnesian invasions in mind: 'Curse you, war, for many reasons, including the fact that I can't now punish my slaves.' If a slave might not be beaten by anyone else, he might certainly be beaten by his master. Within perhaps a year of the establishment of the permanent Peloponnesian post at Dekeleia (midway between Athens and the Boiotian frontier) in 413 'more than 20,000 slaves had deserted, most of them skilled hands' (Thucydides 7.27.5). Given that the deserters can have had little ground for confidence that they would be very well treated by the Peloponnesians and Boiotians, this is strong evidence of discontent. Even if we allow that half the deserters were mine-workers, that still leaves 10,000 others, whose conditions were less frightful. It was obviously hardest for domestic slaves to desert, and in some cases there will have been little inclination. A newly purchased domestic slave was welcomed into the *oikos* like a bride by the mistress showering nuts and figs over him. He was thereby admitted to the religious life of the family, and the gesture was not hypocritical. The slaves of Alkestis regarded her as a mother (*Alkestis* 769f.). Finally, for the slaves that lived apart there was the prospect of earning their freedom. Such slaves will have had no motive to revolt and little to desert.

Third, what did the Athenians think about the institution? In Aristophanes' *Frogs*, the slave Xanthias ('Ginger') is represented as brave, clever and, up to a point, loyal. In Plato's *Menon* (82ff.) Sokrates, who in reality may not have attached great value to mathematics, is made to test the geometrical understanding of an uneducated slave-boy. Whether the experiment proves as much as Plato thinks it does is a question, but it certainly proves the rationality of a not untypical domestic slave. (Like Homer's Trojans, the slave is made to speak Greek simply to facilitate communication; it is not implied that a barbarian slave would have done less well for any reason but ignorance of the language.) We may therefore wonder how most Athenians managed to convince themselves that slavery was natural in that all (and only) barbarians were slaves by nature. 'Barbarians are slaves, but Greeks are free,' says Iphigeneia in a play of Euripides (*Iphigeneia in Aulis* 1401). A partial justification was afforded by the belief that subjects of an absolute monarch like the Great King of Persia were *eo ipso* slaves. Furthermore, the triumphant outcome of the Persian Wars, the more glorious for having been generally unforeseen, reinforced the notion, derived from the experience of the colonists from Old Greece who during the period from about 750 to 550 had settled round the shores of the Mediterranean, that barbarians were inferior to Greeks in courage and culture. Again, the life they led would sap the self-respect and initiative of nearly all slaves. The ultimate justification was no doubt the crude doctrine that might confers right.

If only barbarians were designed by nature for slavery, it should have followed that Athenians did not enslave other Greeks. But although Plato (*Republic* 469bc) drew the correct conclusion, most Athenians did not. In 427 the Assembly voted, on the advice of Kleon, to execute all the citizens of the rebel city of Mytilene, and to enslave the women and children (Thucydides 3.36.2). This decision was reversed the next day. But in 416 a similar decision was carried out, and with less justification: Mytilene had left the Athenian alliance at a time of crisis, Melos, as far as we know, merely refused to join it in time of peace.

One might have expected the free poor of Athens to feel, and to express in the Assembly, resentment of the competition of slaves; for it can hardly be doubted that the existence of slave labour did depress their earnings and so lengthen their hours. But this did not happen, partly because they assumed that the profits of empire would continue to supplement their incomes by providing pay for rowing in the fleet and for holding public office. To ensure that they did, almost any means, including the execution and enslavement of Greeks, were justified. And in partial defence of the Assembly it should be added that, as Xenophon (*Education of Kyros* 7.5.73) put it: 'It is the universal and unchanging custom of men that when a city is captured in war, the citizens' persons and property belong to the captors.'

There were some thinkers and poets in Athens who rejected racialism, nationalism and snobbery, although we need not suppose that they themselves owned no slaves. 'One thing only', says a character in Euripides' *Ion* (854ff.), 'brings disgrace on a slave – the name. In all else an honest slave is a match for a free man.' And in a fragment of Euripides: 'I count an honest man my friend, even if he lives in a remote part of the world, and I never set eyes on him.' These sentiments were in line with the teaching of some of the itinerant professors called Sophists. Hippias, who believed in the natural kinship and amity of all Greeks, if not all men (Plato, *Protagoras* 337cd), regarded as God-given or unwritten only those laws and customs that were observed universally (Xenophon, *Reminiscences* 4.4.19); so presumably he denied special excellence to the laws and customs of any particular city. Antiphon the Sophist (44, fragment B, column 2) somewhat obscurely said: 'We respect and revere the sons of noble fathers, whereas we neither respect nor revere the sons of a humble house. In this we have become barbarous to one another, since by nature we are all of us in all respects equally adapted to be barbarians or Greeks.' By contrast, Sokrates appears to have accepted slavery without question.

A fourth question is: how did slavery affect Athenian attitudes to other matters?

In the first place, it further clouded the evaluation of different contributions to society, by adding to the age-old belief that to earn payment (*misthos*) from another man (though not perhaps from the community) was degrading the newer belief that the typical occupations of slaves were degrading. The admired style of life was to derive a large enough income from landed property to be able to afford the panoply of a heavy infantryman (hoplite) if not horses, and to have leisure for political, if not intellectual, activity. Inheriting landed property may not seem to thoughtful people to be a praiseworthy achievement, but most of those who do inherit property manage to convince themselves of the superiority of their own kind. This belief may be bolstered by a further belief, that alternative styles of living are physically and morally harmful. In such a context developed the notion of the 'banausic' occupation. This was essentially a sedentary, indoor occupation, very likely involving the use of fire. Such an occupation was held by some to deform and weaken both body and soul (Xenophon, *Oikonomikos* 4.2). Xenophon makes Sokrates condemn (*Reminiscences* 4.2.22) smiths, carpenters and cobblers as for the most part 'slavish' because of their ignorance of beauty, goodness and justice. This condemnation of the life of the artisan was not a condemnation of all manual work: the respect which Euripides and Aristophanes expressed for the small farmer working his own land (*autourgos*) was shared, at least up to a point, by the gentleman farmer if not by Plato and Aristotle. It might, however, easily develop into such a condemnation. One of the marks of the objectivity of Thucydides is his ready recognition, the more striking because he was a member of the upper class, that it was on the well-disciplined skill of her oarsmen that the power of the city rested. Most members of the upper class, although willing enough to serve as generals, or at least trierarchs, were more inclined to the hostile opinions later voiced by Plato in *Laws* (706a–707c).

Secondly, the presence in the community of large numbers of slaves, not all of them ignorant barbarians, was a constant reminder of the fact that only the naval and military strength of the city stood between its citizens and their families and the same fate. The enslavement of Hekabe, queen of legendary Troy, was a symbol of present possibility. This radical uncertainty about status helps to explain the pessimistic tone of much Athenian moralising. Solon had said, 'Call no man happy until he is dead' (Herodotos 1.86.3). Little was heard of the last being first; the emphasis fell on the possibility of the first being last.

Thirdly, the chasm between slave-owners, actual or potential, and slaves was so wide as to help to explain the brutal frankness of much that was said in the Assembly about the relationship between Athens and her subject allies. As the essential fact about a slave seemed to be that he had to take the orders of his master, so the essential fact about the subject allies seemed to be that they had to take the orders of Athens (see chapter 4).

It would enormously increase our understanding of Athens, if we could establish how numerous the different elements of the population were. Unfortunately, it is unlikely that this will ever be possible. In arriving at approximate figures for citizens and metics, some of the relevant considerations, most of them derived from Thucydides book 2, are these:

(i) At the outbreak of the Peloponnesian War, when Athens had 300 seaworthy triremes (compare Aristophanes, *Akharnians* 545), there were presumably as many trierarchs each year, and each year some seventy-five other very rich men will have been needed to discharge the major festival liturgies. No one was required to perform more than one liturgy in a single year, or, apparently (Demosthenes 20.8), to perform liturgies in successive years. So there must have been at least 750 very rich men in Athens. Multiplying by four (to allow for women, children and old men no longer running their households), we get a liturgical or upper class of 3,000. This class may be taken to correspond to the highest of Solon's four orders of Pentakosiomedimnoi, Hippeis, Zeugitai, Thetes.

(ii) Corresponding to Solon's Hippeis, we may assume a much larger upper-middle class of those occasionally called on to discharge minor festival liturgies, together with their families, of, say 12,000.

(iii) Athens had 1,000 cavalrymen, recruited from the youngest and fittest men in the top two Solonian orders.

(iv) In 431 Athens had an effective hoplite strength of 14,000, including 1,000 serving in garrisons at home and abroad. Fighting in hoplite armour was very strenuous, and we may assume that of the men in the top three Solonian orders aged from twenty to forty-nine, and so liable for call-up as hoplites, many were unfit for active service. In computing the total number of men aged from twenty to forty-nine, we must allow for the 1,000 cavalrymen, some 1,500 unfit for active service, and some 1,500 exempt (men under fifty who were discharging liturgies or serving as councillors or magistrates). This gives us 18,000.

(v) In 431 there were apparently 16,000 men available for manning the thirteen or more miles of walls. From this number, we must subtract some 6,000 metics (see (ix)), some 1,500 citizens aged from twenty to forty-nine but fit only for manning the walls, and the 1,500 exempt from active service. This gives us some 7,000 citizens aged eighteen or nineteen or fifty to fifty-nine. Adding those 7,000 to the 18,000 aged twenty to forty-nine, we get 25,000. Multiplying by four, we get 100,000 for the total number in the top three Solonian orders – Pentakosiomedimnoi, Hippeis, Zeugitai.

(vi) In 431 most Athenians had houses in the country, though this did not preclude some of them from having a *pied-à-terre*, or something better, in Athens or Peiraieus.

(vii) Estimating the number of Thetes is very difficult, partly because we do not know what proportion of the sailors were Thetes or what proportion of the Thetes were sailors, and partly because we do not know the rate at which men rose, or were raised by the community, from the order of Thetes to that of Zeugitai. But only a few thousand Thetes seem to have lived in the country, and they may not have numbered more than about 70,000 in all.

(viii) We are told that in 445/4 14,240 Athenians (nearly all of them Thetes, we may assume) received the corn given by Psammetikhos. Multiplying by four gives some 57,000, which tallies well enough with a total of 70,000 in 431.

(ix) The effective hoplite strength of the metics was at least 3,000 (Thucydides 2.31.2). The total number of metics aged twenty to forty-nine with hoplite armour was perhaps half as many again: 4,500. Therefore, adding another 1,500 to give the total number of men with hoplite armour aged from eighteen to fifty-nine, we get 6,000. Multiplying by three-and-a-half, we get some 20,000.

(x) Bearing in mind what the Old Oligarch (1.12) says about the navy's dependence on the metics and the fact that most freedmen will have become metic Thetes, it seems reasonable to assume as many metic Thetes as hoplites.

From now on we shall be mainly concerned with the citizens, and first with the social and economic setting of their cultural achievement.

For primitive people an enormously important question is 'Who are my kin?' and in fifth-century Athens the question was still important, though less so than it had been.

At the end of the sixth century Kleisthenes had carried legislation creating a new political structure of some 140 demes, grouped in thirty *trittyes* or thirds or ridings (ten in each of three regions – Asty (Urban), Paralia (Coastal), Mesogeios (Inland)), and ten *phylai* or tribes, each composed of three ridings (one from each region). Each tribe was named after an Attic hero. Most *trittyes* were named after the principal or only deme within them.

The *trittyes* of three tribes may be tabulated thus:

	V *Akamantis*	VI *Oineis*	VIII *Hippothontis*
Asty	Kholargos	Lakiadai	Peiraieus
Paralia	Thorikos	Thria	Eleusis
Mesogeios	Sphettos	Pedion	Dekeleia

The Roman numerals give the place of each tribe in the official order of tribes. Akamas, Oineus and Hippothoön were sons of Theseus, Pandion (a legendary king of Athens) and the sea-god Poseidon. Kholargos was the deme of Perikles, and Lakiadai that of Kimon. The name 'Pedion', meaning 'Plain', conceals the *trittys*, and deme, of Akharnai.

The rural *trittyes* appear to have been more or less natural units, and sometimes, as perhaps in Akamantis, the Coastal and Inland *trittyes* of one tribe were adjacent. More often, however, they were not, and the tribes may appear to us artificial. The rural demes, on the other hand, were certainly natural units, and they were now given their own political structure. Each year the demesmen appointed their own chairman or demarch and lesser officials. The deme stood to the *polis* as local to national and as microcosm to macrocosm. In the country many Athenians would rarely look beyond their own deme, but those with political ambitions would gain useful experience in the deme and be eager to represent it on the Council in Athens. To keep the new tribes, and consequently the new tribal regiments, roughly the same size, Kleisthenes made membership of a deme hereditary and independent of any change of residence.

Though his legislation had important social implications, Kleisthenes did not tamper with the immemorial kinship structure. In this the basic unit was the household (oikos), consisting of master (kyrios), mistress, children, elderly parents, slaves, animals, allotment of land (kleros). A number of oikoi whose kyrioi traced their descent from a common, legendary, ancestor constituted a clan (genos). Larger than the genos was the phratry (phratria, brotherhood), containing both genos-members (gennetai) and their social inferiors. Finally, a number of phratries constituted one of the four old Attic or Ionic tribes (phylai). It was supposed that these four tribes had been founded by the sons of Ion, who was himself the son of Apollo.

After the legislation of Kleisthenes, the significance of the kinship structure was mainly religious. Though it was a source of embarrassment not to belong to a phratry, membership was no longer a necessary condition of citizenship. On the other hand, it was only the phratry-lists that recorded the status of the wives and young sons of citizens (Isaios 8.18f). The principal phratry festival was the Apatouria or Gathering of Fathers, which lasted for three days (Dorphia, Anarrhysis, Koureotis). At this festival the members of a phratry met to worship Zeus Phratrios and Athenaia Phratria (Plato, Euthydemos 302d) and also Zeus Herkeios (Protector of the Fence) and Apollo Patroös (Father of the Community). On the third day, probably named after the symbolic shearing of the young men's hair, the 'brothers' voted on the enrolling of sons born to members during the previous year, of newly 'adult' young men (about sixteen), and of newly married wives.

As we have seen, only citizens could own land, and land was their main source of income. Being a large land-owner involved privileges and duties.

Solon had converted Athens from an aristocracy to a timocracy. Whereas previously eligibility for high office had depended on birth, it was thenceforth to depend on yield from landed property. Solon divided the citizen body into four parts, defining his four orders or census-classes in terms of measures, dry or wet (medimnoi or metretai – these were measures of capacity equal to about 1½ bushels and 8 imperial gallons respectively) of grain, wine or oil. (That he considered only agricultural wealth, and only these forms of it, tells us much about the state of the Athenian economy at the beginning of the sixth century.) Men so rich that their land yielded 500 or more measures Solon called Pentakosiomedimnoi – a new degree of prosperity perhaps earning a new word. Those whose land yielded 300–500 measures were Hippeis (cavalry). Those whose land yielded 200–300 measures were Zeugitai (hoplites). Those whose land, if any, yielded less than 200 measures were Thetes.

The main purpose of defining these four orders was to make it possible to define eligibility for the chief magistracies in terms of the orders. In accordance with the assumption that only the richest men could be relied on not to embezzle public money, Solon laid it down that the chief financial officers of the community, the Treasurers of Athena, should be drawn from the first order; but the chief magistrates of all, the nine Arkhons, could probably be drawn from the first two orders. Furthermore, the supreme court and council of the Areopagos, so called from its place of meeting, was thenceforth to be recruited from ex-Arkhons. One sign that the orders still counted for something in the fifth century is that in 458, by which time both Arkhons and Areopagos had lost most of their old importance to the generals and the popular jury-courts, the Arkhonship, and therewith the Areopagos, was opened to Zeugitai. Another is the amendment to a decree (ML 49), specifying that membership of a new colony should be open to Zeugitai as well as Thetes.

At the outbreak of the Peloponnesian War, the annual public income of Athens is believed to have been some 1,000 talents made up of 600 talents from overseas (including the tribute paid by the subject allies) and 400 talents of internal revenue. The 400 talents included the price of mining concessions in Laureion together with the mining royalties, rents paid for the use of other land or property owned by the community, harbour dues at Peiraieus (1 per cent on incoming and outgoing goods), a tax on foreigners trading in the Agora, court fees (these were sums payable by both plaintiff and defendant in cases in which the plaintiff was seeking his own interest; both fees went towards paying the jurors, but the winning party was reimbursed by the loser) and fines, the proceeds from the sale of confiscated property, and the *metoikion*.

Two other internal sources of revenue were of greater social significance: *eisphorai* and liturgies. An *eisphora* was an extraordinary war-tax, voted by the Assembly and levied on property. But on what kinds of property? Had it been levied on landed property only, metics would have been exempt, but they were not (Lysias 12.20). Solon had been able to ignore wealth that was not agricultural, but that would not have been realistic by the time of the Peloponnesian War. The basis of the tax was the individual's declared assessment of his taxable capital. (There was no public register of landed, or other, property.) *Eisphorai* were probably voted at least four times during the Peloponnesian War, starting in 428. Citizens resented direct taxation as an infringement of their independence, and we may assume that there was much reluctance to pay, but not necessarily that the burden was one that we should regard as heavy.

The other internal source of revenue was the (to us) curious institution of the liturgy (*leitourgia*, public service). It seems curious to us because it managed to do something that no modern tax-collector attempts – to make the tax-payer proud of his payment. In theory, and to a large extent in practice, the richest men in Athens were willing to perform various public services to the best of their ability, rather than in accordance with the letter of the law (Lysias 21.5). The services were either military or civilian. The one military liturgy was the trierarchy. A citizen appointed trierarch was for one year in at least nominal command of an Athenian warship. (He did not, like a councillor or juror, have to have reached the age of thirty.) The generals assigned him a trireme (some triremes being in much better condition than others, and some being destined to see much less action than others – Thucydides 2.24.2) together with its tackle. It was the trierarch's responsibility to maintain the vessel in good trim, and to engage and train, though not to pay or feed, the crew. The trierarchy was the most expensive of the liturgies, sometimes costing the best part of a talent. It would appear that at the beginning of the Peloponnesian War the Council must have appointed 300 trierarchs a year, whose expenditure on her warships saved Athens perhaps 100 talents a year.

The civilian liturgies seem all to have been connected with religious festivals. They include *arkhitheoria, gymnasiarkhia, hestiasis*, and, most important of all, *khoregia*. An *arkhitheoros* was responsible for leading and financing a delegation to a foreign religious festival – to one of the four Panhellenic festivals, which were held at Olympia, Delphi, Nemea and the Isthmos, or to Delos, birthplace of Apollo. A gymnasiarch was responsible for training and paying a team of runners for the inter-tribal torch-races that formed part of the Panathenaia, Hephaistia and Prometheia. A *hestiator* was responsible for feasting his tribe on the occasion of the Great Panathenaia or the principal festival of Dionysos, the City Dionysia.

A *khoregos* was an impresario (literally, a chorus-leader): he was responsible for selecting, training, paying or providing with ration-money (Old Oligarch 1.13), and costuming the fifteen members of a tragic chorus, the twenty-four members of a comic chorus, the fifty members of a dithyrambic chorus, or a team of pyrrhic dancers. In each case, strange though the notion of overt competition in a religious service may seem to us, he was competing with other *khoregoi* for victory. Pyrrhic dances were war-dances involving energetic play with a hoplite shield and leaps in the air, performed by men and by boys at the Panathenaia. Dithyrambs were hymns, in honour of Dionysos originally, sung at the Panathenaia, at the City Dionysia (by a men's chorus and a boys' chorus from each of the ten Kleisthenic tribes), and at Apollo's festival of the Thargelia (by a men's chorus and a boys' chorus from each of five pairs of tribes). Finally, *khoregoi* were responsible for the dramatic choruses, tragic and comic, at the Lenaia and City Dionysia. Part of an inscription recording the winners at the City Dionysia is preserved, and the entries for some years are complete. We can see that the order of information was fixed:

1 Arkhon (dating by year was done by naming the Arkhon then in office).
2 Boys' dithyrambs: winning tribe and *khoregos*
3 Men's dithyrambs: winning tribe and *khoregos*
4 Comedies: winning *khoregos* and poet
5 Tragedies: winning *khoregos* and poet and, from 449, winning protagonist or principal actor, who was not necessarily the protagonist of the winning poet.

Although internationally famous poets sometimes wrote the dithyrambs, their names were not recorded.

Just as a trierarch might well know little or nothing about warships, so a *khoregos* might be no expert on music or dancing; all that was necessary was sufficient will to win. We may compare the determination of a lord mayor of London to make his procession memorable. Xenophon (*Reminiscences* 3.4.3f.) makes Sokrates say of an ambitious *khoregos* that, although 'ignorant of singing and the training of choruses, he nevertheless managed to discover the people who were best at those activities', with the result that every time he was *khoregos*, his chorus won. According to Plutarch (*Nikias* 3.3), the wealthy Nikias won often and never lost.

Khoregoi had to be citizens, except in the case of the Lenaia, where they might be metics (and where alone aliens might dance in the chorus). In the case of tribal activities, such as the dithyrambic contests at the City Dionysia or *hestiasis*, *khoregoi* or *hestiatores* were appointed by their tribes, and otherwise by magistrates, as the Arkhon appointed the *khoregoi* for the dramatic contests at the City Dionysia.

Just how particular *khoregoi* were chosen from those eligible is unknown. Mistakes might occur: a man might already be performing another liturgy, or be less prosperous than had been supposed at the time of his appointment. Rectification could follow either through adjudication by a jury-court presided over by the magistrate concerned, or through the mechanism of exchange (*antidosis*), whereby if A were appointed to a liturgy but considered that B was better able to discharge it than himself, he could challenge B either to take on the liturgy or to exchange property. (The existence of this institution shows that there was no public register of property.)

The twenty *khoregoi* needed for the two dithyrambic contests at the City Dionysia were appointed by the tribes a month after the previous festival, but not for another three months did the new Arkhon take office. On taking office in midsummer, he received the *khoregoi* as the magistrate in charge of the whole festival, and he supervised their drawing of lots for choice of poet and *aulos*-player or aulete, neither of whom had to be an Athenian. The poet might or might not train the chorus himself. The *khoregoi* now had eight months in which to prepare. Assisted by tribal officials, they had to choose fifty singers from their tribe, and designate one of them leader (Demosthenes 21.60). In the case of boys, it might be necessary to bring pressure to bear on reluctant fathers (Antiphon 6.11). It seems that the services of a talented songster might be in demand for all three dithyrambic contests in the year for several years on end. Those chosen would need a room, in the house of the *khoregos* (Antiphon 6.11) or elsewhere, in which to practise. Apparently, members of a men's chorus were exempt from military service while they were in training.

The willingness of the *khoregos* to spend heavily on costumes for himself and his chorus would influence the outcome of the competition, and, partly because of the larger numbers involved, to produce a men's dithyrambic chorus was more expensive than to produce a tragic chorus. The victorious *khoregos* received, on behalf of his tribe, a bronze tripod. This he might set up at his own expense on a monument, with a suitable inscription. In 476 Simonides of Keos had been poet for a successful *khoregos*, and he composed three elegiac couplets for the inscription. In English prose they run: 'Adeimantos was Arkhon at Athens when the Antiokhid tribe won the handsome tripod; on that occasion Aristeides, son of Xenophilos, was *khoregos* of the well-trained chorus of fifty men; and because of that training glory attended Simonides, the 85-year-old son of Leoprepes.'

The Basileus appointed the seven *khoregoi* for the Lenaia, and the Arkhon, on coming into office, appointed the eight dramatic *khoregoi* for the City Dionysia (Aristotelian *Constitution of Athens* 56.3). Like the twenty dithyrambic *khoregoi*, these eight *khoregoi* had eight months in which to prepare. They were responsible only for the fifteen or twenty-four members of the chorus, together with their aulete and, if he were not the poet himself, their trainer, and not for selecting, paying, training or costuming the actors.

About a hundred civilian liturgies were performed each year, at an average cost of hardly less than 1,000 *drakhmai*, which is to say that by this method the community raised the equivalent of some 16 talents a year. In a speech (Lysias 21) made in his own defence, a young man describes his uniquely heavy expenditure on liturgies in the decade from 411 to 402. If we take his figures and halve them, we get an expenditure of nearly 7 talents by twenty-eight *khoregoi* on the contests at the City Dionysia:

Boys' dithyramb	$1{,}500 \times 10 = 15{,}000$
Men's dithyramb	$5{,}000 \times 10 = 50{,}000$
Comic chorus	$1{,}600 \times 5 = 8{,}000$
Tragic chorus	$3{,}000 \times 3 = \underline{9{,}000}$
	$2|\ \underline{82{,}000}$

41,000 *drakhmai*

It is harder to estimate the direct expenditure of the community on these contests, but it may have been a little less. The dithyrambic tripods were expensive, but it is not quite certain that at Athens victorious dithyrambic poets received a bull as they did elsewhere. All competing dramatic poets received honoraria (Aristophanes, *Frogs* 367) of unknown value. Whether the prize of the winning poet amounted to more than a crown of ivy is not known. If, as is probable (pseudo-Plutarch 841f.), one of the comic protagonists or principal actors was chosen at the festival of the Anthesteria only a few weeks earlier, it appears that the actors rehearsed for a very much shorter time than the choruses. On the other hand, although the actors did not eclipse the poets in importance until the fourth century, they were greatly gifted and presumably well paid. The value of the winning tragic protagonist's prize is unknown.

The system of civilian liturgies worked well. Xenophon (*Reminiscences* 3.3.12) makes Sokrates say: 'whenever a national chorus is formed, like the one we send to Delos, no chorus from anywhere else is a match for it . . . .'

It would be naive to ascribe the undoubted zeal of many performers of liturgies solely to piety or philanthropy. The institution reflected the competitive spirit of the society. Most rich Athenians rose to the bait of honour. They could take a pride in the visible fruits of their expenditure such as no modern tax-payer can take when the drop or drops that he has contributed can no longer be distinguished in the national bucket. Their role resembled that of our sponsoring firms. The ambitious *khoregos* hoped to achieve brilliance and popular favour that might help to secure election to office or, if the need arose, acquittal in a jury-court. 'My reason', says a defendant for whom Lysias wrote a speech (25.12), 'for spending more than the community required was that you should regard me as more of a benefactor, and that, should some misfortune befall me, I might give a better account of myself in court.'

We should be surprised if a rich man in a modern dock tried to introduce the subject of how much he had paid the state in income tax or given to charity. We should be glad when the judge ruled that such evidence was irrelevant, and we should in any case feel that it was as much evidence of good luck as of good will. In another speech of Lysias (26.4) the point is made that heavy expenditure on liturgies is a means whereby an enemy of the people can win the trust of the people. In general, Athenians attributed riches and especially newly won riches, to good luck rather than to divine favour (human fortune was so obviously mutable), but provided that the rich spent enough of their riches on the community and the poor, the poor were well satisfied. The story of the Widow's Mite (Mark 12[41-4]) would not have been appreciated by anyone except Sokrates.

It was fortunate for the self-esteem of the Athenian upper class that this was the attitude of other Athenians to riches. The power of the city now rested not on the 1,000 cavalry, nor on the 14,000 hoplites, but on the oarsmen. It is true that the generals, who were also admirals of the largest navy in Greece, were members of the upper class, but most members of the upper class were prominent neither in action nor in debate. All they could do was to spend heavily on maintaining the warships rowed by the oarsmen or on providing popular entertainments, many of them, as Plutarch (*Perikles* 11.4) allows, 'not uninspired'.

Only a critic as crude as the Old Oligarch (1.13) could look on the dithyrambic and dramatic contests and the preliminary training for them merely as circumstances in which the rich had to pay the poor for singing and dancing. There arise also questions about the quality of performance and about communal involvement in the arts. Not all the 16 talents, if that was the sum, raised in civilian liturgies went on strictly 'cultural' activities – there were also the torch-races and the feasts, but, as we have seen, more than a third of the sum did go on the cultural contests at one festival. There were in addition dramatic contests at the Lenaia and dithyrambic contests at the Thargelia and Panathenaia. That magistrates, *khoregoi*, poets, trainers and performers were working, nominally at least, to the greater glory of the gods is true, but other gods than those of Athens would have been satisfied more easily.

· 3 ·

Radical Democracy

Constitution

The legislation introduced by <u>Kleisthenes in 508</u> established, for the citizens, a form of democracy that may be called 'moderate' by contrast with that introduced by <u>Ephialtes in 462</u>, which may be called 'radical'.

The main fact about radical democracy is this: all major matters of public policy were settled by the voting at meetings, regular or extraordinary, of the Assembly (Ekklesia). All citizens of good standing who were present at the meeting-place on the Pnyx were entitled to vote. There was a Council (Boule) of 500 to draw up the agenda for the Assembly, but it can hardly be said to have controlled the Assembly because the convention that the Assembly could pass decrees only on matters put before it by the Council in preliminary resolutions (*probouleumata*), though usually observed, was not very cramping, since the Assembly could amend or reject any such resolution and indeed instruct the Council to submit a *probouleuma* drafted on specified lines.

It is difficult for anyone living under a system of representative democracy which entitles him every five years or so either to vote for the man who has just finished representing him and 50,000 other electors (or for the successor that his party is putting forward in his place) or for one of a handful of alternative candidates, to get the feel of direct democracy. In Athens, questions of peace and war, of diplomacy, strategy and finance, some of them fairly complex, were resolved at open-air meetings attended by several thousand people.

Since the meetings were held in the open air, they might occasionally be broken off in the event of heavy rain. In peace-time, if a big issue was to be debated, an attendance of 6,000 (a quorum for a number of purposes) could be counted on. How even the most forceful speakers made themselves heard, speaking from a low platform to thousands of people sitting on the hillside before them, is a question. By the latter part of the fifth century there may have been as many as forty regular meetings a year. Big issues might take two days to resolve (Thucydides 1.44.1).

All meetings began with a consecrating ritual. Then the president for the day instructed the Herald of the Council and People to read out a *probouleuma*. If it made a recommendation and was not merely raising a matter, he next ascertained by a show of hands whether the Assembly wished to accept it as it stood or debate it. In the latter event he instructed the herald to ask 'Who wishes to speak?', as he did if the *probouleuma* merely raised a matter. All the citizens had the right to speak (*isegoria*), but we may be sure that only a well-endowed and confident minority dared to avail themselves of the privilege. It was a help to be good-looking, rich and well-born, but even with such advantages it was unwise to speak on technical questions if one was inadequately informed (Plato, *Protagoras* 319bc; Xenophon, *Reminiscences* 3.6). In the Funeral Speech, Thucydides (2.40.2) has Perikles distinguish between the few who can devise policies and the many who can judge them. Those who spoke regularly and built up a following were called 'the speakers' (*rhetores*) and became the nearest thing in Athens to professional politicians. Their speeches in the Assembly largely determined national policy, and yet they commonly held no public office and so were not accountable in the same way as magistrates. This, however, did not make them irresponsible: their prestige depended upon their recommending policies that proved successful. Thucydides (8.1) records that in 413 the Assembly was angry with the speakers who had joined Alkibiades in promoting the disastrous expedition to Sicily. Any speaker whose policy was adopted might be prosecuted for deceiving the people if that policy failed. Even the most persuasive speaker lived a precarious life: although one Assembly might decide for a policy of his, another, perhaps differently composed, might decide against it, and he had the support of no party to fall back on.

If we wish to know what debating in the Assembly was like, we cannot do better than read Thucydides', no doubt abridged and recast, versions of the speeches of Kleon and Diodotos in the second debate about the Mytileneans (3.36–49) and of Nikias and Alkibiades in the second debate about the Sicilian expedition (6.8–26), in their contexts. Perikles was the greatest orator: the comic poet Eupolis (fragment 94), writing long after his death, said, 'He alone of the speakers left his sting in his audience.' But though Thucydides gives us two or three of his speeches in the Assembly, he gives no opposing speech.

Legislatures must try to maintain consistency in their legislation, but it is not entirely clear how the fifth-century Assembly did this. In the fourth century a distinction was drawn between general laws (*nomoi*) and particular decrees (*psephismata*), and those, whether councillors or ordinary citizens, who moved decrees that were inconsistent with existing *nomoi* (or ill drafted or irregularly carried) were liable to face a prosecution for illegality (*graphe paranomon*) that any citizen who wished might bring. The earliest datable instance of the bringing of a *graphe para-*

nomon occurred in 415 (Andokides 1.17). This kind of prosecution may go back to 461, but just how it worked in the fifth century is not known.

To the sovereignty of the Assembly all the magistrates, at home and abroad, numbering several hundreds in all, had to bow. Their subordination was ensured in a variety of ways. Most civilian magistrates were appointed by the use of the lot (sortition) and did not enter office conscious of massive popular support. On a certain day, some months in advance, lots were drawn to determine which of those eligible who had submitted their names as wishing to hold a certain office should hold it. Most magistrates were members of annual boards or colleges of ten, all the members being equal in power. No magistrate appointed by sortition could hold the same office twice (rotation). The use of sortition was not, as in Acts 1[26], a way of committing the issue to heaven. It should rather be seen as a natural consequence of applying the principle of rotation to most of the numerous boards of magistrates. The Assembly could hardly be expected to take a keen interest once a year in deciding which citizens should have their turn at serving on all the different boards for the ensuing year. Furthermore, the scope of these magistracies was closely defined and made as small as was compatible with reasonable efficiency.

The sphere of finance affords a striking instance of this aspect of radical democracy. Instead of a chancellor of the exchequer assisted by junior ministers and the Treasury staff, we find a multiplicity of boards, normally ten-strong and annual: the exactors (Praktores), who collected fines; the sellers (Poletai), who sold confiscated property, mining rights, and rights to collect indirect taxes; the receivers (Apodektai), who received the revenue of the state; the paymasters (Kolakretai), who paid the jurors; the Treasurers (Tamiai) of Athena and, from 434, the Treasurers of the Other Gods, who looked after the financial reserves of Athens, which were stored in temples; the Treasurers of the Greeks (Hellenotamiai), who received the tribute from the subject allies.

A college of ten was responsible for the regulation of the markets in Athens and Peiraieus (Agoranomoi). Another college, known as the Eleven and composed of one member from each of the ten tribes and a secretary, supervised the state prison and the execution of death-sentences. The Eleven also dealt with various kinds of flagrant wrong-doing, including the theft of clothes from gymnasia – by execution without trial in the event of a confession.

The Arkhons (as the Arkhon, Basileus, Polemarch and six Thesmo-thetai were known collectively) antedated democracy and did not form a normal college. From 457/6 citizens in the top three Solonian orders were eligible for office. In 487/6 a hybrid method of appointing the Arkhons had been introduced: sortition, after direct election of perhaps ten candidates by each tribe. Later, they were appointed by double sortition; but the change of 487/6 had already destroyed the political importance of the office.

The Arkhon, literally 'ruler', who was still nominal head of state and after whom the year was named, managed the City Dionysia and was in charge of legal cases concerning households, property and inheritance among citizens. The Basileus, literally 'king', managed the Mysteries, the Lenaia and torch-races, and he was in charge of cases concerning religion, and especially cases concerning irreverence or homicide. The Polemarch, literally 'commander-in-chief', though he had been superseded in that capacity by the board of ten generals, arranged the public funeral ceremony in the Kerameikos for men killed in action, and he was in charge of cases concerning metics. The Thesmothetai were in charge of a wide range of cases not falling within the jurisdiction of the other Arkhons and especially cases concerning offences against the community. As we shall see, it was one mark of their subordination to the people, that the presidency of the three Arkhons, the Thesmothetai and the other magistrates in court was not more important than their preliminary hearings (*anakrisis*): it was the business of the magistrate(s) concerned to discover by interrogation just what was being alleged and just what points were in dispute. If the case fell within a magistrate's jurisdiction, he had to bring it before a jury-court.

The Assembly conceded something to expertness: it appointed its ambassadors, its architects, its boards for the supervision of public works, its doctors, its generals and other important military officers, such as the taxiarchs, who commanded the tribal regiments, by direct election rather than by sortition. Some of these appointments were extraordinary, but the chief military officers were elected annually. There was, furthermore, no bar on re-election. In a period of almost continuous warfare the competence of the board of ten generals (Strategoi) was obviously a matter of great national importance. It is true that the poet Sophokles was elected general for the year 441/0, which saw the outbreak of the revolt from the alliance of the island of Samos, but a peaceful year had been expected (Athens had been at peace with Persia since 449 and with the Peloponnesians since 446).

In theory all ten generals enjoyed equal powers, but in practice a general like Kimon or Perikles, who had been elected year after year, acquired higher standing, and was therefore able, for a time at least, to guide Athenian policy in a single direction. Kimon and Perikles combined the roles of general and speaker, but after the death of Perikles such versatility was found more rarely, and tension between generals and speakers was to weaken Athens. Many of the new speakers came from a manufacturing background, whereas most of the generals continued to come from the great houses. Alkibiades was as versatile as his guardian Perikles had been. He first made his mark in the Assembly in

420, when, as Thucydides (5.43.2) tells us, he was still young 'but honoured for the standing of his ancestors', and he was elected general for 420/19. Long hours spent in *palaistra* or gymnasium no doubt helped to reveal and develop strength and confidence in upper-class young men, and the Assembly believed, not altogether without reason, that military talent was commonly inherited. 'As for social standing,' said Perikles in the Funeral Speech (Thucydides 2.37.1), 'when a man is distinguished for something, his advancement in public life depends on merit rather than on rotation; but as for poverty, a man who can benefit the community is not debarred from doing so by the obscurity of his standing.' This was more nearly true in Athens than anywhere else, but in the fifth century no poor man became either a speaker or a general, and these were the pre-eminent roles in society.

For the first half of the fifth century, one general was elected *by* the Assembly *from* each tribe. But about 441 the rules appear to have changed, with some such result as this. Any candidate polling more than a certain minimum vote was deemed to have been elected *from* the whole people (*ex hapanton*) – that is, without prejudice to the electoral chances of other candidates from his own tribe. The tribe(s) to be unrepresented would be the one(s) whose most successful candidate(s) polled fewest votes. A likely reason for the change was a desire to save the city from being deprived of the services of any other very capable man in Perikles' tribe (V Akamantis). One result was no doubt yet higher standing for any candidate who was elected *ex hapanton*. There is no need to invoke extraordinary constitutional powers to explain Thucydides' famous words (2.65.9) about Perikles towards the end of his life: 'and what was nominally a democracy was turning into government by the leading citizen.'

High standing could not prevail over the constitution. Any magistrate could be removed from office by vote of the Assembly on any one of ten occasions during the year. In the second year of the Peloponnesian War the Assembly voted to reverse Perikles' policy of making no concessions to Sparta, and instead to sue for peace. Their overtures came to nothing, and after a fighting speech from Perikles the pacific mood passed. Nevertheless, they voted to refer the case of Perikles to a jury-court, which convicted and fined him (on a charge of embezzlement, according to Plato (*Gorgias* 516a)), and so kept him from office until the fine was paid. The situation in 430, with a plague raging, was extraordinary, but it was normal practice for the Assembly, and not the generals, to decide whether to go to war, whether to stay at war, what military expeditions, more or less precisely specified, to undertake and with what forces and under which generals.

Before taking up office, magistrates, who presumably had, like councillors and jurors, to be at least thirty years old, underwent a preliminary vetting (*dokimasia*) by Council (in the case of Arkhons) or jury-court, and on giving up underwent a final examination (*euthyna*). As part of the process of *euthyna* those magistrates who had handled public money had to submit their accounts to the board of thirty auditors (Logistai). The minimum age, the fact that *dokimasia* might involve an enquiry into character, the fact that *euthyna* might expose any misconduct or incompetence in office, all combined to keep away from public office the hothead, the knave and the fool. A man appointed by sortition to a board of ten was required to perform, with his colleagues, limited functions for a year and no more. He had little scope for malpractice. From him the Assembly required just good will and average ability, and usually got them. Sokrates' criticism of sortition was not cogent. The vital question was not whether ten average men could be expected to perform the functions of, say, the Praktores, but whether mass meetings could run an empire.

The large number of civilian magistracies (perhaps five hundred), tenable for one year only, must have ensured that a modicum of political experience was quite widely diffused among the citizens, though most such office-holders will have held similar office before: but there was more experience to be gained by serving on the Council.

Strictly speaking, membership of the Council of 500 might be described as 'the most democratic of the magistracies', but it is convenient to contrast magistrates and councillors.

Quite certainly, direct democracy could not have worked without a council of some kind to prepare the Assembly's business and execute its decisions. But what kind? The 200 or so ex-Arkhons who composed the original supreme court of the Areopagos would never have done, if only because they were life-members. Membership of the Council of 500 was by no means for life. In the fourth century no one could be a member for more than two years, and the two years were not to be consecutive. Before the Peloponnesian War, when the population was much larger, it may well have been that no one could be a member more than once. (No fifth-century case of a second term is known.) If it was so, each outgoing 500 and the public clerk will have had much to explain to the next 500. Calculation suggests that more than half the Athenians who reached the age of fifty had served on the Council, and any ex-councillor who had been regular in his attendance knew a great deal about public affairs.

Everything possible was done to prevent the Council from acquiring a will of its own. It was intended to be representative of the whole people. Fifty councillors were appointed from each of the ten tribes by the use of sortition, each deme being represented in proportion to its population. (When the population reached 40,000, the smallest, one-councillor, demes should have been about eighty strong.) Thetes were

probably debarred from serving, and it may not always have been easy
for demes to find enough representatives. It is inconceivable that a small
farmer, for example, could have been compelled to devote the larger
part of a year to serving as a councillor. Volunteers, of some standing
in most cases, must have come forward, but some of them will have
needed pushing. Sokrates, for example, would not have let his name go
forward against his will, but it seems likely that only pressure from other
members of his deme would have induced him to do so. The principle
of rotation must have ensured that men of standing who were eager to
serve had their chance sooner rather than later. This method of
appointment, combined with the size of the citizen body (Thucydides
8.66.3), must have ensured that at the start of their year of office few
councillors knew even a tenth of the other councillors.

Every day, except for major festival days and Assembly days, the
Council met, usually in the council house on the west side of the Agora.
By 411 councillors were paid for every day that they attended (Thucydides 8.69.4). It is probable that Perikles introduced pay for councillors
after he had introduced pay for jurors but before the outbreak of the
Peloponnesian War: councillors were exempt from military service
(Lykourgos, *Against Leokrates* 37), and from 431 that would have been
incentive enough for men to put their names forward. If the rate was 4
obols a day, the maximum cost to the community may be calculated:

$$\frac{500 \times 300 \times 4}{6 \times 6,000} = 16\ 2/3 \text{ talents}$$

There was no legal sanction against members who failed to attend.
Meetings can rarely have been brief, even though the Council had a
standing committee, the Prytaneis, to do for it much what it did for the
Assembly.

The Prytaneis at any given time were the fifty representatives of one
of the ten tribes, and they served for a tenth of the year (about thirty-
six days). Although for most purposes Athens used a lunar calendar, the
Council's year was, until 407, a roughly solar one, beginning at about
the summer solstice. Each period of thirty-six or so days was called a
prytaneia. Which should be the first tribe to serve was settled by sortition,
and at the end of that *prytaneia* and of each of the next seven *prytaneiai*
sortition was used to settle which tribe should serve next. During their
term of office the Prytaneis worked and dined in the round-house
(Tholos), a circular building with a conical roof, south of the council
house, which must be distinguished from the town hall or Prytaneion.
Every twenty-four hours sortition was used to select one of their number
to be president (Epistates). From one evening to the next he held the
keys of the temples in which lay the financial reserves of the city. He

was assisted by a 'third' of the Prytaneis, picked by himself. He and his assistants slept in the round-house on his night of office. If there was a meeting of Council or Assembly on his day, he presided, assisted by the other Prytaneis. No one could be Epistates more than once; so more than half of the Council had to hold the office. A politically inexperienced Epistates, presiding over the Assembly in the first *prytaneia*, might find himself in difficulties. If he put an illegal motion, or if standing orders were breached in some other way, all the Prytaneis were apparently held responsible. In 406, in the debate on the conduct of the generals after the battle of Arginousai, Sokrates, as one of the Prytaneis, tried in vain to prevent an illegal motion being put.

It was the business of the Prytaneis to convene the Council, to draw up its agenda, and to introduce to it magistrates and, in suitable cases, private citizens who wished to address it. They were also the first to receive ambassadors and messengers. It was the primary business of the full Council to draw up the agenda of the Assembly. Religious matters came first, and then foreign heralds and embassies were heard. As we have seen, it was the generally observed convention that the Assembly could pass decrees only on matters put before it by the Council, but the Council's meetings were normally open to the public (Aristophanes, *Knights* 625ff.), and there is no sign or likelihood of the Council's having tried to prevent the Assembly from debating and deciding any matter of general concern. If the Council's preliminary discussion of a matter (*probouleusis*) issued in a resolution (*probouleuma*), it might contain a recommendation for action or might simply raise a matter for debate. In the former case, it was open to the Assembly to accept the resolution as it stood, to accept it with amendment, or to reject it. The prescript of a decree commonly began: 'Resolved by the Council and the People, with tribe T as Prytaneis . . . .' The Prytaneis convened the Assembly as well as convening the Council, and they perhaps advertised its regular meetings five days in advance.

There was a legal aspect to the Council's probouleutic work. By the process of *eisangelia*, approximately our impeachment, any person, including any Councillor, might at any time, and without fear of reprisal, lay information before the Council charging any citizen with a grave offence against the state. If the Council did not reject the information, it might itself try the case and impose a fine of up to 500 *drakhmai*. If it thought the case too serious to be dealt with by such a fine, it might refer it to the Thesmothetai for trial before a jury-court or it might refer it to the Assembly by drafting an appropriate *probouleuma*. The Assembly might then try the case itself, as it tried that of the generals in 406, or it might refer it to a jury-court, as it referred the case of Perikles in 430. If someone laid such information directly before the Assembly, as happened in 415 when Alkibiades was charged with profaning the Mysteries (Andokides 1.11), the Council would have to draft a *probouleuma* before the Assembly could try the case.

In addition to its original probouleutic role, the Council had acquired important executive and supervisory roles. The Old Oligarch noted (3.2) that the Council's work was never done: it was concerned with war, revenues, legislation, day-to-day problems, the allies' affairs, collection and receipt of tribute (ML 46), dockyards, and shrines. To lighten its own burden, the Council appointed sub-committees of ten to deal with such matters as the construction of warships and the conduct of various religious ceremonies. The Council supervised and co-ordinated the activities of such financial boards as the Treasurers of Athena, the Treasurers of the Other Gods, the Treasurers of the Greeks, the sellers, the receivers and the paymasters. Only the Council could see the whole financial picture. Only it knew whether extra revenue was needed or extra expenditure could be afforded. It is no exaggeration to say that on the vigilance and zeal of the Council depended the welfare of the community. Nevertheless, the Council's recommendations were not always accepted by the Assembly, nor was the Council exempt from *euthyna* or final examination after its year of office.

As we have seen, though public policy was discussed in the Council, it was largely determined by speeches made in the Assembly, but speeches made in the courts might also have important political consequences.

At the end of the sixth century there was only one popular court, the Heliaia – the Assembly sitting in a judicial capacity. It was possible to appeal to the Heliaia from the judgment of an Arkhon. In due course, partly because the legislation of Ephialtes transferred much of the jurisdiction of the Areopagos to the Heliaia, and partly because judicial business grew as Athens and Athens' overseas involvement grew, it became necessary to subdivide the Heliaia into a number of jury-courts (*dikasteria*). And then to these *dikasteria* passed most of the cases formerly reserved for the judgment of the magistrates, the magistrates becoming no more than the presidents of the new courts.

A little is known of the court-houses that had to be built in consequence. Two of them, the Metiokheion and the Kallion, seem to have borne the names of well-known contemporaries of Perikles. Metiokhos and Kallias will either have paid for the buildings themselves or been chairmen of the boards for the supervision of the work. Excavation in the north-east of the Agora suggests that the court-rooms were no more than walled enclosures.

The *dikasteria* were manned by panels of jurors (*dikastai*), hundreds strong, drawn from a pool of 6,000 (perhaps 600 from each tribe) selected annually by lot from those who volunteered. Like Councillors, jurors had to be thirty years old. Six thousand – not less, that is, than one citizen in seven – were taken to be representative of the whole people, and so, conveniently, was each *dikasterion*. There could, therefore, be no appeal against the verdict of a *dikasterion*.

At a trial the accuser or plaintiff spoke first, then the accused or defendant. In many kinds of case the sequence was: accuser, accused, accuser, accused. The length of time allowed to each party depended on the kind of case. Even a capital case was decided in a single day (Plato, *Apology* 37a). A water-clock was used to ensure that neither party overran his time. Each party was expected to speak for himself, if he could, but he might hire a speech-writer, and he might call relatives or friends to speak in his support.

Just as public policy was determined by mass meetings, so were questions of legal guilt and innocence. The presiding magistrate did little more than keep order. Unlike a modern judge, he did not sum up or instruct the jury in the law after the hearing: the jurors voted as soon as it was over, putting a pebble into one or other of two urns. A man was guilty or innocent if a bare majority thought so; an even vote acquitted.

Cases in Athenian law were either private or public, which is not our distinction between civil and criminal. We classify murder as criminal, but in Athens the prosecution of a murderer remained, as it had always been, a matter for the victim's family. A public case concerned an offence or dispute deemed to affect the community as a whole.

One kind of public case was the *eisangelia*. The commonest kind was a *graphe* (once the only kind of written charge). In the absence of a director of public prosecutions, a public case could be brought by anyone who wished other than a slave or disfranchised citizen. This gave scope to the professional accuser (*sykophantes*), who might blackmail by threatening to prosecute or might actually prosecute to gratify himself or another. Two other sorts of public case – *apographe* and *phasis* – gave him further encouragement. In an *apographe* the accuser listed property which he alleged that a public debtor was withholding from the sellers. If he won his case, he received three-quarters of the value of the property in question. In a *phasis* the accuser might denounce a guardian for failing to lease an orphan's estate as instructed in a will, or he might denounce an evasion of customs duty (Aristophanes, *Knights* 300ff.). If he won, he received half the fine imposed or property confiscated. Some check on the professional accuser's operations was afforded by the rule that if the accuser in a public case (other than an *eisangelia*) dropped a charge once made or failed to secure one-fifth of the votes when it came to a verdict, he was liable to a fine of 1,000 *drakhmai*.

In a public case, the verdict of an Athenian jury, despite the fine-sounding oath which the 6,000 jurors swore each year, represented not so much a considered answer to the question whether the accused had or had not broken such-and-such a law in the respects alleged as an immediate answer to the question whether he had or had not benefited the community, and as Aristophanes suggested in *Wasps* (917), the jury was inclined to think: '*L'état, c'est moi.*' The jurors assigned to the courts that tried important public cases, and especially the court of the Thesmothetai, exercised considerable control over those prominent in public life, who lived in constant danger of prosecution.

A private case (*dike idia*), concerning alleged harm done to an individual, could be brought only by the person claiming to have been harmed or, if the case were one of homicide (*dike phonou*), by the nearest male relative. It was for the Basileus to decide before which court to bring a homicide case. Cases of alleged deliberate homicide committed by the hand of the accused (not to mention cases of alleged wounding, arson or destruction of sacred olive trees) came before the Areopagos. This court, composed of the 200 or so ex-Arkhons who had passed their final examination, met, like other homicide courts (Antiphon 5.11), in the open air, on the hill of Ares, on any of the three days before the last day of the month. Any one of those days on which they did meet to try a case of homicide was accounted 'polluted': a man was on trial for doing something grossly offensive to the gods, and if he was found guilty he would be sentenced to death by attachment to a wooden board, and his property would be confiscated. Because they had all been Arkhons, the Areopagites had legal experience, and Xenophon (*Reminiscences* 3.5.20) makes Sokrates rate them superior to any other Athenian court. Irrelevance, tolerated in other courts was not tolerated in the court of the Areopagos (Lysias 3.46).

Other kinds of homicide were tried by courts of fifty-one Ephetai. It is probable that they had to be fifty years old and that they were selected by lot, perhaps from the Areopagos.

The Ephetai met outside the Palladion, a temple of Pallas Athena that lay in the south-east of the city, to try cases of (a) unintentional homicide, (b) instigation of, or complicity in, homicide intentionally or unintentionally committed by the hand of another, and (c) the killing of a metic, a foreigner or a slave belonging to another. The penalty for unintentional homicide was exile for life, unless the dead man's family pardoned his killer. The penalty for instigation or complicity was the same as that for committing the kind of homicide in question. The penalty for killing a non-citizen may have been left to the jury, but must normally have been less severe than that for killing a citizen.

The Ephetai met outside the Delphinion, a temple of Apollo and Artemis, the twin divinities of Delphi, that lay near the Palladion in the south-east of the city, to try cases of homicide admitted by the defendant but claimed by him to be lawful. The first speech of Lysias, for example, was written to be delivered by one Euphiletos who had killed Eratosthenes when, so he claimed, he had caught him in bed with his wife. Homicide was lawful in such cases as these: killing in defence of oneself, one's property or one's womenfolk; the accidental killing of an opponent in an athletic contest or of a fellow-soldier mistaken for one of the enemy or of a patient receiving medical treatment; killing public enemies of certain kinds.

The Ephetai met in Phreatto, perhaps in Zea, to try anyone who, having been exiled for committing an unintentional homicide for which he had not yet been pardoned by the dead man's family, was accused of committing another homicide intentionally. The court sat on the shore, and the accused, arriving in a boat, made his defence from it. Not often can it have happened that a man exiled for committing an unintentional homicide for which he hoped to secure pardon was confident enough of securing acquittal on a further charge of intentional homicide to return to Athens and risk the possibility of being condemned to death.

There were, of course, many kinds of private case concerned with offences less grave than homicide, such as battery, slander, theft and damage to property.

After a jury had returned its verdict, it might have to decide on a penalty or on damages or compensation. In some public cases the penalty for the offence was fixed. If a defendant had been found guilty of an offence for which the penalty was not fixed, the jury had to decide between a penalty proposed by the prosecutor and one proposed by the defendant. It might be a nice matter for the defendant to decide what was the lowest penalty he could propose without provoking the jury. The legal penalties that a citizen might incur ranged from execution or exile for the gravest offences, through disfranchisement (*atimia*), to fines, which were much the commonest penalties. The known methods of execution were attachment to the board or poisoning with a cup of hemlock. To the penalties of death and exile might be added confiscation of property, demolition of house, denial of burial in Attike or disfranchisement of descendants. Disfranchisement involved the loss of all, or only some, of the following rights: the right to enter temples and the defined area of the Agora; the right to engage in public service as magistrate, councillor or juror; the right to speak or vote in the Assembly; the right to speak in court. To disfranchisement might be added confiscation of property. Though men might be held in prison pending trial or execution or payment of a fine, imprisonment was not a common penalty. If the building 100 yards south-west of the Agora is correctly identified as the state prison, administered by the Eleven, there was not enough room for long-stay prisoners.

In any one year at least 7,000 Athenians were engaged in public service as magistrates, Councillors or jurors – not less than one citizen in six. Up to 6,000 might attend an important meeting of the Assembly. How were these thousands composed? How fully did the poor participate?

We can be certain that Athenians of the lower class lived near subsistence level. They could not be expected to devote much time to public affairs unless they were compensated for loss of earnings. In the Funeral Speech Thucydides (2.40.2) makes Perikles claim: 'The same people attend to public affairs as well as their private affairs, and despite the variety of their occupations, they have an adequate understanding of public affairs.' We may wonder how true this was of the poor.

We know what sort of people the generals and speakers were. It is harder to say what sort of people attended the Assembly in peacetime or served as minor magistrates, Councillors, or jurors. Attendance at the Assembly was unpaid in the fifth century. There was at least one regular meeting (*kyria ekklesia*) every *prytaneia*. The quorum for a valid ostracism, held in the Agora, was 6,000, and there is no sign that it was difficult to gather that number on the occasions when Thoukydides, son of Melesias, and Hyperbolos were ostracised (about 443 and 417–415) or indeed on earlier occasions, when the population was smaller, but we do not know how often the quorum was not reached after the Assembly had voted to hold an ostracism. On the Pnyx there would hardly have been room for more than 6,000 and we may regard such an attendance as close to the maximum. Distances that were long in relation to the available transport may have kept many small farmers away from Athens, especially at busy seasons. Though the Thetes did not outnumber the Zeugitai, they did mostly live in Athens or Peiraieus and so, if not at sea with the fleet, they were within easy walking distance of the Pnyx. There is some evidence that the Skythian archers used a ruddled rope to drive gossips out of the Agora and up to the Pnyx on the occasion of a regular meeting of the Assembly (Aristophanes, *Akharnians* 19–22). We cannot improve on the disparaging account of the composition of the Assembly given by Xenophon (*Reminiscences* 3.7.6), who makes Sokrates say that it was composed of fullers, cobblers, carpenters, smiths, farmers, merchants, and traders in the Agora. We do know that the proportion of the citizens who attended was never high, but we do not know the frequency of meetings or the, no doubt varying, ratio among those who did attend between farmers and artisans or retailers.

It was probably Perikles who established the principle of payment for civilian service by introducing payment for jurors – 2 obols a day, raised to 3 in 425, but not raised again. Unfortunately, we cannot date the innovation, which is attested – on the Athenian scale, at least – for no other Greek or Roman city, or be sure of Perikles' intentions. For all we know, the date could have been any year between 465 and 450, but there are reasons for narrowing the range to 461–457. Perikles may have wanted to ensure that enough jurors came forward, or to acquire a strong following in the Assembly, or to do both. According to Aristophanes in *Wasps* (661f.), produced in 422, 6,000 jurors earned 150 talents a year. He must be assuming that they all worked 300 days a year:

$$\frac{150 \times 6,000 \times 6}{6,000 \times 3} = 300$$

This is no doubt a theoretical maximum of jury service, never attained in practice: no courts sat on major festival days or on Assembly days, nor did they all sit on all the other days. We may assume that there was less litigation in the 450s than in the 420s, but it is improbable that there were then anything like as many as 6,000 Athenians able and willing to give up anywhere near 300 days a year for jury service without compensation. So it is likely that Perikles' first concern was to ensure that enough jurors came forward. Two obols was perhaps half what a skilled workman earned then and Aristophanes' picture of jurors' pay functioning rather like an old age pension may be near the mark. There is no sign of a clash between jury service and military service. Pay for Councillors was very likely introduced soon after pay for jurors, and pay for Arkhons probably accompanied the opening of the Arkhonship to Zeugitai in 458. By the death of Perikles all magistrates appointed by lot were probably being paid.

While it is reasonable to assume that many of the 6,000 jurors were recruited from the ranks of the elderly poor and especially from retired sailors, it appears that Thetes were debarred from the Council as they were, at least in theory, from all magistracies. If Councillors were paid 4 obols a day, and if it was possible to serve twice in the fifth century, we may conclude that it would otherwise have been difficult to obtain enough volunteers. If it was easier to obtain enough civilian magistrates than enough Councillors, the explanation may be that the work of most magistrates was much less exacting: it could not fall to them to preside over a turbulent Assembly, nor had they nearly so much to do. Even after the introduction of pay, many Zeugitai must have been reluctant to abandon their normal occupation for a full year.

In a famous passage in *Gorgias* (515e) Sokrates is made to say to the ambitious Kallikles: 'I am told that Perikles made the Athenians lazy, cowardly, garrulous and grasping by being the first to institute payment for public service.' What Plato means by saying that in this way Perikles made the Athenians 'cowardly' is not clear. Can he be referring to Councillors' exemption from military service? It was perhaps Councillors' pay that he thought made the Athenians 'garrulous': it encouraged regular attendance by Councillors. The claim that pay made them 'lazy' and 'grasping' is hardly plausible. One could be a Councillor at most twice, and hold any magistracy to which appointment was made by sortition only once (and not concurrently with any other magistracy); and neither Councillors nor magistrates will have been highly paid. The total number of Councillors and civilian or domestic magistrates in any one year perhaps amounted to 1,000. (There were also some hundreds of overseas magistrates, but little is known about them.) One could serve more or less continuously as a juror, but jurors were paid little more than was necessary for subsistence.

Ration-money for soldiers must have been introduced before the Peloponnesian War, and pay for sailors may have been introduced as early as 480, but it would have been even less plausible to suggest that these kinds of payment made the citizens lazy, cowardly, garrulous and grasping. The rate for soldiers and sailors was normally ½ *drakhme* a day. (This rate was not high, and though it may have been easier for sailors to obtain regular employment, throughout the campaigning season, most soldiers could expect to be called up for no longer than it took to make a sortie into the territory of Megara.)

Cohesion

The citizen of fifth-century Athens was a member of many social groups, but the two fundamental ones were household (*oikos*) and community (*polis*). The *polis* was an association of *oikoi*. The Athenian *polis* was formed during the eighth century, as the population soared, by the process called *synoikismos*, uniting of *oikoi*. The principal sign, discoverable by archaeology, of the formation of a *polis* is the construction of a monumental temple to a patron deity. The recognition by the heads of neighbouring *oikoi* that there were advantages to be derived from the acceptance of laws and legal machinery transcending individual *oikoi* and clans (*gene*) was the origin of Greek civilisation. Though Perikles claimed in the Funeral Speech that Athenians attended to the affairs of both *oikois* and *polis*, the tension between private and public was not, and could not be, finally resolved.

Homeric values antedated and survived the formation of the *polis*. According to that system of values, the hero strove to win fame in his lifetime (*kydos*) and a fame that would survive his death (*kleos*). While he was alive, what mattered most to him was the esteem or honour or status (*time*) accorded him by others of comparable standing, and that depended on his power (*dynamis*) and his exploits. He did not, of course, operate in isolation. Behind him lay his *oikos* – his family, his free dependants, his slaves, his animals, his inanimate possessions, his land

and therewith his ancestors in their tombs. He aimed for self-sufficiency (*autarkeia*) and he could almost achieve it. All that he lacked was immediate access to metals suitable for making tools and weapons. In Homeric society the good man was the man who could preserve and even augment his *oikos*. Ideally, he would be descended from a god. Failing that advantage, he needed at least to have inherited a substantial *oikos*, and to be strong, courageous, prudent and hard-working. Odysseus, like Penelope and Nausikaa, was quite willing to do manual work, for the *oikos*. The good (*agathos* or *esthlos*) man was useful (*khrestos*) to his family (*oikeioi*) and to those who were close to him (*philoi*). The abstraction corresponding to *agathos* was *arete*, which was far-removed from *agape*, the impartially distributed benevolence of Christianity. It was more akin to courage, prowess, merit, worth or success. Opposite in meaning to *agathos*, *esthlos* and *khrestos* were *kakos, poneros* and *deilos*, the last being derived from *deos*, meaning 'fear'.

The survival of Homeric values in fifth-century Athens was ensured by the fact that Homer was the staple of education. The desire to be highly esteemed (*philotimia*) and to win posthumous glory spurred to action the leading men of Athens as it had spurred Achilles and Hektor.

Xenophon (*Oikonomikos* 7.15) describes the prudence of both husband and wife as the maintenance of existing property in the best condition and the honourable acquisition of as much more as possible. Though self-sufficiency was now much harder to achieve, it remained a theoretical aim.

So long as the community appeared to do more for its households than its households were required to do for the community, the leading men were patriotic. To count as a good member of the community (*agathos polites*), it was necessary to benefit the community; but, under favourable circumstances, it was possible to benefit the community and still be a net gainer. Thucydides (1.70.6) makes the Corinthians testify to Athenian patriotism before the war: 'Their bodies they devote to their community as though they were not their own, and their minds, which are most truly their own, to achievement on its behalf.'

Virtually all we know about Athenian values we learn from upper-class male authors. If they were writing plays or forensic speeches, they had to take some account of popular sentiments, but from other evidence we can recover pure upper-class sentiments.

If we examine the vocabulary of the 'Old Oligarch', an anonymous upper-class pamphleteer, writing apparently in the 430s, but not necessarily in old age, we may draw up a table of terms that he thought applicable to his fellow citizens, those in the first column to the few upper-class people like himself, and those in the second column to the many.

Laudatory	*Pejorative*
khrestos, useful, good	*poneros*, troublesome, worthless; *poneria*
gennaios, well-born, noble	*penes*, poor (but not destitute); *penia*
plousios, rich	*demos*, common people, Thetes (1.2, 2.14)
dynatos, powerful	*demotikos*, popular, vulgar, common
beltistos, best	*kheiron*, worse, bad
akribeia, precision, care	**akolasia*, indiscipline
dexios, right-handed, clever	**adikia*, injustice, unfairness
aristos, best	**amathia*, ignorance, boorishness
arete, prowess, merit, worth	**ataxia*, indiscipline
sophia, skill, knowledge	*aiskhros*, shameful
eudaimon, fortunate	**apaideusia*, lack of education or culture
dynamenos, powerful, influential	*mainomenos*, mad
beltion, better, good	*okhlos*, rabble

* The prefix *a* indicates a lack

It is clear enough that this vocabulary is continuous with Homer's: and, like Homer's, the terms in it are sometimes used more descriptively than evaluatively (as for us to call a man an aristocrat is not necessarily to commend him, even if we know that *aristos* means 'best') and sometimes more evaluatively than descriptively (as for us to call a man mad is not necessarily to imply that, if he fell into the hands of consultant psychiatrists, he would be certified). It is clear enough also that, though the lower class might have been willing to apply to itself some of the terms thought applicable to it by the Old Oligarch – *penes, penia, demos, demotikos, amathia, apaideusia*, used descriptively – it could hardly have accepted the others.

Now the Old Oligarch concedes (1.2) that it is fair that in Athens the poor and the common people should do better than the well-born and rich because they row the ships and so give the community its power (here, as at 2.14, he is identifying the common people with the Thetes), and the petty offices give the community much more power than the hoplites, the well-born and the good. In other words, the paradoxical fact emerges that, from the community's point of view, the nominally useful are less useful than the nominally useless. (The nominally useful were not of course completely useless: both hoplites and cavalry retained important roles; most, if not all, of the generals and politicians came from the upper and upper-middle classes; and the richest men retained their important liturgical role, as trierarchs and *khoregoi*.)

The lower class would have shared at least this element in the Old Oligarch's moral thinking. The Chorus in Aristophanes' *Wasps* are retired sailors turned jurors. More than once they make the point that they make in these words (1091–1101):

> In those days, I was so frightening as to fear nothing, and I crushed the enemy, sailing against him with the fleet. For in those days we were not concerned to be ready to make a good speech or denounce someone, but about who would prove to be the best oarsman. So, because we captured many cities from the Persians, we are chiefly responsible for the arrival in Athens of the tribute, which the young men are purloining.

Here then is one moral principle that was shared by most Athenians: those who do most for the community should receive most from it.

Another principle, accepted by almost all but upper-class admirers of Sparta or Lakonizers, is this: as Greeks are superior to other men (in courage, intelligence and political organisation), so is Athens superior to other Greek communities. This superiority was first demonstrated in the Persian Wars and especially on the field of Marathon. In *Wasps* (711) Bdelykleon, who wishes to disparage the jurors' 3 obols a day, argues that, if the tribute paid by the subject allies were devoted to maintaining 20,000 of the common people of Athens in style, they would be 'enjoying themselves as befitted their country and the victory monument at Marathon'. In the Funeral Speech Perikles claims that both politically and culturally the rest of Greece learns from Athens.

A third principle that would have been generally accepted is this: the good life includes inheriting an estate prosperous enough to make a man as nearly self-sufficient as possible and quite free to devote himself, if he wants, to politics. That such a life presupposed heavy dependence on slaves would have seemed a drawback only to a handful of eccentrics. All citizens were proudly aware that only they could own land or take part in politics, and even the poorest of them might hope that one day they too would become slave-owners. In these circumstances, it is hardly surprising that no distinctive lower-class ideology emerged. There is no sign of an attack on inherited wealth *per se*, though its abuse might be attacked.

There was, therefore, a wide area of agreement on questions of value, and this agreement, sustained by pay for public service and other advantages of empire, made possible a measure of political stability and freedom from faction (*stasis*) denied to most other Greek communities. Nevertheless, as the vocabulary of the Old Oligarch seems to show, at least some members of the upper class felt more contempt for the lower

class than most members of the British upper class now feel for the
working class. In any society, some modes of living must be more highly
approved than others, although the language of disapproval is not always
as strong as it was in the circle of the Old Oligarch. All Athenians were
free to speak and vote in the Assembly or watch in the theatre or be
initiated into the Mysteries of Eleusis or shop around the Agora, but the
lives of aristocrats and Thetes were very different, the lives of some
Thetes hardly differing – in material terms, at least – from those of the
more fortunate slaves.

It is possible briefly to characterise the life styles of seven occupational
segments of Athenian society. (Finer distinctions could well be drawn,
especially within the sixth segment.) To some extent these seven segments
cut across Solon's four orders or census classes – Pentakosiomedimnoi,
Hippeis, Zeugitai, and Thetes, which, if the top two orders are combined,
correspond very roughly to our upper, middle and lower or working
classes. In general, membership of one segment rather than another was
hereditary: fathers taught their sons to live as they themselves lived. But
financial failures did occur, and members of the second segment were
often *nouveaux riches* or the sons of *nouveaux riches*.

The nobles of fifth-century Athens belonged to the houses that had
emerged from the Dark Age in a dominant position, politically and
religiously. They were the Eupatrids ('sons of good fathers'), who had
achieved the *synoikismos* centred on Athens. Their estates mostly lay in
the plain around Athens, and they had monopolised political power until
Solon. Unconvincing though their genealogies may seem to us, they and
their descendants thought of themselves as sprung, ultimately, from gods.
A fifth-century noble would not, however, have voiced such a claim in
the Assembly or in a law-court; there the only acceptable claim on behalf
of one's ancestors was that they had done the state some service within
what we should call the historical period. So even in a fourth-century
court a descendant of Harmodios might refer to the killing of the tyrant
Hipparkhos in 514. There were also houses that had risen to prominence
since the emergence of the Eupatrids. The members of the clans (*gene*),
round which phratries formed, included, but were more numerous than,
the Eupatrids.

A high proportion of the most famous Athenians of the fifth century,
most of them nobles, belonged to Urban demes: Aristeides, Kallias,
Thoukydides, son of Melesias, Sokrates (Alopeke); Thucydides, son of
Oloros (Halimous); Perikles (Kholargos); Plato (Kollytos); Sophokles
(Kolonos); Andokides, Aristophanes, Kleon (Kydathenaion); Miltiades
and his son Kimon (Lakiadai); Hyperbolos (Perithoidai), Alkibiades
(Skambonidai). But the so-called Urban area stretched from Aigaleos to
Hymettos, and of the nine demes in question only three – Kollytos,
Kydathenaion, Skambonidai – lay inside the Themistoklean city wall.

Ownership of land worth more than about 4 talents put a man in the liturgical class, whose members could achieve great éclat as trierarchs or *khoregoi*. 'Wealth we use', said Perikles in the Funeral Speech, 'as an opportunity for achievement rather than as something to boast about.' Boasting might be unattractive, but neither Perikles nor any other Athenian wanted his achievements to go unremarked.

Ownership of (relatively) well-watered land made possible the breeding of horses, with a view to hunting or competing in the chariot-races at the Panhellenic games. (From the Archaic Age onwards the upper class remained more internationally minded than the rest of the community.) Personal names incorporating *hippos* (horse) seem often to have been upper-class names. From young men able to provide their own horse was recruited the community's thousand-strong force of cavalry. This force had some military importance, and it also figured prominently in religious processions, especially that of the Great Panathenaia. In 416 Alkibiades entered seven chariots at Olympia, winning and also coming second and fourth. To win the four-horse chariot-race at a Panhellenic festival conferred the greatest prestige at home. To win any event conferred enough prestige to justify talented athletes in spending long hours practising in *palaistra* or gymnasium. Even those without much talent would spend some time wrestling or running for the sake of general fitness. This was a point of resemblance between the upbringing of upper-class young Athenians and that of young Spartans, like the homosexuality that was bound to flourish in such circumstances. Another point of resemblance was the wearing of long hair.

In addition to any expenditure on horse-breeding, the upper class also spent heavily on dowries for their daughters and other female dependants, on funerals and, from about 435, on grave-reliefs. Some upper-class expenditure was of greater social utility. Kimon, a member of the rich Philaid clan, not only performed many liturgies but also subsidised the poor members of his deme, Lakiadai, and was responsible in one way or another for many public buildings and other works. (A marked feature of fifth-century Athens is the transition from private to public enterprise in this sphere.)

The possession of a sizable estate made possible not only expenditure of the kinds described but also a political career. Without the leisure afforded by an assured income, a political career, as opposed to occasional participation in politics, was impossible. Such a career might be assisted by the spending of time and money on instruction in rhetoric by Sophists (see chapter 8).

Certainly, members of the upper class had more education of the traditional, 'musical', kind than their social inferiors: they were better acquainted with Homer and the other poets, more skilful at dancing and at accompanying themselves on the lyre, and more capable of singing the next line of a drinking-song (*skolion*) at a *symposion* or drinking-party (Aristophanes, *Wasps* 1222). Before the formation of the hoplite phalanx in the early seventh century the nobles had been a fighting aristocracy; after its formation they became a social aristocracy. Some nobles might excel at Olympia, others as speakers on the Pnyx or as generals at sea; the typical milieu of most of them was the *symposion*, at which a select few reclined in oriental fashion to enjoy themselves. Upper-middle-class Athenians followed their example as far as they could.

Since their style of life approximated to the generally accepted ideal, aristocrats could hardly help despising other styles; and though they were envied, they were accepted as being indeed *kaloi kai agathoi* – brave and fair descendants of illustrious, if not divine, ancestors. There were fewer than a thousand nobles and they married girls from families of the same standing as their own. (Aristocratic houses allied by marriage might be expected to combine politically.)

Distinguishable from aristocratic and other large landowners were a small number of rich men like Nikias, Kleon, Hyperbolos, Kleophon and Anytos, who rose to political prominence after the death of Perikles, although they could boast no illustrious ancestors. Nikias' fortune rested on his mining interests and his thousand mining slaves. The fortunes of the others rested on the large-scale manufacture of goods – leather, lamps, lyres – by slave labour. Though no Athenian was economically self-sufficient, the obvious need of these men to sell their products like retailers (*kapeloi*) exposed them to some contempt. Yet despite the onslaughts of Aristophanes and indeed Thucydides on the upstart 'dema-gogue' Kleon and his successors, there is reason to suppose that Kleon married an aristocratic wife, and Anytos was certainly a respected figure. In Plato's *Menon* (90a) Sokrates says that Anytos' father 'got his money not by luck, through a gift . . . but made it by his own skill [*sophia*] and hard work: furthermore, he was accounted a modest and agreeable member of the community, not insolent, arrogant or offensive. . . .' This suggests that members of the community did not necessarily resent or despise the commercial success of other members, but that such success was not always good for their characters. Finally, as we can see from the opening pages of Plato's *Republic*, the shield-makers Kephalos and his sons, who were metics, were on the best of terms not only with Sokrates, who was a Zeugites, but also with Plato's elder brothers, who were aristocrats.

A third occupational segment was formed by the farmers or small-holders who worked their own land (*autourgoi*), growing mainly olives, vines and figs. If a farmer was also to grow barley on any scale, he would need a yoke of oxen. Market-gardening flourished because of the mildness of the climate. Farming proper was hard work on the thin, stony soil of Attike – but there were two slack periods each year, and many farmers had at least one slave, very likely a girl. The ambition of these farmers was to enjoy in peace and at home the pleasures of eating, drinking and making love, but at any rate at the beginning of the Peloponnesian War they accepted the need to abandon their farms to the invaders for a month or more each year. Thucydides (2.16) stresses the intensity of local loyalty: each man's village was his *polis*; but town and country were interdependent and not sharply demarcated. Craftsmen needed to sell to farmers, retailers needed to buy from them: farmers needed to sell in the Agora of Athens or to retailers. Furthermore, it was hard to say whether a market-gardener living just outside Athens, or one living in Athens but owning a garden outside, belonged more to the town or the country. In dress and in vocabulary the countryman proper was conspicuous in town, and though he needed the retailer, he expected to be cheated by him.

A fourth, small, occupational segment was formed by the fishermen of Attike, equipped with boat, net and trident. In the diet of the urban population fish was second in importance only to bread, and a section of the Agora was known as the Fish (Aristophanes, *Wasps* 789, *Frogs* 1068). The fishermen's lot was as hard as that of the farmers.

A fifth segment was formed by those overseas traders, exporters and importers (*emporoi* or *naukleroi*), who were not metics. The principal export was silver; of less importance were olive oil and wine, contained in earthenware vessels, and also painted pottery. The imports included, in addition to a wide variety of luxury goods, salt fish, slaves, iron, copper, timber (for ship-building) and above all corn. '*Emporoi* love corn,' says Sokrates in Xenophon's *Oikonomikos* (20.27). The great Solon had been an *emporos*, and *emporoi* enjoyed a prestige denied to the uniquely important group of middlemen with whom the corn-importers among them had to deal – the corn-sellers (*sitopolai*), but they were mostly metics (Lysias 22.5).

The sixth segment comprised local traders or retailers (*kapeloi*), craftsmen or artisans (*kheirotekhnai*), and most of those who provided services. It included figures as diverse as greengrocers and fishmongers, cobblers and masons, barbers and most diviners, teachers and most doctors. Many of them made something, the skill (*tekhne*) involved being much harder to acquire in some cases than in others, and all of them sold something. Typical *kapeloi* were sellers of bread, barley-groats, fish, vegetables, wine or wool. Their reputation was low: they were regarded as dishonest. In a speech of Demosthenes (57.30), we read: 'Euboulides traduced us not only contrary to the decree about the Agora, but also contrary to the laws, which enjoin that anyone who reproaches any citizen, male or female, with doing business in the Agora shall be liable to the penalty for slander.' The decree was probably designed to curb the excesses of commercial rivalry, the law to curb expressions of anti-commercial prejudice.

Prominent among the craftsmen were cobblers, carpenters, stone-masons, potters, smiths and makers of various kinds of weapon and armour. In most cases the workshop, like the bakery, was also the place of sale, so that producer and salesman were usually identical. Carpenters, however, would have to go to the dockyards for much of their employment. Not all craftsmen were Zeugitai; some were Thetes. 'Don't you see', asks Kallias in Xenophon's *Symposion* (4.4), 'plenty of carpenters and builders who build houses for many other people, but cannot do so for themselves and live in rented houses instead?'

The standard of craftsmanship in Athens was extremely high, as so much of the surviving architecture, sculpture and painted pottery testifies, but craftsmen were not very highly esteemed. Of all the potters and painters whose names can be found on Athenian pots, not one is mentioned in a literary source. According to Herodotos (2.167), the only Greek community in which craftsmen enjoyed any standing was Corinth. Sedentary, indoor occupations, and especially those in which fire was used, were considered by some upper-class people to deform and weaken both body and soul (Xenophon, *Oikonomikos* 4.2), and the skills involved were branded 'banausic'. It was no accident that the only craftsman among the gods, Hephaistos, was the only god who was lame. Even more obviously than the members of the second segment, those of the sixth had to sell their products or services, and thus were closer to the despised hired men (*misthotoi*), with nothing to sell but their labour. Furthermore, though slaves were not prominent in trade, they were prominent in all crafts (if not always at the highest level of craftsman-ship), and all crafts might therefore be regarded as fit only for slaves.

It is important, however, not to take the opinions of Xenophon, Plato or Aristotle on manual work in general or on crafts in particular as typical of Athenian thinking on the subject. Xenophon's complete rejec-tion of manufacture in favour of agriculture was not universally shared. Aristophanes for one did not share it. As two passages show (*Peace* 296f., *Wealth* 899ff.), he recognised as respectable two other occupations in addition to the farmer's – those of the *emporos* and the craftsman. All three occupations, together with the fisherman's, involved hard physical work; by comparison, intellectuals, such as doctors, diviners and teachers, were idle (*Clouds* 316, 334). Underlying this distinction was a recognition that only those capable of hard physical work could fight effectively for the community, and the price of defeat might be slavery. Plato makes Sokrates say (*Menon* 91d) that Protagoras alone made more money as a Sophist 'than Pheidias, whose work was so outstandingly fine, and ten other sculptors put together'. Now while it is true that Athens did not reward Pheidias as highly as we might think he deserved, it is noteworthy that Sokrates chooses a manual worker, albeit an artist (as we should say) rather than an artisan, as his example of someone who claimed with obvious justice to possess useful knowledge; and, until his exile in 438/7, Pheidias was a friend of the leading man in Athens. It is reasonable to suppose that many potters and sculptors were on good terms with their aristocratic patrons. Finally, Sokrates claims in Plato's *Apology* (22cd) to have found more knowledge in the craftsmen of Athens than in the politicians or poets.

The seventh and last occupational segment comprised all Thetes other than those already located in the sixth segment. Because of the upper-class viewpoint of our sources, it is hard for us to reconstruct the life of the Thetes. We may assume that some thousands still lived on the land as tenant farmers or hired labourers, but most of them must have lived in lodging-houses in Athens or Peiraieus. Many of them could find unskilled employment in land transport (for which there must have been increased demand while the building-programme lasted), in and around the dockyards, and as merchant seamen. Agriculture provided some seasonal employment: helping with the olive harvest (*Wasps* 712) resembled our hop-picking before the advent of mechanisation.

Athens' 1,600 unmounted archers were probably Thetes, but the community had no other light-armed force. Military service for the Thetes was normally naval service – as oarsmen, deckhands, or petty officers. Unfortunately, we do not know how many of the community's sailors during the Peloponnesian War were citizen Thetes and how many were metics or *xenoi*. Before the war, according to Plutarch (*Perikles* 11.4), sixty ships were regularly in commission for eight months of the year. Unfortunately again, Plutarch's account of the rivalry in the mid-440s of Perikles and Thoukydides, son of Melesias (*Perikles* 11–14), is suspect, but if he is right about the naval training programme, and if we may assume that the sixty ships were manned exclusively by citizen Thetes, and that the rate of pay was ½ *drakhme* a day, then some 12,000 Athenians earned 240 talents altogether:

$$\frac{60 \times 200 \times 240}{6,000 \times 2} = 240$$

Rowing, even for short spells, is, of course, strenuous work, and it is doubtful whether many Thetes would have been able to go on rowing above the age of forty or perhaps forty-five. They might hope for promotion to the rank of petty officer, but only a very small proportion could achieve it: there were 170 oarsmen and only half-a-dozen petty officers on a fully manned trireme. After retirement up to 6,000 of them could draw the juror's pay of, from 425, ½ *drakhme* a day.

It seems that a fairly desirable career-sequence would have been:

oarsman, petty officer, juror. But for such men, despite the agreed value of their naval service to the community, life was hard. The Chorus-leader in *Wasps* says (300f.): 'Out of this mini-pay I have to get barley-groats, fish and firewood for three.' The three are himself, his wife and his son – he cannot afford a slave. Perikles alludes to poverty twice in the Funeral Speech: 'As for poverty, if a man can benefit the community in some way, he is not hindered by the obscurity of his status. . . .' 'It is not disgraceful for a man to confess poverty; the real disgrace lies in not trying to escape it.' Clearly the Old Oligarch did think that poverty was disgraceful, and Jason was saying nothing controversial when he told Medeia (Euripides, *Medeia* 561): 'A poor man is shunned by all his friends.' Equally clearly it would not have been easy for a Thes with his limited education to benefit the community except at sea, or to escape his poverty.

Although the community provided water from fountain-houses, roads of a sort, an adequate, but not free, supply of corn, some meat (at public sacrifices), some sort of medical service (Aristophanes, *Akharnians* 1030; Plato, *Gorgias* 455b, 514de), gymnasia and baths (Old Oligarch, 2.10; Aristophanes, *Clouds* 837, 991, 1044–1054), occasional allotments of land overseas (in colonies independent of Athens and in *kleroukhiai* still part of Athens – see chapter 4), modest pay for various kinds of public service, an obol-a-day pension for the disabled (Lysias 24), and eventually, Kleophon's *diobelia* (2 obols or $1/3$ *drakhme* a day for the poorest members of the community – ML 84), it appears that Perikles would have agreed with Jesus: 'The poor you have with you always.' It was up to energetic Thetes to help themselves, if they could.

After consideration of these seven occupational segments of the Athenian community, the diversity of that community is apparent, and so is the inadequacy of many generalisations, ancient and modern, about 'the Athenians'. Relations between segments were not always harmonious, nor were their different aspirations fully compatible. It is, however, remarkable that in the half-century from 461, when Ephialtes, the architect of radical democracy, was assassinated, to 411, when the first of two short-lived oligarchic reactions set in, there was so much harmony. In 457 a Spartan force in Boiotia was encouraged to stay there by some Athenians who hoped to put a stop to radical democracy and the building of the Long Walls (Thucydides 1.107.4), but no more is heard of them.

One fact about all seven segments is that they were composed of households. To determine how patriotic most Athenians were, it is necessary to consider how much more or less households in different segments gained from the community than the community required of the households. The community was originally formed to preserve households – by providing arbitration between households in conflict and also defence against external attack. In historical times the preservation of households was a main concern of the law of Athens. It was vital to maintain the number of citizens capable of fighting and the number of citizens capable of performing liturgies. We may consider first the advantages of membership of the community as they would have appeared to the heads or *kyrioi* of households in at least the top six segments.

With very few exceptions, all and only adult male members of citizen households were full members of the community, entitled to own land. As members of the Assembly, they all had the right not only to vote but also to speak (*isegoria*) on all matters of public concern. From the age of thirty, they all had the right to serve as jurors. Probably from the same age, most of them had the right to hold most magistracies.

'As for legality,' claims Perikles in the Funeral Speech, 'there is equality for all in their private disputes' (*isonomia*). No doubt the Arkhon's court, for example, did usually return a just verdict in any private dispute about property, even though Philokleon might boast in *Wasps* (583–6) that a jury would happily disregard a father's sealed will, leaving his brotherless daughter and his property to a particular man.

Despite the use of rotation and sortition in the appointment of minor magistrates, the most important magistrates, the ten generals, were elected directly, with no restriction on re-election. Kimon and Perikles were re-elected general year after year. 'As for public esteem,' Perikles goes on, 'when a man is in any way distinguished, he is generally advanced in public life, not in rotation, but on merit.' (It is noteworthy that what Perikles has to say about radical democracy is defensive: able men *do* have scope (2.37.1); ordinary citizens *do* have an adequate understanding of public affairs (2.40.2). He does not say that radical democracy is more efficient than oligarchy or preferable in some other way.)

'Live as you please' was a slogan of radical democracy, and it is one that still appeals to disciples of J. S. Mill. In the Funeral Speech, Perikles claims:

> We play our part in the community as free men, both in public life and also in everyday life, because we avoid mutual suspicion; we are not angry with our neighbour if he enjoys himself, nor do we indulge in resentment which, though not harmful, is unpleasant to observe.

In any other city, Sokrates, had he tried to live as he lived in Athens, would have been silenced much sooner.

But liberty was combined with the rule of law. 'In our private life', Perikles continues, 'we associate without giving offence; in public life we act lawfully, chiefly through fear, obeying the magistrates of the day and the laws, especially those which are ordained for the protection of the injured, and those unwritten laws whose sanction is admitted disgrace.' Three hundred Skythian archers, public slaves, were used by the community to keep order in the Assembly, Council and courts. Within at most fifteen years of Perikles' speech, a process was introduced for prosecuting anyone who proposed in Council or Assembly a resolution contrary to an existing law in form or content (*graphe paranomon*). Perikles' words about obedience to the magistrates of the day and to the laws echo words in the oath sworn by young hoplites. Anyone who wished might prosecute on behalf of an injured party in a public case. No body of laws, and certainly not the law of Athens, attempts to cover all forms of wrong-doing. There is no need to legislate against misconduct that is adequately deterred by moral and religious upbringing. The written laws supplement, but do not replace, the unwritten.

Athens could afford to celebrate many more festivals than any other Greek community (Old Oligarch 3.2, 8). In these festivals, purely religious activity (as we might judge) was combined with social, political, artistic and, often, athletic activity, much as it is in southern European countries today. What had begun as agrarian magic had turned into a succession of colourful public holidays. 'Furthermore,' Perikles goes on, making his only reference to religion, 'we provide the mind with the most relaxation from business, by holding contests and festivals all the year round.'

The power of her navy made sea-borne attack by Athens' enemies almost unthinkable and ensured the safety of her seaborne trade. Naval power created the Athenian empire, from which the most conspicuous advantage derived was the annual receipt of tribute from the subject allies (see chapter 4). We may think of the tribute as paying at least for the Athenian navy, ships and men, and of any surplus being combined with Athens' own internal revenue to help pay for administration, for the maintenance of public buildings, for the community's share in the provision of festivals, and for the jurors, Councillors and magistrates (Thucydides 6.24.3). To help maintain the morale of its armed forces, the community wisely undertook to look after the war orphans. In the Funeral Speech, Perikles says of the Athenian dead: 'The community will maintain their children at public expense from now until they come of age.' Other benefits mentioned earlier were appreciated more by the lower class than the upper, but all alike, from Thetes to trierarchs and generals, could bask in an international esteem (*time*) such as no household or clan could ever achieve by itself. The ten generals were the admirals of the largest navy in Greece, and the trierarchs were its captains.

On the other side of the balance-sheet, we find the community intervening to ensure that the number of viable households was maintained. This involved restricting the freedom of *kyrioi* in many ways. A father could be prosecuted for neglecting his estate through idleness or mental incapacity. In the Funeral Speech Perikles, knowing that most of the mothers had been married in adolescence, says to the parents of the dead: 'Those of you who are still young enough to have children must bear up in the hope of having other sons: those born hereafter will enable households to forget those who are no more, and the community will benefit twice over – it will not be depleted and it will be safer. . . .' Either in his lifetime or posthumously by will, the *kyrios* of a household with no legitimate son could adopt as his heir a citizen (with at least one brother, who could continue the other household), usually a kins-man, but a legitimate son had an almost inalienable right to his father's estate, and, if there was more than one son, to an equal share. From 451/0 (in the interest, apparently, of racial purity), the community required *kyrioi* to marry Athenian girls if they wanted legitimate offspring, and, in theory at least, no one could propose a resolution in the Assembly or be elected a general unless he had legitimate offspring (Deinarkhos 1.71).

The obsolescent institution of ostracism, devised originally to break political deadlocks, entitled the community to deprive one household a year of its *kyrios* without the necessity of proving that he had broken any law: the victim went into exile for ten years, but his property was not confiscated, and when he returned, his rights were undiminished. The community did confiscate the property of perpetrators of heinous crimes like treason, intentional homicide, sacrilege or other forms of gross irreverence.

Under the strategy devised by Themistokles and adopted by Perikles, Attike was treated as expendable, and in the Arkhidamian War (431–21), and more especially after the Peloponnesians occupied Deke-leia in 413, both large landowners and smallholders suffered heavy losses, material and psychological.

The hoplites of Athens could no longer perform their original function. As we have seen, in the Archaic Age, before Athens had a navy, military service was closely bound up with citizenship. The mass of citizens formed the hoplite phalanx, the chief function of which was to defend the city's agricultural land. In the Classical Age all those who could provide their own armour had to be ready to serve as hoplites, up to the age of forty-nine, or even fifty-nine if necessary. What public arrangements were in force for training the hoplites of the fifth century is not known, but preserved on a fourth-century stone slab from Akharnai are the words of a much older oath sworn by young hoplites:

> I will not disgrace these sacred arms, and I will not desert the comrade beside me, wherever I may be stationed in the line. I will defend our institutions, both sacred and secular, and I will hand on

my fatherland not smaller but bigger and better, to the best of my own ability or with the help of all. I will obey those who for the time being exercise authority reasonably and the established laws and those which they will establish reasonably hereafter. Should anyone seek to demolish them, I will prevent it, to the best of my own ability or with the help of all. I will honour the cults of our fathers. Witnesses are the gods Aglauros, Hestia, Enyo, Enyalios, Ares . . . Zeus, Thallo, Auxo, Hegemone, Herakles, the boundaries of the fatherland, wheat, barley, vines, olive trees, fig trees.

There are a few minor points to note. The 'sacred arms' are the shield and spear presented by the community in the late fourth century (Aristotelian *Constitution of Athens* 42.4). Before the reforms of Ephialtes, it would have been for the Areopagos to decide if the conduct of magistrates or their legislation was reasonable. Two of the non-Olympian deities cited as witnesses are martial (Enyo, Enyalios) and two are agrarian (Thallo, Auxo); originally, the soldiers had mostly been peasants and the peasants had mostly been soldiers. The major point to note is that the oath, embodying much of the Athenian conception of good citizenship, had been rendered partly obsolete by Themistokles and Perikles. The hoplites of Athens could no longer defend their agricultural land: so widespread was the enmity that Athens had incurred in acquiring her empire. Furthermore, it was not the military service of the hoplites, called up by the generals and taxiarchs, but the naval service of the Thetes – paid manual work, devoid of mystique, that they, like metics and *xenoi*, might choose to do at a trierarch's invitation – that gave the city its power (Old Oligarch 1.2). Status and contribution were uneasily diverging.

As the right to hold public office was transferred from the few to the many, political as well as military service was demanded. 'We are unique', claims Perikles in the Funeral Speech, 'in regarding the man who takes no part in public life not as quiet, but as useless.' One reason why the man who took no part in public life was not commended but condemned was that, since the Athenians were not prepared to allow permanent officials to become powerful, they had to carry on the manifold business of government themselves, unpaid at first, later paid just enough to compensate for loss of earnings. (Such compensation could not have been much inducement to, say, a self-employed cobbler, dependent on goodwill.)

Taxation was normally indirect, taking the form of imposts on trade, for example, and in that form was not resented. Nor did the richest citizens resent being called upon to perform liturgies. But when tribute from the subject allies and Athens' own internal revenues combined did not suffice to finance the Peloponnesian War, the community had

recourse to direct taxation in the form of *eisphorai*, which were resented
as an infringement of independence. It is likely that Kleon was a member
of the Council in 428 (Aristophanes, *Knights* 774), and took a prominent
part in exacting the 200 talents raised on that, first, occasion. Furthermore, in legal cases involving rich men and the community, the jury-
courts could not be counted on to be impartial. A state prosecutor might
say with some plausibility (Aristophanes, *Knights* 1359f.): 'Jurors, your
daily bread depends on your convicting the defendant.' Similar sentiments are attested in Lysias (27.1, 30.22, 22.22). In *Wasps* (575) the
veteran juror Philokleon boasts of snubbing the rich. Again, generals
were prosecuted and convicted on what we should regard as insufficient
grounds, like Perikles in 430 and Phrynikhos in 412 (Thucydides 8.54.3).
The leading men of Athens lived in constant danger of prosecution
for deceiving the people or taking bribes or embezzling or 'giving up'
(*prodosia*).

Despite the claims made by Perikles for Athenian tolerance, eccentri-
city was not popular. He himself, after divorcing his wife, chose instead
of remarrying to have as his concubine Aspasia of Miletos, and was
exposed to endless gossip in consequence. The flamboyant behaviour of
his ward Alkibiades engendered so much envy and distrust as partly to
explain why the community twice (in 415 and again in 406) dispensed
with his services when his leadership might have saved it from disaster.
Sokrates was executed in the end. Two institutions that tended to induce
conformity were the jury-courts and the comic theatre, in neither of
which was undue attention paid to relevant fact. In Aristophanes' *Wasps*
(900) Philokleon exclaims that a defendant has the look of a thief, and
in a speech of Lysias (16.18) a young aristocrat thinks it advisable to
point out to the jury that long hair like his harms neither individuals
nor the community. In comedy, named or thinly disguised contemporaries were exposed to savage satire, apparently unchecked by the law of
slander. In Plato's *Apology* (18c), Sokrates alludes to the damage done
him by comic poets over many years, and he singles out Aristophanes
(19c). Traditional morality might enable an eccentric to ignore envy
(Pindar had taught that it was better to be envied than pitied), but it
did not enable him to ignore defamation or ridicule. In *Wasps* (1023ff.)
Aristophanes is anxious to explain that his success as a comic poet did
not go to his head, and he adds that if any lover (*erastes*) urged him to
satirise a favourite (*eromenos*) with whom he was angry, he always
refused to do so; but clearly comedy could serve to bring the wayward
into line.

Despite its concern for the preservation of households, the community
expected its members to be more self-reliant than does a modern welfare
state. Very many of the functions nowadays performed by the police or
some other department of local government were either performed by

the individual for himself or not performed at all. In time of adversity, a household would need the help of neighbours, relatives or friends. The machinery of government being slight, that help might be insufficient against a powerful opponent – an Alkibiades, for example.

Ideally, there should have been no political grouping intermediate between the household and the community. To take a stand (*stasis*) in advance, instead of listening to the debate in the Assembly and voting for whichever policy seemed best in the light of it, would be to reject the rational basis of democracy. As Perikles put it in the Funeral Speech: 'If we cannot all devise policies, we can at least assess them, and we do not regard discussion as detrimental to action, but rather taking necessary action unguided by preliminary discussion.' In fact, although political leaders had their henchmen, nothing very like a political party, held together by an ideology, did emerge. According to Plutarch (*Perikles* 11), after the death of Kimon, Thoukydides, son of Melesias, organised the *kaloi kai agathoi* for political action, but the passage is suspect.

For some years after the ostracism of Thoukydides in about 443, though there were, as there had long been, associations (*hetaireiai*, from *hetairos*, 'comrade') outside the tribal structures, they were not, so far as we know, politically significant: to judge from the historian Thucydides, the community was united behind Perikles when he led it into the Peloponnesian War. Such groups might have merely religious or social aims (as the evening wore on, the views expressed at elegant *symposia* were decreasingly likely to be those of *agathoi politai*, good citizens), but they might also serve to provide mutual assistance in the courts or at election time (Thucydides 8.54.4). Since oaths of loyalty were sometimes required of members, another, less favourable, word for such a group was 'conspiracy', and, as we know from the comedies of Aristophanes, accusations of conspiracy were rife during the Arkhidamian War.

Shortly before the Sicilian expedition sailed, in 415, there occurred the celebrated outrage known as the mutilation of the Hermai. It proved to be the work of a *hetaireia* of upper-class young men. This mutilation was a planned operation, not merely, like some previous mutilations, the aftermath of a drunken revel. One purpose was to bind the *hetaireia* more tightly together, all the members being accomplices in the same crime. Another purpose may have been to stop the expedition sailing – Hermes was the god of travellers – but that cannot be proved.

After the destruction of the expedition had shaken the community's nerve and suggested to many of its richer members that it was time to put an end to radical democracy, some *hetaireiai* were certainly active politically, for it was through them that the short-lived oligarchic revolution of 411 was effected. They made assassination part of politics for the first time since the death of Ephialtes.

Traditional morality offered little encouragement to a Greek to stay loyal to the community in time of adversity. Treason and corruption were commoner than they are in Britain today. From the time that Megabazos carried Persian influence to the northern frontier of Thessaly, about 512, any Greek politician or group in difficulties might seek Persian help. In Athens there were always some Lakonizers as well. The fact that Thucydides (2.65.8.), in explaining the ascendancy of Perikles over his fellow-countrymen, emphasises that it had become manifest that he was utterly incorruptible (like his political mentor, Ephialtes) suggests that that was something unusual in a leading public figure, and no doubt it was. A fourth-century orator (Hypereides 5.25) explained the usual practice to a jury thus: 'Gentlemen, you readily allow generals and speakers to make large sums . . . but on one point you insist: the sums are to be made in advancing your interests and not in opposing them.'

Traditional morality prescribed primarily the preservation, if not the advancement, of your household; secondarily, the preservation, if not the advancement, of your community, but only if that was compatible with attaining the primary objective; thirdly, the practice of justice, fairness, moderation and restraint, but likewise, only if that was compatible with attaining the primary objective. There was a laudatory word for 'loving-the-community' or 'patriotic' (*philopolis*). According to Thucydides (6.92.4), Alkibiades felt able in the winter of 415/14, when he was doing what he could to help the Spartans destroy his country, to describe himself as 'truly patriotic'. 'The patriotism that I feel is not for the circumstances in which I am wronged, but for those in which I exercised my rights in safety.' In fact Alkibiades had not been wronged: he had been recalled to stand trial on a charge of which he was probably guilty – taking the leading part in blasphemously parodying the Mysteries. But even if he had been wronged, we might think that an insufficient justification of his treason. And yet behind Alkibiades in Sparta lay Homer's Achilles sulking in his hut at Troy. On a child of traditional morality at loggerheads with his community emphasis on the power and the glory of his community would make little impression.

This was the appproach of Perikles in the Funeral Speech. For those who die fighting for their country, praise that never grows old. Let the living contemplate the reality of the community's power, and so fall in love with it. Such was the politician's picture. More attractive was the poet's. Aristophanes' *Clouds* (303–312) hail Attike as:

> the home of sacred Mysteries,
> where the Hall of Initiation
> is opened in holy rites;
> of offerings to the Heavenly Gods;
> of high-roofed temples and statues;
> of sacred processions honouring the Blessed Ones;

> of garlanded sacrifices and feasts
>   at every season;
> and, in the spring, of Dionysian joy,
>   with contests of singing dancers
>   and the loud music of pipes.

More prosaically, the poet's picture comprises: the Eleusinian Mysteries (Athens' special access to the divine); the Olympian gods, resident in their splendid temples, and honoured with processions and sacrificial meals; and the great festival of Dionysos with its contests in dithyramb and drama.

But what if the community loses its power? What if it can no longer afford to put on its national festivals as splendidly as it could once? And what if it wrongs an aged *kyrios* with a distinguished war record, who never broke a law, and who once risked his life trying to uphold legality in a frenzied Assembly?

A day or two before he was to be executed, Sokrates rejected the suggestion of his friend Kriton that he ought to escape from prison (which would not have been too hard to arrange). Kriton urged the claims of Sokrates' friends and children. Sokrates preferred to urge the claims of the community. Breaking with traditional morality, he had earlier reached the conclusion that it was wrong to treat anyone badly, even someone who had treated you very badly (49c). (He does not say what he thinks of the institution of punishment, but we do know that he was not a pacifist.) It would be supremely wrong to treat the community and its customs and laws badly. They had much more claim on him than had his parents. It was thanks to them that his father had married his mother and begotten him, and subsequently maintained and educated him. His duty to the community exceeded his duty to his parents: he had more reason to be grateful to it than to them. In the case of the laws, though not of his parents, his sole and life-long duty was obedience.

Not only had he a duty to obey the laws, he also had an obligation. Provided that it is right, one has an obligation to do what one has freely undertaken to do, and Sokrates had freely undertaken to obey the laws. He had done so by choosing to remain in Athens, although he was free to leave. Furthermore, it had always been open to him to try to change the laws by persuading a majority of the Assembly.

One of the laws of Athens was that there could be no appeal against the verdict of a jury-court, the large juries being deemed representative of the community. Sokrates believed that the jury that had tried his case had treated him badly by returning a mistaken verdict, but he did not regard that as justifying any attempt to prevent the execution of the sentence. To make such an attempt would be to do what he could to undermine the laws. And though, in general, individual breaches of the laws do little to undermine them, Sokrates was right in thinking that if *he* tried to frustrate the purpose of the laws, he would be, as it were, contradicting his life's message.

By his life and death, Sokrates poses in sharp terms the question whether a cohesive community is more likely to result from households responsive to public opinion or individuals responsive to conscience.

· 4 ·

The Imperial Ethos

In his Last Speech (Thucydides 2.64.3) Perikles says to the despondent Athenians: 'even if we should one day have to give ground (and everything tends to decline), it will still be remembered that we ruled over far more Greeks than did any other Greek state.' Perikles here makes a mistake like that made by Lincoln in the Gettysburg Address: what Athens is remembered for is not her empire. But we shall misunderstand that empire unless we realise that, whatever material advantages it conferred on rulers or ruled, the number of Greeks subject to them was a source of deep satisfaction to most Athenians. Athens maximised her own freedom by abridging the freedom of other Greeks. (There was no comparable satisfaction to be derived from ruling over barbarians.) According to the Athenians in Sparta in 432, honour was the second of three motives that from the anti-Persian alliance produced the empire (Thucydides 1.75.3), and whatever other emotions it may have aroused abroad, there can be no doubt that the Athenian Empire did arouse admiration. In Greek thought, power was the prime source of glory. Earlier in his Last Speech (2.63.1), Perikles had spoken of 'the city's imperial dignity, in which you all take pride'. That pride, shared by almost all, though not by the extreme right or by Sokrates, was attended by a confidence without which the cultural achievement would hardly have been possible.

Was this imperial pride tinged with feelings of guilt?

Our knowledge of the imperial ethos derives from Thucydides and especially from his speeches, in so far as corroborated and supplemented by Aristophanes, the Old Oligarch and the surviving imperial decrees of the Assembly. If Aristophanes, writing for the mass audience, did not plainly accept the empire, if the Old Oligarch, realistic or cynical as he was, did not show grudging admiration for the efficiency with which the empire was administered, if the tone of the imperial decrees was not as peremptory as it is, we should have to suspend judgment, but, in fact these diverse sources agree well enough. It remains, however, to consider the consistently hard-boiled tone of the most relevant speeches in Thucydides.

In reading any speech in Thucydides, it must be remembered that the historian does not claim (1.22.1) to be doing more than 'keeping as close as possible to the general intent of what was actually said'. The point of 'as close as possible' is that if he had not himself heard the speech, he would have had to rely on others who had heard it, but who might have misrepresented its general intent. Clearly we are entitled to assume, if we believe that Thucydides was truthful and did not subsequently lose sight of what he had written in 1.22.1, that whenever he attributes a speech to a certain party, that party made a speech (or perhaps a series of speeches) with the same 'general intent'. But if we give a low interpretation to 'general intent', we are entitled to believe that Thucydides sometimes suppressed arguments that were used but that he thought inappropriate, and that he sometimes supplied arguments that were not used or made explicit but that he thought would have been appropriate or were implicit. This would explain the consistency of tone and even phrasing in the speeches of diverse characters.

When the speech was a contribution to a debate about foreign affairs, as opposed, for example, to a funeral speech, the arguments that Thucydides thought appropriate were unsentimental assessments of what was expedient, and what was expedient might or might not be honourable or just. Moral considerations could not outweigh, but they might reinforce, considerations of expediency. Thus the unsentimental Diodotos, arguing against the execution of all the men of Mytilene, says (3.47.3): 'But if you destroy the common people of Mytilene, who did not take part in the revolt and who, on getting possession of arms, surrendered the city of their own accord, you will in the first place be killing your benefactors, and that is unjust.' In view of what Thucydides says at the beginning (3.36.4) and end (3.49.4) of the debate, it is virtually certain that some speakers argued from compassion, but Thucydides seems to have regarded such emotional argumentation as inappropriate in a debate on foreign affairs.

At first reading, the following passage from Perikles' Last Speech (2.63.1f.) may seem surprising:

> Do not think that the struggle concerns only the exchange of freedom for slavery. No, it concerns also the loss of your empire and the danger arising from hatred incurred in its exercise. Nor is it any longer possible for you to retire from the empire, if indeed there is anyone who, fearful in the present situation, would play the part of such honest inactivity. For your empire is now like a tyranny. Its acquisition is counted unjust; its surrender would be dangerous.

In this short passage Perikles admits that the empire was hated, tyrannical and unjustly acquired. Was it so, and even if it was, would Perikles have said so in a speech to the Assembly?

The empire posed a clear threat to many states outside it, and though the common people of many states inside it will have disliked Athens less than they disliked their own oligarchs, it cannot be doubted that the empire was widely hated. The Old Oligarch (1.14) regarded it as inevitable that the ruler should be hated by the ruled.

Tyranny – rule by a single usurper or his descendants – was abhorrent to democratic Athens, and it may seem strange that Perikles should compare the empire to a tyranny. But in Aristophanes (*Knights* 1111–4) the Knights tell Demos: 'Fine [*kalos*] is your empire when all men fear you like a tyrant.' And the language of some imperial decrees is certainly dictatorial. In the early 440s (or possibly the late 420s) the Assembly approved a decree requiring the subject allies to use only Athenian coins, weights and measures. Among the provisions was (assuming a probable restoration) this (ML 45): 'If there are no Athenian magistrates, the magistrates of each community shall carry out the provisions of the decree; and if they do not act in accordance with the decree, such magistrates shall be prosecuted in Athens and the penalty shall be disfranchisement.' Athenian magistrates were quite likely to be present. It was not stretching language to call such treatment of once free Greeks 'tyrannical'.

As Sokrates found, few people have an entirely clear idea of justice or injustice, but most people are likely to think that to take away rights long unchallenged is unjust. No one in Thucydides denies that the novelty of Athenian rule over other Greeks is unjust, but 'just' and 'unjust' in Greek were not such a powerful pair as 'fine' and 'shameful'.

The mass audience that heard decrees like the Coinage Decree read out in the Assembly or heard songs like that in Aristophanes' *Knights* sung in the theatre was also the mass audience that heard the beguiling flattery of embassies from smaller cities like Leontinoi or Egesta in the Assembly (Aristophanes, *Akharnians* 633–640; Thucydides 6.8.2) and fulsome praise of Athens in funeral speeches in the Kerameikos and in tragedies in the theatre; but it is not likely to have been shocked by Perikles' Last Speech, and we must not call that speech 'cynical' or we shall have no word for the speech of Kleon to the Assembly in 427 or of the Athenian ambassador Euphemos to the assembly of Sicilian Kamarina in 415 (Thucydides 6.82 ff.).

Thucydides assimilated not only the style of his speakers but also their arguments to his own. It is hard to believe that even the Athenian Assembly could have followed arguments as dense or as general as he sometimes offers. Nevertheless there is no reason to doubt that in the original of the Last Speech Perikles did make such realistic references to the empire. Whether such realism of thought and speech owed something to the Sophists or whether the second, more destructive, generation of Sophists derived their hard-boiled realism from the imperialist politicians, it appears to have been characteristic of Athenian political debating in the latter part of the fifth century. Both the Athenians at Melos in 416 and Euphemos at Kamarina in 415 renounce 'fine words' (Thucydides 5.89, 6.83.2).

Before the Peloponnesian War it appears that most Athenians would have said of their empire that though it was unjustly acquired, it was nevertheless a source of honour. As the struggle went on, less and less was heard of honour and more and more of the other two motives.

The prime motive that produced the empire was fear (1.75.3) – fear perhaps of Persia, but more likely of the Spartan alliance. Under pressure from her alliance, Sparta had in 479/8 invited Athens to remain an open city on the pretext of denying the Persians a base should they return. By tricking the Spartans, Themistokles had made it possible for Athens to rebuild her walls nevertheless (Thucydides 1.89.3). It would have been foolish to offend the Spartans by such trickery had armed intervention by Sparta not seemed at least possible.

Once the Athenian alliance had begun to turn into the empire, Athens had to fear revolt as well as the increasing hostility, already noted, of states outside the empire, such as Aigina, Corinth and Megara, which with reason felt their independence threatened by Athenian naval activity. In the early 450s Athens subdued Aigina, called by Perikles 'the eyesore of the Peiraieus', and she became a tribute-paying ally. In the late 430s the fears of Corinth and Megara coincided with Spartan fear of the growing power of Athens to precipitate the Peloponnesian War (Thucydides 1.23.6). (Although the behaviour of Athens might be regarded as provocative, it was the enemies of Athens who broke the Thirty Years' Peace of 446 (Thucydides 7.18.2).)

Another Athenian fear, antedating the formation of her alliance and indeed the Spartan alliance, was fear for her food supply. From the time of Solon she had been dependent on imported corn, and became increasingly so as her population grew during the fifth century. In this respect she was unique among cities of Greece. The corn route from the Crimea was her lifeline. She had to ensure that the merchant-men bringing her grain could do so unmolested. Hence her warships, which had a limited range of operation, needed a chain of friendly, or at least neutral, harbours reaching to the Bosphoros and beyond. Fear for her corn supply helped to bring the empire into existence, but while the empire remained strong, the fear was veiled. A related fear was fear for her supply of timber, which came mainly from Thrace.

In his Last Speech Perikles also told the Athenians: 'Your naval resources are such that neither the King of Persia nor any other nation on earth can stop you sailing where you like.' By the terms of the Thirty Years' Peace, Sparta had conceded to Athens thalassocracy or mastery of the sea. So long as she retained that mastery, the chronic inability of

Attike to sustain her population would not matter: the subject allies who paid the tribute were mostly islanders, incapable of combining forces against Athens (Old Oligarch 2.2) or denying her fleet the use of their harbours; the fleet could therefore ensure the continued payment of the tribute, by which it was itself financed, and also ensure the safety of merchant shipping, especially that bringing corn from the Crimea, Egypt and elsewhere, in exchange, chiefly, for Laureion silver, whether coins or bullion. And barring unforeseen reverses, like the plague that struck first in the spring of 430, and distant and lengthy entanglements like those in Egypt (in the 450s) and Sicily (415–13), there was no reason why Athens should lose that mastery.

The strategy devised by Themistokles and adopted by Perikles was, despite the scepticism of the rest of Greece (Thucydides 7.28.3), almost as sound as it was simple. Long walls linking the walls of Athens and Peiraieus created a stronghold that was large enough to contain the population of Attike and also impregnable – siegecraft being still primitive, and there being little prospect of treachery. A springtime invasion by the Spartan alliance, or even the permanent occupation of a fortress in Attike, would be destructive, but not in itself very dangerous. The danger to health from overcrowding inside the walls was not foreseen, and we know too little about the state of medicine at that time to be able to say that it was foreseeable.

The other dangers were psychological. Most Athenians still lived in the country and would naturally be distressed if their property was destroyed by invaders. Country folk cannot have found it easy to adjust to the ways of the city. Again, a strategy that amounted to an admission that the hoplites of Athens, though capable of suppressing revolting allies (Old Oligarch 2.1), were not capable of protecting Attike against her enemies, would entail a serious slump in hoplite morale, since a man's standing depended on his contribution to the defence and welfare of his household and community. While the Spartans were in Attike, only for some of the younger hoplites was there the prospect of active service, as marines or *epibatai*, ten per vessel: we do not hear of Thetic *epibatai*, who must have been armed at public expense, until 415 (Thucydides 6.43). (Members of the upper class who were of military age and were not serving in the 1,000-strong cavalry would serve as hoplites, but their morale would be less seriously affected than that of the Zeugitai as long as they could afford to play their normal liturgical role, especially as trierarchs. The 1,000 members of the upper class who did serve in the cavalry were hardly affected because of their active role in curbing invaders (Thucydides 2.22.2).)

The third motive that produced the empire was advantage (1.75.3). (Of the three successive motives – fear, honour and advantage – honour is the odd one out: it alone rises above the prudential.)

The most obvious advantage – as the world, if not Sokrates, judged – that Athens derived from her empire was the tribute paid by the subject allies, and paid after the Coinage Decree in the silver coinage of Athens. If we can believe the few figures we have, the public income of Athens at the beginning of the war was 1,000 talents a year (Xenophon, *Anabasis* 7.1.27), of which 600 talents came from overseas and 400 from internal sources. (In *Wasps* (660), produced in 422, Bdelykleon gave the total annual revenue as nearly 2,000 talents. His case would have seemed stronger if he had magnified the true figure, but in 425 the assessment of tribute had been trebled (ML 69), and he may not have been far wide of the mark.) The text of Thucydides (2.13.3) says that the 600 talents came in tribute from the allies, but the evidence of inscriptions is that the amount received in tribute cannot have exceeded 400 talents. It is not, however, impossible to believe that 200 talents came from other imperial sources. The 400 talents that came in as tribute matched Athens' own internal revenue and made possible the financing of her huge fleet, which cost far more than did the military operations of the Spartan alliance.

In addition to the annual income from the subject allies there was the alliance reserve, transferred from Apollo's custody on Delos to Athena's on the Akropolis in 454, if not earlier. This reserve, consisting partly of spoils won from the Persians and partly of surplus tribute, amounted to 5,000 talents or more at the time of transfer. After the conclusion of peace with Persia, the decision was taken to use the reserve to finance the rebuilding of the temples burnt by the Persians. From that source, now administered by the Treasurers of Athena, came the money to pay for the marble Parthenon, the gold and ivory Parthenos and the marble Propylaia.

Every extension of the empire brought not only an increase of power and glory but also an increase of tribute. Thucydides (6.24.3) thus describes the mind of Athens in 415 at the time of the second debate on the projected expedition to Sicily:

All alike fell in love with the expedition: the old men thought that either they would crush their opponents or at any rate, with so great a force, would not come to grief; the men of military age longed to see distant sights and spectacles, and were confident of a safe home-coming; the mass of servicemen expected to draw pay in the short run and to win additional power which would make it possible to draw pay for ever.

Since the reserve had been used to finance the Periklean building-programme, imperial revenues had come to be regarded as available for any purposes of state. The more money there was to spend on paying citizens for public service, the more nearly would be realized the Periklean ideal of an *emmisthos polis* – a community in public service (Plutarch, *Perikles* 12.4).

A second advantage that Athens derived from her empire was additional territory. In 476 Kimon recovered Eion-on-Strymon from the Persians, and it was occupied by Athenian settlers. He then cleared Skyros of pirates, and it too was occupied by Athenian settlers. In the middle of the century, Athenian settlers were probably sent to Lemnos and Imbros, both member-states of the alliance. Settlers like these, who retained their Athenian citizenship, perhaps because they formed only an addition to an existing community, were known as *kleroukhoi* or lot-holders, anglicised as 'cleruchs'. At about the same time Perikles led 1,000 cleruchs to the Thracian Khersonese or Gallipoli. These five settlements not only provided poor citizens with land, but also helped to protect the corn and timber routes. Other, smaller, settlements were planted on the territory of, probably restless, allies, such as Naxos, Andros and perhaps Karystos in the south of Euboia. In 446, after the suppression of the revolt of most of Euboia, the people of Hestiaia were expelled, and 1,000 Athenians settled there.

A sign of Athens' continuing interest in Thrace was a joint settlement of 10,000 Athenians and allies at Ennea Hodoi, upriver from Eion, in about 465. Allied participation in this semi-autonomous colony was necessary because Athens herself could hardly have spared more than a thousand or two able-bodied men. The colony was successfully established, but when the colonists ventured further inland they were virtually annihilated by the native Edonians at Drabeskos. An inscription of about 445 (ML 49) records the decision to send a colony of Zeugitai and Thetes to Brea, somewhere in Thrace, but its fate is not known. In 436 Athens established a Panhellenic colony, led by Hagnon, on the site of Ennea Hodoi, now renamed 'Amphipolis'. Again, the Athenian colonists were in a minority, but though, like Eion, Amphipolis did not pay tribute, she made an important contribution to the imperial revenue. A similar Panhellenic colony had been founded in the west, at Thourioi, in 443. These two colonies may be called 'Panhellenic' in that most of the colonists were not Athenians, but they were – initially at any rate – friendly to Athens.

It is evident that between the middle of the century and 436 Athens exported several thousands of her poorer citizens. The choice of site appears to have been determined by strategic considerations. Why were poor Athenians willing to go to these sites at a time when Attike was not being ravaged? It would be a striking commentary on the value of Athenian citizenship, if thousands of the poorer Athenians were willing to abandon those rights for ever. Cleruchs, who are sometimes hard to distinguish from colonists, did not cease to be citizens of Athens. But what of the Athenian colonists of Brea, Thourioi and Amphipolis? Did they for ever forfeit their Athenian citizenship? No one knows, but it seems unlikely.

Did cleruchs, even if sent out, have to remain on their lots? In 427, after the suppression of the revolt of most of Lesbos, Thucydides (3.50.2) says of the Athenians:

> They did not impose tribute on the Lesbians, but they divided the land, apart from that of Methymna, into three thousand lots; three hundred of them they consecrated to the gods, and to the remainder they sent out cleruchs of their own, chosen by sortition; the Lesbians agreed to pay a rent of two hundred *drakhmai* a year for each lot and worked the land themselves.

Athens could hardly have spared 2,700 able-bodied men in 427, and even if she could have, nothing more is heard of Athenian cleruchs on Lesbos, even when Thucydides could have been expected to mention them, had they been there. It looks as though these cleruchs soon became absentee landlords.

Very few Greek states had enough cultivable land. Athenian cleruchs may have been welcome in the Khersonese, but on Naxos, Andros, Euboia and Lesbos they must have been bitterly resented, even if oligarchs had been removed or the tribute was reduced. No less bitterly resented must have been the private acquisition of allies' land by richer Athenians. This is attested in Thasos (ML 79) and Euboia, for example.

A third area of advantage, which the possession of the empire certainly enlarged, lay in trade and tourism. If, roughly speaking, the alliance-cum-empire paid for the fleet and the Periklean building-programme, Athens' imports of corn were paid for with her silver and the proceeds of trade and tourism. Solon had allowed foreign craftsmen to settle in Athens (Plutarch, *Solon* 24.2). Themistokles had begun to realise the commercial, as well as the naval, possibilities of Peiraieus. As we have seen, metics, though subject to a poll-tax, enjoyed a more or less respected place in the community. By the middle of the fifth century, when Hippodamos had replanned Peiraieus, Athens-cum-Peiraieus was a centre of both commerce and tourism. Whether for short stays or long, thousands and thousands of visitors, Greeks and non-Greeks, poured constantly into Peiraieus, if not Athens, for a variety of purposes, and paid for doing so in a variety of ways.

The empire rested on the efficient management of the naval installations of Peiraieus (three harbours with their ship-sheds, the main jetty in Kantharos), 300 sea-worthy triremes (in 431), gear (wooden and hanging), raw materials (timber, pitch, leather, canvas, papyrus, bronze), manpower (trierarchs, petty officers, oarsmen, deck-hands, marines, archers). The provision of ships, together with the necessary gear and sheds, was the responsibility of the Council. The whole dockyard area was supervised by an annual board of ten magistrates and guarded by 500 men. It was a source of great pride to the Athenians, and in the fourth century Demosthenes (22.76) classed the ship-sheds with the Propylaia, the Parthenon and the stoas.

The growth of Peiraieus as a naval base was matched by its civil and commercial growth. More and more people, both native and foreign, were living there, many of them connected with the dockyards in one way or another, and many of them engaged in commerce. Thalassocracy enabled Athens to import not only vital commodities but also, as we learn from the comic poet Hermippos (fragment 63), such luxuries as fish from the Hellespont, beef from Italy, cheese from Sicily, frankincense from Syria, ivory from Libya, slaves from Phrygia and Thessaly, dates from Phoenicia, and rugs and cushions from Carthage. Perikles summarised the position in the Funeral Speech: 'So great is our city that we import the products of the whole world and enjoy foreign goods quite as freely as our own.' If self-sufficiency had been a goal once, it was hardly so now. It should, however, be added that not all the goods imported into Peiraieus were consumed locally: there must have been much re-exporting to smaller cities round about.

To the international port of Peiraieus, where those who could pay might buy almost anything, flocked merchants, craftsmen and sailors from all over the eastern Mediterranean, bringing with them their own customs, dress and dialect or language (Old Oligarch 2.8). Plato's *Republic* opens with an account by Sokrates of how he had the previous day walked down to Peiraieus with one of Plato's brothers to attend the first festival held in honour of Bendis, the hunting goddess of the Thracian immigrants (this was in 429) and of how he was persuaded to visit the home of the Syracusan metic Kephalos. The supposedly autochthonous Athenians had no need to travel in order to observe customs not their own.

To Athens itself came a steady stream of foreign embassies, of Greek intellectuals and tourists, and of allied litigants and delegations. It was a tendency of Athenian imperialism to have cases that arose in allied cities but were of concern to Athens tried by Athenian courts. 'The common people of Athens', noted the Old Oligarch (1.17), 'derive the following advantages from having trials involving allies held in Athens: first, the 1 per cent tax at Peiraieus brings in more for the city; second, anyone with rooms to let does better; third, so does anyone with a vehicle or a slave for hire; fourth, heralds do better when the allies stay here.' (Heralds were attached to boards of magistrates and to law-courts.) When their cases came up, there were court fees to be paid, which went towards the jurors' pay.

Every spring, in time for the City Dionysia, delegations from the cities of the empire were required to bring their tribute to Athens (Aristophanes, *Akharnians* 504–6), where they were to take it to the council house (ML 46). They were also invited to attend the festival. According to Isokrates (8.82), a decree was passed requiring the tribute money for the year to be carried into the *orkhestra*, talent by talent, when the theatre was full. What the delegates felt about that display or about the new public buildings financed by the alliance-cum-empire or about the tragedies and comedies (compare an Afghan delegation at the Bolshoi Ballet) may be conjectured. Most Athenians were certainly very proud of it all.

The advantages derived by Athens from her empire are evident, but as we have seen, it was not the habit of Thucydides in reporting, or apparently of Athenian speakers in contributing to, debates on foreign affairs to consider any advantages that Athens conferred on others. In the Funeral Speech (2.40.4f.), however, Perikles does allude to advantages conferred by Athens: 'In doing good, too, we are unlike other states: we make our friends by conferring, not by deriving, benefits. . . . We alone give help without fear for the consequences – not from a calculation of what is expedient but with the confidence of free men.' The language is as fine as it is general, but it hardly refers to the subject allies. What does refer to them is the proud claim that Athens alone of her contemporaries gives her subjects no cause to complain that their rulers are unworthy to rule them (2.41.3).

Although at the time of the formation of her grand anti-Persian alliance in 477, Athens certainly had benefited the member states, and although subsequently she was prepared to help Ionian or other cities outside the alliance who appealed to her (as Egesta was to do in 416), Perikles does not attempt to show that after the conclusion of peace with Persia (by the Peace of Kallias, 449) the alliance-cum-empire was conferring benefits on the subject allies.

The Athenians at Sparta in 432 can explain convincingly enough how and why Athens was offered the anti-Persian hegemony. They then claim that the transformation of hegemonial alliance into empire was 'inevitable', human nature being what it is. But, as they admit at the start (1.73.1), the most they can prove is: 'It is reasonable (or natural) for us to hold what we have gained.' 'Reasonable' perhaps but not strictly 'inevitable', and certainly not 'just'. 'Praiseworthy are those', say the Athenians (1.76.3), 'who so far comply with human nature as to rule others, and yet prove more just than the extent of their power requires.' In peacetime at least Athens' treatment of her allies was more respectful of justice than it needed to be (and so not strictly inevitable). On the whole, we may believe that an Athenian jury-court was more merciful, at least to the ordinary East Greek, than had been the Persian satrap. Paradoxically, the Athenians argue, Athens' very moderation made her rule more resented than had been that of Persia, which in any case was imperfectly remembered.

Moderate in administration, Athens could claim to be moderate also in taxation. It is probable that the burden of the tribute fell, not very heavily, on those in the cities of the empire best able to bear it. Before the Peloponnesian War only five cities are known to have paid more than 15 talents in any one year. The maximum, 30 talents, was paid by Aigina and Thasos alone.

To be subjected in any degree to the jurisdiction or taxation of another state was a painful infringement of autonomy, but in this case there were corresponding advantages. In the early fourth-century funeral speech of Lysias, very likely never delivered, the Athenians who died fighting in the seventy years down to the battle of Aigospotamoi in 405 are said to have kept the allies free from civil strife, because they did not believe that the many should be slaves of the few and instead compelled all to live on an equality. Furthermore, the Great King of Persia no longer coveted what belonged to others, no tyrant arose among the Greeks, and no Greek city was enslaved by non-Greeks.

This passage exaggerates Athenian liberation of Greek cities: under the Peace of Kallias the Greeks of Cyprus had been left to fend for themselves. On the other hand, East Greek cities from Phaselis westwards would have been foolish to think that the Peace of Kallias ended the Persian danger. It ended the diminishing hope of exacting reparations from Persia, but not the need for a permanent, powerful and costly navy. The maintenance of such a navy would have been too costly for Athens alone. Hence her continuing need for tribute. In return for their tribute, the subject allies were spared any further expenditure on defence against Persians, Phoenicians or pirates. (Of course, the Persian or Phoenician threat was not felt very acutely in, say, Aigina.)

In *Akharnians* 541ff. Aristophanes makes Dikaiopolis say to the audience: 'Suppose a Spartan had sailed out, denounced a Seriphian puppy-dog as contraband and sold it, would you be sitting back at home? Far, far from that! In double quick time you would be launching three hundred triremes.' Seriphos was a small island member of the alliance, less than a hundred miles from Sparta. Such behaviour by Athens may be viewed in at least three different ways: unfavourably, with the poet, as expressive of absurd bellicosity; neutrally, as expressive of the city's restless energy; favourably, as expressive of proper concern for a weak dependent. The Athenian empire presented all these aspects. A few years earlier, in 430 or 429, the Assembly had decided (ML 65) to send an embassy to Perdikkas, King of Macedon, telling him to respect Methone's frontiers and freedom of movement by land and sea.

Athens' suppression of piracy promoted her allies' trade. Much of the tribute, paid by the richest of the allies, returned to the poorest of them

in the form of pay for naval service: as more and more of Athens' Thetes
rose to become Zeugitai, she became less and less able to man even a
third of her 300 triremes with her own citizens. She could just do it,
using metic Thetes as well (Thucydides 1.143.1; Old Oligarch 1.12); to
do more, she needed volunteers from her alliance. Normally, her fleets
were manned by a mixture of citizen Thetes, metic Thetes and subject
allies. Immigration into Athens being unrestricted, thousands of poor
men from the over-populated cities of the empire, and especially from
the islands, decided to take metic status in Athens between the Peace of
Kallias and the outbreak of the Peloponnesian War. Service in the fleet
was not the only kind of employment open to them. The building-
programme demanded much additional labour, skilled and unskilled.
The sons of these metics knew no other home-town than Peiraieus or
Athens.

The degree of social cohesion achieved in Athens in the half-century
from 461 to 411 was unusual: in most Greek cities there was at least
tension between the few and the many. Being democratic herself, Athens
had a natural preference for democracy among her allies, as her oligarchic allies will have realised. Though we cannot trace the process in
detail, it is clear enough that within the alliance oligarchy steadily gave
ground to democracy. When oligarchies revolted, as Samos did in 440
and Mytilene in 428, suppression of the revolt was normally followed
by the establishment of democracy. How heavily these new democracies
depended on Athenian magistrates and troops cannot be determined.

In the Mytilenean debate, Thucydides (3.47.2) makes Diodotos claim
that in all the cities of the empire the common people favour Athens.
Though some allowance should perhaps be made for rhetorical exaggeration, the claim appears, from Thucydides' own narrative, to be broadly
true. If the popularity of the Athenian empire could have been assessed
by counting citizen heads among the allies, the historian might not have
written elsewhere (2.8.4f.) that in 431 'men much more strongly
favoured Sparta ... such was the indignation felt against Athens by
most men, some wishing to be released from the empire, others fearful
of being incorporated in it'. This judgment can hardly be upheld, unless
'men' are understood to be men of the same social standing as
Thucydides himself.

That the fifth-century empire was advantageous in many ways to most
of the subject allies is probable; that it was, as far as we know, left to
a metic to make that claim in the fourth century is not entirely to the
discredit of fifth-century Athens.

· 5 ·

Schooling, Literacy, Books and History

To understand a culture, one needs to know how its beliefs, values and techniques are transmitted from generation to generation. Before the coming of literacy, this is mostly done orally, though often informally or indirectly. Aristophanes makes his heroine Lysistrate say (*Lysistrate* 1124f.): 'Since I have often listened to my father and other old stagers talking, I am not badly educated.' (Miss Beale and Miss Buss would have been horrified to hear her say that.)

To understand the culture of Athens we need to know the processes of oral instruction and also the inroads that literacy had made on their domain.

We must begin with the influence on the young child of mother, nurse and, later, *paidagogos* (in households rich enough to be able to afford slaves to perform the two latter roles). Since, as we shall see, the mother is unlikely to have had much education herself, and likely to have been young, her influence was presumably mainly psychological and moral. If she contrasted her restricted scope unfavourably with her husband's freedom (Euripides, *Medeia* 232–247), her attitude to any son of hers is likely to have been ambivalent. When the lullaby stage was passed, it was time for improving fables, such as those ascribed to Aesop. Then the mother would introduce her child to such myths, legends and genealogies as she knew. The size of her repertoire would depend on what she herself had learnt as a child, which would have been reinforced by subsequent participation in the religious life of the city. There will have been few books, if any, in most houses, and certainly no illustrated books; but in some houses visual assistance to oral instruction in myth was provided by painted pottery, which commonly depicted mythological scenes. It is important to realise that instruction in myth was not just being told stories: it was also instruction in politics, morals, religion, science and history, all in one.

The nurse will usually have been older than the mother, and thus more experienced, if not better educated. She might attempt to impose discipline with the help of such bogeys as Empousa, Lamia and Mormo. The primary duty of the *paidagogos* was to escort any son of the family to school. How much else he might do is unclear, but since, like the

94

nurse, he was a slave, compelled on many occasions to say in effect 'Do not do as I do; do as I say', his influence must have been limited. According to the Platonic *First Alkibiades* (122b), Alkibiades' guardian, Perikles, assigned as his *paidagogos* a Thracian slave too old for other work.

The influence of the father, away from home for much of the day, must have been largely indirect, but the growing child will have become steadily more aware of his father's role as family priest. Regular venera-tion of Zeus Herkeios (from *herkos*, fence) or Ktesios (from *ktema*, possession) and of Hestia, goddess of the hearth, must have ensured that those deities figured early in the oral instruction in myth (though there was not much to be said about Hestia). There were also three deities whose images might stand outside the front-door: Apollo Aguieus (from *aguia*, street), Hermes and Hekate (Aristophanes, *Wasps* 804, 875; *Clouds* 1478; *Lysistrate* 64). These were the deities of travellers by road.

When the time came for the *paidagogos* to take the son of the house to school, 'grammar' formed only about one-third of the curriculum, and, according to Plato's *Protagoras*, as we shall see, the purpose of learning to read was to be able to learn Homer and other edifying poets by heart. Close visual study of texts, so prominent in our academic education, was largely lacking in Athenian education. Though it had been committed to writing for more than two centuries, poetry was still written to be heard. (There are gradations between reading aloud for others to hear and completely silent reading to oneself. That inaudible reading of prose was a familiar accomplishment in fifth-century Athens seems to be established by the behaviour of the Chorus in Euripides' *Hippolytos* (864–876) when Theseus is reading Phaidra's letter and by the behaviour of the Second Slave in Aristophanes' *Knights* (118–128) when the First Slave is reading the Paphlagonian's oracle.)

The other two-thirds of primary schooling consisted of music (mainly learning to sing poetry to the lyre) and gymnastics or athletics (wrestling, running and so on), and since the schooling of most Athenians went no further than this primary stage, to which we shall shortly return, we may suppose that formal instruction in school did little to shake the supremacy of the spoken word.

After a boy had left school, his instruction remained largely oral. His father and uncles would talk to him and introduce him in due course to the principal institutions of the city – theatre, law-courts, and Assembly. In the working of all these, writing played some part, but what chiefly mattered was being able to take in what one heard, some of it (dithyrambic and tragic choruses, especially) being decidedly complex. Citizens picked up news and comment from the busy-bodies in the Agora and at the perfumer's or barber's (Lysias 24.20), not by reading. Other, more philosophical, exchanges might occur at gymnasia or drinking-parties.

Vocational training, like political initiation, was normally given by fathers to their sons. In Sparta, according to Herodotos (6.60), there were castes of heralds, *aulos*-players, and cooks, and, though, as we should expect, there was more flexibility in Athens, the same tendency prevailed. Technical manuals were beginning to appear, but the bulk of vocational instruction was certainly transmitted orally, from father to son.

Such in outline were the processes whereby Athenian culture was transmitted. We may now consider in more detail the role of schooling, literacy and books within the oral context.

One might have expected a democracy to take a keen interest in education – 'We must educate our masters.' But in fact the Athenian state did not run schools of its own, and did not subsidise or enforce attendance at private schools, or inspect them. Fathers wishing their sons to have a 'liberal' education – one fit for the son of a free man – sent them to private day-schools, if they could afford to. The schools would be chosen carefully, since anybody might open one; which partly accounted for the low esteem in which schoolmasters were held. Demosthenes (18.265) put teaching letters on much the same level as being an under-secretary of the Assembly or the junior actor in a team of three.

In his sketch of the old education (*Clouds* 961–983), Aristophanes' Right describes the heroes of Marathon (Marathonomakhai) as having been instructed as boys, between, that is, about seven and fourteen, in music and athletics. To get their instruction the boys of each urban district had to visit music master and trainer.

It was the first job of the music master (*kitharistes*, *kithara*-player, a *kithara* being a heavy seven-stringed lyre) to teach his pupils to play the ordinary lyre. When they had learnt to do that, he taught them improving lyric poetry, which he himself had set to music, and taught them to sing it (Plato, *Protagoras* 326ab). In due course they would be able to sing to their own accompaniment. If the lyre or *kithara* was the characteristic instrument of Apollo, that of Dionysos was the *aulos*. As the lyre stood to lyric poetry, so stood the *aulos* – more like an oboe than a flute, despite the conventional translation – to elegiac poetry, but instruction in the *aulos* seems to have been less common: you cannot accompany yourself on a wind-instrument. If *aulos*-playing was required at drinking-parties, it was normally provided by slave-girls. Learning to sing and play the lyre was considered an essential part of a liberal education. To be unable to play the lyre was to be uneducated (Aristophanes, *Wasps* 959). Ability to take part in a dithyrambic or dramatic chorus, which would involve dancing as well as singing, was a valued accomplishment, but not a rare one, as we can see from the requirements of the big festivals. At the City Dionysia the dithyrambic contests required 1,000 singers. Gentlemen were also expected to be able to join in after-dinner drinking-songs (*skolia*; *skolios*, crooked, of the course of the singer's myrtle-wreath around the *andron*), though Sokrates and other intellectuals preferred to converse (Plato, *Protagoras* 347c-e).

The other form of instruction mentioned by Right was that provided by the trainer (*paidotribes*, boy-rubber – an allusion to the use of olive oil in massage). The trainer normally kept what was in origin a wrestling school (*palaistra*) somewhere within or near the city walls. It consisted of an open quadrangle with adjoining undressing-room and wash-room. Just as it was the music master's business to prepare boys for participation in musical contests at festivals, so it was the trainer's business to prepare boys to compete in athletic contests. There were events for boys and for beardless youths at the Great Panathenaia, and there were events for boys at the Theseia.

The life of an Athenian boy was in many ways healthier than that of his British equivalent of today. Because of the climate the Athenian was in the open air more, and he did not wear constricting clothes or shoes, and he did not over-eat. Consequently, the remedial function of physical training was less in evidence. And the original connection with military training, which had no doubt been the earliest form of education in the community, was nearly severed. 'As for education,' said Perikles (Thucydides 2.39.1), 'our enemies seek to attain courage through arduous training from early youth, but we live as we please. . . .' Whatever the public arrangements for hoplite training may have been, the contribution of the private trainer was no more than general fitness. According to *Protagoras* (326bc), boys were sent to the trainer so that they might 'not be compelled by physical deficiency to play the coward in battle or on any other occasion'. In Plato's *Gorgias* (452b) a trainer defines his function as 'making men physically fair and strong'. He was expected to have some knowledge of surface anatomy and diet, and to be able to prescribe exercise appropriate to a given physique. Bearing his badge of office, a forked rod, he would introduce his boys, who would be segregated from the young men (Plato, *Lysis* 206d), by easy stages to wrestling, boxing, running, long-jumping (more useful than high-jumping in countryside divided by more water-courses than walls or hedges), and throwing the discus and javelin. (Even this last exercise had little relevance to hoplite training, though it was relevant to cavalry training.) The elements of complex activities were practised to an *aulos* accompaniment. That *palaistrai* were more than mere institutes of physical training is apparent from the descriptions given in Plato's *Kharmides* and *Lysis*. At the beginning of *Lysis* a young man tells Sokrates that the usual occupation of his friends and himself at a newly built *palaistra* is conversation. *Palaistrai* were social centres, where Sokrates was quite free to converse with anyone who was willing to converse with him and who was not required by the trainer.

At some stage there had been added to elementary education a third constituent, provided by what we might call the Greek master (*grammatistes*, teacher of letters). Aristophanes does not mention him in *Clouds*, but that can hardly be because he thought that he was still a rarity when the Marathonomakhai were at school, say in 500. He is plainly in evidence on a famous red-figure cup painted by Douris at about the time of Marathon. It may be that the poet sensed the connection between the work of the *grammatistes* and the intellectual developments that he so much abhorred, and wished to sharpen the contrast between old and new. In the course of time the *grammatistes* became the *didaskalos*, the teacher *par excellence*.

Since gauging the extent and depth of literacy in the second half of the fifth century is so important for understanding the culture, it will be well to sketch more of the background first.

Mycenaean syllabic writing went out of use in about 1150. Greece remained illiterate until Greek traders who had settled in the Levant adopted and adapted the alphabetic writing of the north Semites in the middle of the eighth century. If an alphabet is a set of written signs representing more or less all the phonemes of a spoken language, then the Greek alphabet is the first. The earliest surviving Greek inscriptions, scratched on pots or sherds, are mostly personal, but since the new alphabet was easy to learn, it spread rapidly and was soon put to more public uses – on gravestones or dedications to gods. Its commercial and legal possibilities, too, were soon realised in the mercantile cities of Old Greece. At Athens in about 621 Drakon had codified and published (on wood) the Athenian laws relating to homicide and other offences. Early in the sixth century Solon had codified and published, also on wood, a complete corpus of law.

A century later such documents had begun to be published on stone. No documentary inscriptions survive from the period of the tyrant Peisistratos or his sons, but there is reason to suppose that a standard text of Homer, designed to curb the vagaries of rhapsodes reciting at the Great Panathenaia, was prepared in Athens at the behest of Peisistratos or his son Hipparkhos (Platonic *Hipparkhos* 228b). At the same time official, and unofficial, collections of oracles in writing were being formed by oracle-utterers (*khresmologoi*) like Onomakritos (Herodotos 7.6.3). In 510 the Spartan king Kleomenes carried off the oracles that he found in Athena's temple on the Akropolis (Herodotos 5.90.2).

The earliest extant Athenian decree published on stone (ML 14), relating to Salamis, is dated by modern scholars to about 500. Only three other decrees, all concerned with religious matters, survive from the period before the reforms of Ephialtes. Thereafter the official documents published on stone came to include much more than just the texts of laws. They were often lengthy, and both for that reason and because of the care taken over the carving, must have been costly. It is not easy to believe that such expenditure would have been incurred unless most of the citizens had been able to read the inscriptions. Nor would the recurrent phrase 'for the inspection of anyone who wishes' have been compatible with extensive illiteracy. The masons must have worked from master-copies written on papyrus, but the systematic filing of those master-copies in the old council house may not antedate the end of the fifth century.

In addition to the use of permanent public inscriptions, we must consider the use of temporary public notices written on wooden boards coated with gypsum (*Wasps* 249, 848) – perhaps announcing proposed additions to, or alterations of, the laws; perhaps announcing meetings of the Assembly and the agenda of the Council; certainly announcing forthcoming trials; certainly announcing call-up for military service. In Aristophanes' *Peace* (1183), produced in 421, taxiarchs are attacked for arbitrarily altering the lists of those liable for call-up, with the result that a member of the tribe Pandionis, standing by the statue of Pandion, suddenly sees his own name. (It is not known just where the statues of the ten Eponymous Heroes stood in the fifth century.) We do not know how early in the fifth century this method of publishing such information was adopted, but we may assume that by the time it was adopted, in preference to the use of a herald, the great majority of Athenians could read.

Ostracism, which was probably introduced by Kleisthenes in 508, presupposed that most of the citizens could at least read names. If most, or even many, of the citizens had been unable either to inscribe an *ostrakon* for themselves or even to read an inscribed *ostrakon* handed to them, the opportunities for deception would have been intolerably great.

The earliest Greek schools of which we are told (on Ionian Khios, where 120 boys learnt their ABC, and on Dorian Astypalaia in the southern Cyclades attended by sixty boys) do not antedate the first decade of the fifth century. Nevertheless, if we reflect on the existence of a sizable school on such an insignificant island as Astypalaia in the 490s, on the dangers of introducing ostracism to a population not largely literate, on the Douris cup, on the use of inscriptions on stone from the beginning of the fifth century, then we can hardly doubt, despite the silence of Aristophanes, that the Marathonomakhai had had at least the chance of attending schools run by *grammatistai*. The most literate fathers would have been out of the house for most of the day, many of the mothers would have been barely literate themselves, and evidence for literate Greek-speaking slaves giving instruction in the home seems to be lacking. Hence the need for *grammatistai*.

We may take it that by the mid-fifth century at latest most Athenian boys of the upper and middle classes attended for a period a school run by a *grammatistes*, and that the *grammatistes* was steadily gaining in importance over the *kitharistes* and *paidotribes*. To judge from the Douris cup, a *grammatistes* and *kitharistes* might share the same premises. The activities of the two were clearly related, even though Homeric poetry, once sung by bards to the four-stringed *phorminx*, was now spoken in the schools of *grammatistai*, as it was on the platform by rhapsodes. (Every full Greek word was spoken with a melodic or pitch accent.)

The first thing to be learnt from the *grammatistes* was the shape, name and value of each letter. When a boy could recognise and write the letters and knew their values, he was ready for syllables – first vowel or consonant and vowel, then more complicated syllables. Eventually, since by this method only slow progress was possible, he would be able to read and write such a polysyllable as 'A – GA – MEM – NON'. (There were no small letters for him to learn.) He was then ready for lines of poetry. In *Protagoras* (325e–326e) Plato makes the great Sophist say:

> when boys have learnt to read and write, and are ready to under-
> stand the written word as well as they formerly understood the
> spoken, their masters set before them the works of good poets to
> read as they sit on their benches, and they make them learn them
> by heart. These works are full of guidance, and full of stories,
> eulogies and panegyrics of the good men of old. The intention is
> that the boy should be eager to imitate them and long to be like
> them.

Several points about this passage may be noted. First, the 'good poets' – narrative and encomiastic – were mainly epic poets, and above all, Homer and Hesiod. In the Douris cup, the *grammatistes* is reading a line from a lost epic as he hears the boy reciting it. Second, the poets' writings were treated in some respects like sacred texts: apart from the obsolete words, they were assumed to be intelligible enough for criticism at this stage to be otiose or worse. The objective was to train the character rather than to sharpen the sensibility. Third, the value of learning by heart was unquestioned. According to Xenophon (*Sympo-sion* 3.5), Nikias compelled his son Nikeratos to learn the whole of Homer – *Iliad* and *Odyssey*, that is – in the hope that he would turn into a good man. (When we consider how much less writing there was to remember then, the feat, which was accomplished by all rhapsodes, is not quite so astonishing as it at first seems. Again, although the 28,000 lines did not rhyme, they were metrical (the basic scheme of the hexameter line was that of six dactylic feet (-⌣⌣) less the last syllable: -⌣⌣/-⌣⌣/-⌣⌣/-⌣⌣/-⌣⌣/-⌣) and included much repetition of phrases and lines. And we may further assume that learning was assisted by the Athenian boy's ability to identify with the characters he was reading about. He was totally absorbed in what he read, and every recitation he gave was a reenactment of the events his lines described.) Fourth, Athenian parents and teachers did not hesitate to use compulsion, often of a crude physical kind. Protagoras had shortly before mentioned that nurse, mother, *paidagogos* and father might enforce their moral education of a boy 'with threats and beatings'. Not until the time of Quintilian does antiquity offer us a reasoned rejection of corporal punishment as an educational instrument.

As we noted above, the Athenian state declined to interest itself in the provision of education. Those fathers who could afford to do so sent their sons to school (the fees can hardly have been very high), escorted by a *paidagogos*, who spent the school hours sitting at the back of the class or in the *palaistra*. It was his business to see that the boy reached his school safely and behaved himself there. What then of the boys from homes with no slaves, or at any rate no *paidagogos*? There must have been many such. Did they learn all they knew orally, from their fathers and their fathers' friends? All we can say is that by the second half of the fifth century illiteracy was decidedly rare, and that a father who could not afford much schooling would probably be more concerned that his son should be able to read, write and reckon than that he should be able to sing or wrestle. In *Wasps* (959f.) Philokleon assumes that grammar is a more basic subject than the lyre, and it is the *kaloi kai agathoi* that Aristophanes elsewhere (*Frogs* 729) describes as 'brought up on wrestling and dancing and music'. Such a father would likewise be less concerned to have his son's character improved by Homer than to have him able to keep records and accounts. In Aristophanes' *Clouds* (19), Strepsiades kept accounts, although he was not a tradesman. In *Wasps* (538, 559, 576) Bdelykleon took full notes on his father's speech. At a lower social level, the Sausage-seller was more or less literate. He had not, of course, been to a *paidotribes* (*Knights* 1238f.) or even apparently to a *didaskalos* (1235f.): he was schooled in the Agora (636). There is a reference to his rustic counterpart in Lysias (20.11): 'Whereas *he* was poor and kept sheep in the country, my father was educated in the city.' There is no sign of village schools. It is not surprising to find deficiencies of script or spelling on the surviving *ostraka*.

So far we have been mainly concerned with primary schooling, though we noted in passing that there were young men as well as boys to be found in *palaistrai*. The chief requirement of future hoplites was general fitness, which would also contribute to good looks. No doubt some adolescents, including those who aspired to become poets, continued with their kitharists. The elderly Sokrates took lessons from a kitharist called Konnos, whose other pupils were boys (Plato, *Euthydemos* 272c). There seems to be no good evidence of literary education provided by *grammatistai* at the secondary stage. Plato's Protagoras (338e) says that the main part of a man's education is being good on poetry, which he defines as being able to distinguish good poetry from bad and being able to give one's reasons, but his ordinary schooling hardly enabled an Athenian to do that. The teaching of arithmetic at the primary stage, presumably by the *grammatistes*, is not directly attested, but we know that various branches of mathematics were, at some stage, school subjects for at least some boys, because Plato (*Protagoras* 318de) makes Protagoras say:

> The other Sophists ill treat young men who have escaped school subjects [*tekhnai*, an odd use] by forcibly immersing them once more in such subjects – arithmetic, astronomy, geometry and music.

Xenophon (*Reminiscences* 4.4.7) makes Sokrates couple '2 × 5 = 10' with the spelling of his own name as examples of definite knowledge. In Aristophanes' *Wasps* (656) Bdelykleon invites his father to 'calculate roughly, not with counters, but on your fingers'. A study of spelling, involving such questions as 'How many letters are there in "Sokrates"?' or 'What is the fourth letter in "Sokrates"?' would be facilitated by a study of arithmetic. It seems probable that the *grammatistes* gave some, elementary, instruction in arithmetic. How any boy was able to learn astronomy or geometry at school is not clear.

In general we may assume that no lower-class boy had any secondary schooling, and that few middle- or upper-class boys had any secondary schooling that was at all intellectual, though the richer the father the more prolonged the schooling: 'the sons of the richest men go to school earliest and leave latest' (*Protagoras* 326c). *First Alkibiades*, as well as telling us about the incapacity of Alkibiades' *paidagogos*, sums up (106e) his schooling as having consisted of grammar, the lyre (but not the *aulos*) and wrestling. Alkibiades was going to school in about 440. Few Athenian boys will have had more schooling in the fifth century. In Plato's *Menon* (94b) Perikles is said to have had his two sons by his Athenian wife taught riding, music, athletics, and the other *tekhnai* (suitable for young gentlemen). After the end of their primary schooling and their release from the surveillance of the *paidagogos*, most middle- and upper-class boys enjoyed a great deal of freedom before they came of age at eighteen and became liable for hoplite service. At the beginning of *Lakhes* (179a) Lysimakhos says that most fathers (middle- and upper-class fathers, that is) allowed their sons to do what they liked when they became lads (*meirakia*). Possible new activities included riding and training in the stylised use of hoplite armour (*Lakhes* 181c). In *Clouds* (916f.) Right blames Wrong for the fact that lads will not go to school.

Though vases afford some evidence of female literacy and perhaps even of girls' schooling, we may be sure that no girls had any secondary schooling. Xenophon makes Sokrates say (*Reminiscences* 1.5.2.):

> If at the end of our life, we should want to entrust someone with the task of educating our sons, or protecting our daughters' virginity, or preserving our property, should we . . . ?

It is clear that much more importance was attached to the protection of girls' virginity than to the enlargement of their minds.

It is not easy to determine the importance of books (papyrus rolls, that is) in fifth-century Athens. There is no evidence of anything like a publishing house, but the comic poet Eupolis (fragment 304) mentions that a part of the Agora was reserved for the sale of books.

If a Panathenaic text of Homer was prepared at the behest of Peisistratos or Hipparkhos, rhapsodes must have needed copies, and so in due course must serious *grammatistai*. Plutarch (*Alkibiades* 7.1) relates two stories of Alkibiades, the first of which at least is credible:

> Once, when he was emerging from boyhood, he accosted a schoolmaster and demanded a volume of Homer. The schoolmaster replied that he had nothing by Homer, whereupon Alkibiades struck him with his fist and passed on. Another schoolmaster told him that he had a Homer which he had corrected himself. 'What!' said Alkibiades, 'Are you teaching boys their ABC when you are competent to edit Homer? You should be educating young men.'

As texts of Homer multiplied, texts of Hesiod and the more personal poets must have come into circulation. Again, actors, though probably not singers, must have been given written copies of their parts, if not of whole plays. What lies behind a modern edition of an Athenian play is simply the plain text, such as was used by the poet-producer himself (he gave the stage directions orally). He put a certain number of copies into circulation among his friends, and some of those copies were in turn copied. Aristophanes (*Frogs* 52f.) makes Dionysos speak of reading Euripides' *Andromeda*, which had been produced seven years before.

The earliest prose works seem to have been those of the Ionian thinkers, travellers and architects – Anaximandros, Anaximenes, Herakleitos, Hekataios and Theodoros. It is possible that Anaxagoras of Klazomenai introduced the idea of prose treatise into Athens. In the mid-fifth century there appeared a number of technical manuals, which, had they survived, would be of the greatest value for reconstructing the culture of Athens – Sophokles 'On Tragedy', Agatharkhos of Samos 'On Scene-painting', Iktinos and Karpion 'On the Parthenon', Meton 'On the Calendar',

Hippodamos of Miletos 'On Town-planning'. Since they have not survived, it is impossible to say how comprehensive they were. They may
not have been more than pamphlets.

These works were contributions to what De Quincey called the literature of knowledge, but there now began to emerge a prose literature of
power. Perikles may have been the first man to speak a written speech
in court. Protagoras and possibly Herodotos gave readings from their
works. In consequence of this new concern with the sound of written
prose, oratory became more elaborate and prose more elegant. Nor were
Sophists content to publish their works merely by reading them; they also
circulated written copies of model speeches and of manuals. Xenophon
(*Reminiscences* 4.2) describes a young bibliophile called Euthydemos, in
whom Sokrates took an interest, as possessing numerous works by the
most famous Sophists. Some of these presumably belonged to the literature of power and some to that of knowledge – in the course of conversation with Euthydemos Sokrates remarks how numerous the medical
works available are.

There were thus two kinds of prose writing as well as poetry available
in book form, but it is unlikely that the demand for books was very
great. No doubt by the time that ostracism was introduced most Athenians could read simple legends, but there is no reason to suppose that
many of them had much further use for reading. At the end of the fifth
century Aristophanes was still mocking Euripides for his large library
(*Frogs* 1409). He also said (1114), rather mysteriously, that everyone
had a book; but 'everyone' need not mean more than the most advanced
members of the theatre-going public. The situation seems to have been
that, though some Athenians had quite a number of books, most had
very few or, more likely, none. Libraries as large as those of Euripides
or Euthydemos were unusual even among the limited number of book-
readers.

But Thucydides had read his predecessors in history, and it is hardly
credible that Aristophanes could have quoted so extensively from
Aiskhylos and Euripides relying solely on his memory of single performances (the plays of Aiskhylos were revived after his death in 456 –
Akharnians 10, *Frogs* 868). The text of Euripides' *Andromeda* was
available, and presumably the same was true of his other plays. Anaxagoras's book, or pamphlet, of which Sokrates had acquired a copy as a
young man (*Phaidon* 97b, 98b), was available for a *drakhme* in 399
(*Apology* 26de), and it was not unique in that; for Sokrates can assume
that the boy Lysis has come across the writings of the natural philosophers (*Lysis* 214b). According to Xenophon (*Reminiscences* 1.6.14),
Sokrates said:

Together with my friends I unroll and go through the treasures

which the wise men of old bequeathed to us in their books, and if
we come across anything good, we excerpt it.

By the end of the fifth century, there were some fluent readers in Athens
and many books for them to read.

It remains to consider further how far the coming of literacy and
books had loosened the hold of oral tradition.

Let us look first at the power of the Greek language itself. A *Weltan-
schauung* is already embodied in the vocabulary and syntax of a language
before it is put to use, though this fact is unlikely to come to light
until the reading habit is well established. The linguistic precision of
Protagoras and Prodikos prepared the way for such observations as
Aristotle made about the Greek equivalents of 'adultery' and 'theft':
they are inherently pejorative. Again, there are many words to mark
distinctions in areas of concern to society, and few or none in other
areas. There is no exact equivalent in Greek of 'blue'. Illiterate people
are very much in the power of the language they inherit.

The use to which a language is put is mainly determined by the
attitudes of those who speak it, and their attitudes are mainly determined
by what they themselves have heard in infancy and childhood. Until
literacy becomes widespread and books are readily available, the individual has little chance against the oral tradition. Anthropologists have
shown that the corpus of oral lore (myth, legend, genealogy, and so on)
on which the young of pre-literate or only partially literate societies are
brought up changes with changes in the circumstances of those societies.
The function of the oral lore is in large part to render intelligible and
bearable the existing order. As that order changes, so the oral lore
changes, and incongruous elements are modified or discarded. In this
way the oral lore spares itself an unequal conflict with awkward facts,
and for this reason, attempts to extract history from oral lore are largely
misconceived.

History is hardly possible without written records more or less as old
as the events they describe. Only when such written records are available
and used can the conception of the past as something separate, and
perhaps radically different, from the present begin to grow. It was not
for some three centuries after the invention of the Greek alphabet that,
thanks to Herodotos, something like our conception of history emerged.
Herodotos was a citizen of Halikarnassos, a city on the coast of Karia
and an original member of the Athenian alliance. Believing that 'there
lived many brave men *after* Agamemnon', he had resolved to record in
a coherent narrative as much of the truth as he could discover about
the exploits of both sides in the Persian War, fought more than a
generation earlier. He also resolved to enquire into the causes of the
Persian War, and the causes he was looking for were mainly secular.

Though not uninterested in legendary antecedents, he began his story proper with what he himself knew: the aggression of the Lydian Kroisos against the Greeks of Asia Minor (1.5.3). (He knew (3.122.2) that Polykrates, tyrant of Samos, had belonged to the race of ordinary men and that Minos, King of Knosos, had not.)

His aims were those of an oral poet, but his methods were very different: he travelled widely, looking at monuments and manners, listening to priests and nobles. The priests were prone to moralise and the nobles to glorify their own families, and without more checking against written records than Herodotos was able or willing to do, his enquiry (*historie*) could not be entirely successful; but then Aiskhylos, writing less than eight years after the battle of Salamis, had introduced into his *Persians* (355ff.) a most improbable tale about a Greek message to Xerxes on the eve of the battle.

A very schematic chronological setting for Herodotos' *Histories* would be:

750 Alphabet invented
700 Homeric poems written down
600 Beginnings of Ionian natural philosophy
595 Solon flourished
545 Fall of Sardes to Kyros of Persia
525 Xenophanes of Kolophon flourished
480 Battle of Salamis fought
450 Peace of Kallias signed
430 Thucydides' *History* begun
415 Herodotos' *Histories* completed

The oral forebears of the Homeric poems had been of the greatest importance in holding together the small Greek settlements in Ionia, and it was inevitable that once alphabetic writing had been invented the Homeric poems should be written down. But to write down oral lore is to freeze it, to start to turn it into museum pieces: rhapsodes are curators, not creators. Once this has happened, thought must assume new forms, such as philosophy in Ionia, tragedy in Athens. Much of Ionian natural philosophy concerned timeless questions, but in the fragments of Xenophanes and others we find evolutionary ideas, which are akin to historical ideas. The Persian War had been the biggest upheaval in Greek history since the fall of the Mycenaean cities (though Herodotos knew nothing of that) and demanded ambitious literary treatment, which Herodotos supplied.

Ignorant though he was of oriental languages, Herodotos did manage to produce a coherent and, as we now know, remarkably accurate account of Graeco-Persian affairs from the fall of the Lydian capital, Sardes, to the Persians to the fall of Sestos in 478 to the Athenians, and at many points he pushed the frontiers of knowledge further back than that. His example was not, however, copied. Thucydides legislated for his successors: serious history was contemporary political history, of people whose language one knew. The use of oral testimony was endorsed, but enquiry into the distant past was rejected as too hazardous. And profoundly grateful to Herodotos as we must be, we have to admit that Thucydides was not very far wrong. Certainly, the chances of pushing back the frontiers of coherent Greek history more than four generations before 430 were and are slight. Indeed it might be said that really coherent Greek history begins only in the late 430s – with Thucydides.

As well as being too hazardous, enquiry into the distant past was also unnecessary. The purpose of history as now conceived was to exhibit the comparatively new activity of politics, that is, the public behaviour of men living in communities with written constitutions. In place of 'myth' (good stories, that is), Thucydides offered his readers political analysis so subtle as to demand reflective reading rather than declamation. The revolution in communication was complete; but only for a tiny intellectual minority.

By skilful use of the traditions of great families and of Panhellenic shrines, Herodotos had been able to push Greek history back to the mid-sixth century. But for most Athenians of his day there was only one notable figure in the period between Theseus and the Persian War, and that was Solon, Arkhon in 594, whose elegiac poems had been written down and preserved. Since, however, they did not treat of his political activities or their context in any detail, what was, and indeed is, definitely known about his career cannot be said to amount to much. The ascription to the man Solon of laws that were manifestly not his (Andokides 1.95, for example) is hardly more extraordinary than the ascription to the hero Theseus of democratic principles (Euripides, *Suppliant Women*). It was supposed that heroes were better endowed than ordinary men; it was not supposed that radical changes in thought had occurred since their day.

Apart from Solon, then, the characters of myth and legend, Agamemnon and Achilles and the others, were much more real to most Athenians than anyone else who had lived before the Persian War. The current myths and legends, and, above all, those canonised by Homer and Hesiod, afforded, as we have said, instruction in politics, morals, religion, science and history. Inevitably, Homer's hold on fifth-century Athens was less tight than had been his hold on, say, seventh-century Khios. Athenians knew that Mycenae had become politically negligible, and the only king in Athens was an annual magistrate, the Basileus. So the story of Agamemnon, King of Mycenae, had lost some of its relevance. Nevertheless, remarkable claims were still made for Homer. In *Republic* (598de) Plato makes Sokrates say:

> Now we must examine tragedy, and Homer its leader, since people tell us that these poets know all arts, and all about human virtue and vice, and all about religion.

Such claims for Homer and the tragedians (recognised by Aiskhylos as dependent on Homer, that is, epic as a whole) are reminiscent of exaggerated claims once made for a classical education. The natural philosophers rejected Homer as a scientist, the Sophists rejected him as a political theorist, Herodotos (2.118) rejected him as a historian, Sokrates and Plato rejected him as a moralist and theologian; but most Athenians accepted him in all these capacities. The sustained fervour of Plato's onslaught in *Republic* would be inexplicable had not most Greeks continued to regard Homer as a reliable source of guidance on almost all questions.

But though it is right to see Homer's works as a kind of '*Encyclopaedia Graeca*', they were much more than that. The reason, says Sokrates (*Republic* 607e), for the Greek 'passion for such poetry' is 'the upbringing afforded by fine constitutions'. (Plato's use of 'fine' is ironic.) Even after the advent of widespread literacy, that upbringing remained primarily oral. From childhood onwards, Athenians were constantly assisting at, if not performing in, passionate reenactments of the words and deeds of Agamemnon, Achilles and the others. In Xenophon's *Symposion* (3.6) Nikeratos says that he listens to rhapsodes almost daily. It is difficult for fully literate stoics to appreciate the impact of such reenactments on superficially literate people for whom the Delphic Apollo's gospel of moderation and restraint was an unrealised ideal. Plato makes a Homeric rhapsode, Ion of Ephesos, say (*Ion* 535c-e):

> When I am describing something pitiful, my eyes fill with tears; when something terrifying or strange, my hair stands on end and my heart throbs . . . when I look down from the platform, I see the audience weeping, gazing wild-eyed, astounded at the words they hear.

The impact of acted tragedy was even greater than that of recited epic. Greatest and, according to Plato, most disastrous was the impact of rhetoric – in law-courts, Council and Assembly (*Gorgias* 452de, *Phaidros* 261ab).

· 6 ·

Religion

No one knows just how Greek religion began, but it is safe to say that in historical times it had two main components, one Indo-European and the other Mediterranean. The Mediterranean component was essentially agrarian – at one stage, a set of magical procedures intended to assist the fertility of earth, domestic animals and women. The Indo-European component, too, was no doubt magical at one stage. Behind Zeus, the weather-god, and his eagle lay the Indo-European rainmaker or bird-shaman of Siberia, first visible in a Lascaux cave-painting. A shaman is a kind of magician or sorcerer, who, after being 'called', going into retreat and acquiring a technique of ecstasy, is supposedly able to go at will on psychic trips, perhaps up to heaven or down to the underworld. To induce his ecstasy, the shaman is supposed to summon and take possession of familiar or helping spirits, especially the souls of dead shamans, who enable him to acquire information or perform feats beyond normal human scope.

An obviously shamanic figure in Greek mythology is Orpheus – his descent into Hades to recover a soul, his musical control over birds and animals, his singing head. Salmoneus, King of Elis, simulated the thunder and lightning of Zeus and was struck by real lightning. More or less shamanic figures in the history of Archaic Greece include Epimenides of Knosos (slept for six years in a sacred cave, made psychic trips, ate special food, said to have claimed to be a reincarnation of the rainmaker Aiakos, and to have lived many times on earth), Pythagoras of Samos (said to have claimed to have lived many times on earth, and perhaps extended the idea by telling his disciples that they would live again), and Empedokles of Akragas (promised his disciple Pausanias medicine to ward off illness and old age, control of wind and rain, and the recovery of a dead man's soul from Hades; claimed to be immortal himself).

There is no clear line marking the end of magic and the beginning of religion, but whenever procedures intended to rouse nameless powers begin to give way to procedures intended to placate and please named and personal gods, the transition from magic to religion is being made. The sorcerer typically utters spells and incantations or performs acts that coerce, the priest utters prayers that may or may not be answered.

When the Indo-European ancestors of the Greeks were still in the magical state of mind, they explained the unexpected frustration of such human purposes as the catching of a certain species of animal by reference to other stronger purposes, projected on to the environment. In these circumstances, there would come forward sorcerers or shamans claiming, and readily believed, to have affinities with, and control over, the species in question.

At this very early stage, the world was small, and no one had the leisure to consider whether it had had a beginning in time or had an end in space. The questions raised were practical questions of survival and not metaphysical ones. The shaman provided, or appeared to provide, the mastery necessary for survival. It is not hard to imagine that a shaman with a magnetic personality and a long record of success would be remembered after his death, would appear in the dreams of the living, would be credited with their subsequent successes in the chase, and would begin to loom larger and larger in their thinking as increasingly tall stories were told of his exploits.

Quite apart from our own experience of story-tellers' exaggerations, we can see clear evidence of the fact of magnification within the corpus of Greek mythology. Tales of contests such as that in *aulos*-playing between Apollo and the Satyr Marsyas would have made no sense once Apollo had reached his Homeric dimensions, but tales of contests in music between rival shamans make very good sense. The power of the gods no doubt grew as human groups grew.

If the gulf in power between Marsyas and the Homeric Apollo was wide, it was no wider than that between the Homeric Apollo and the Homeric Zeus. Zeus had not always existed, had not created either the world or mankind, and had had to fight for sovereignty. In Homer he respected the honours (*timai*) of the other Olympians, as a Dark Age king had respected the honours of his nobles, but it is nevertheless clear that 'the father of gods and men' held in reserve a more than patriarchal power over them all. He was much stronger than the other gods as well as being the eldest of the three sons of Kronos (*Iliad* 13.355, 15.166). No other gods dared to remain seated when Zeus came in (*Iliad* 1.533–535). He alone of the gods had no direct dealings with mortals (other than the objects of his desire): he communicated with them through divine emissaries, or by thundering, or by appearing as an eagle.

It is hard to doubt that Homer here preserves a memory of kings such as were buried in the shafts within the grave-circles at Mycenae. Indeed, apart from his description of Mycenae as 'rich in gold', this is almost all the memory that he does preserve of the exalted position of the *wanax*, revealed by the decipherment of the Linear B tablets.

As we shall see, the attitude of a Greek to his god was very much that of a subject to an absolute monarch, who enforces rules that he does not himself have to keep (Euripides, *Ion* 442f.), and whose behaviour is only partially predictable or explicable. In so far as Zeus is revealed in the bright upper air (*aither*) he is predictable; but in so far as he is revealed in the stormy turbulence of the lower air (*aër*) he is not. The prudent subject will keep his sovereign's rules, especially those requiring the payment of tribute.

The distance from the Siberian shaman through the Indo-European Sky-father and the Zeus of the *Iliad* to the Zeus of Aiskhylos and Pheidias is enormous. According to Strabo (8.353), Pheidias told his nephew Panainos that his Zeus was modelled on the description in *Iliad* 1.528–530, but no one will ever be able to chart all the earlier stages. One has only to think of successive waves of Greek invaders, ending with the Dorians, parting as they broke over mountainous Greece, Crete, the Cyclades and the Anatolian coast, of the syncretism that ensued in unnumbered valleys, between which the only communication, usually sea-borne, was oral, and of the counter-current from the Near East, reflected in the legends of Kadmos, Danaos, Perseus and Pelops. Part of the explanation of the polygynous behaviour of Zeus is no doubt to be found in these facts; his general sovereignty was symbolised by his alliances with local goddesses.

Homer's description of Zeus' appearance, used by Pheidias, may be derived from the appearance of a storm – the dark brows being the underside of the storm-cloud, the flowing hair being the cirrus above – but it is hard to believe that the prehistoric Greeks discerned in the fickle workings of the weather the personality and exploits that their mythology ascribed to Zeus. Zeus often behaves like a shamanistic trickster because that is how he began. (This Indo-European Zeus must be distinguished from the Zeus who was born in a Cretan cave and who was akin to Adonis and Osiris in dying and being re-born.)

Before Homer went to work, epic poetry had already located the Sky-father, at the top of the highest mountain in Greece, Thessalian Olympos, and to his seat above the clouds less powerful gods had been attracted as courtiers from their original spheres – citadel (Athena), for example, or sea (Poseidon) or forest (Artemis) – or from their favourite cities – Athens (Athena), for example, or Aigai (Poseidon) or Paphos (Aphrodite). We may hope to understand something of what a less powerful god meant to the Greeks only if we relate that god to Zeus, the sovereign, and to the other members of the pantheon, looking for resemblances and contrasts.

One stage in the development of the Greek gods that is supremely, and even dangerously, well documented is the Hesiodic and Homeric.

The *Theogony* of the Boiotian poet Hesiod is the earliest surviving attempt to impose order and definition on the shifting chaos of early Greek religious beliefs. He finds room in his pantheon for a wide diversity of divinities: the individual and personal gods of current cult, like Zeus and Athena; their half-forgotten predecessors; groups, like the Fates and the Muses; features of the visible world, like Heaven and Earth, Sun and Moon, Aither, and individual rivers, such as the Nile and the Strymon; personified abstractions – as we should say – such as Persuasion, Strife, Victory, Sleep and Death. (The Greek tendency to describe in personal terms what we regard as things was very strong; how far it reflected a difference in perception, as opposed to linguistic tradition, is hard to say.) Of Homer it may be said that the brilliance of his portrait of the Olympian gods distracted the attention of generations from many important aspects of Greek religion. What he does give us is a portrait of divine society on Olympos, modelled, with extraordinary consistency, on a heroic society on earth, a society in which little matters but honour.

These gods are beautiful and, like their possessions, ageless and deathless. Though not even Zeus is omnipotent, they have much more power, and therefore honour, than men. What they do they do easily and without risk. Indeed the whole life of the gods is easy. For them the spectacle of human life is entertainment – gripping at times and even painful if their own offspring are in trouble, but not ultimately serious. The Christian reader of Homer is struck not only by the humanity of his Olympian gods but also by their inhumanity.

At the beginning of *Iliad* 4, the Greeks and Trojans having agreed that single combat between Menelaos and Paris, the seducer of Menelaos' wife Helen, shall decide the issue, Zeus acknowledges that Menelaos has gained the victory, despite the intervention of Aphrodite to save Paris from death. The way is thus clear for the Trojans to hand back Helen, together with due reparations, and for the Greeks to sail home. Nevertheless Zeus, who claims to hold Troy in higher esteem than any other human city, complies when Hera invites him to order Athena to incite the Trojans to break the truce. (Hera and Athena resented the fact that Paris had once awarded a beauty prize to Aphrodite rather than to either of them.) To counter Zeus' expression of his esteem for Troy, Hera says that should he ever be vexed with her favourite cities – Argos, Sparta, Mycenae – she will not seek to save them from destruction.

In virtue of his sovereignty over gods and men, the Zeus of the *Iliad* has a concern for good order and the *status quo* on earth, which may or may not extend beyond his concern for his own honour, but it certainly matches the concern of earthly kings for good order and the *status quo* within their domains. Both Zeus and Apollo were increasingly associated with order and peace, and, as civilisation emerged from the Dark Age, such a battle as that between the Olympian gods and the superhuman but subdivine Giants came to be regarded as a triumph of civilisation over brute force and not simply as the suppression of a rebellion.

Even if Zeus and, to a lesser extent, Apollo can be shown to have grown more interested in justice and harmony as civilisation developed on earth, it would be hard to claim as much for the Olympians in general, and certainly it could not be claimed that the Olympians were generally benevolent towards humanity. Communities like Troy or Mycenae and individuals like Odysseus in the *Odyssey* or Hippolytos in Euripides' play about him may enjoy the temporary favour of Zeus, Hera, Athena or Artemis, but they cannot count on enjoying it for long.

It was unusual success, in, for example, the chase, that created the shaman. It was the persistence of his presence after death, in dreams and in stories, that magnified him to divine dimensions. But because the new god was only a successful man, writ ever larger as horizons widened, his followers looked to him for success rather than for moral example. He could be expected to share both their tastes and their vices. Fed on special food, ambrosia and nectar, he enjoyed much more power (how much more depended on his status in the hierarchy worked out by Hesiod and others) and did not die or even grow old. (Neither, therefore, could he rise to the moral height of a human hero, since he never risked catastrophe or death.)

Less than two centuries after Homer, Xenophanes of Kolophon came very close to an important truth: the Homeric gods were men writ large. On the other hand, it might be held that the Homeric picture of a world dominated by beings of dazzling power and beauty, towards whom a man might well want to stretch out both arms, with palms upturned, in a gesture primarily of amazement, and who, though respectful of each other's sphere of operation, were yet ultimately unconcerned about the fate of men, matched much of the experience of humanity. Neglecting Aphrodite, Hippolytos adored Artemis, but Artemis did not attempt to save him from destruction by Aphrodite. In Aristophanes' *Wealth* (1117) a slave tells Hermes that the cessation of sacrifice to the gods is justified: 'You looked after us badly in the past.'

When Solon (13.3f) prayed to the Muses:

Grant me prosperity from the Blessed Gods
and from all men good repute always

he gave neat expression to the aspirations of conventional upper-class Athenian piety. The gods, who were indeed blessed, being spared the indignities of weakness and old age, had it in their power to confer prosperity on man or to withhold it. Solon does not hope for communion with them in this world or the next. He hopes for prosperity in this world, which would certainly conduce to the constant esteem of his fellow men.

What materials Hesiod and Homer had to work on can be inferred only to a limited extent. Homer (that is to say, whoever put the *Iliad* and *Odyssey* into substantially the shape in which they have survived to this day) was an artist working on traditional materials – lays and formular phrases – of great antiquity. If we had his materials, we could see further into his mind than we in fact can. We should be able to infer his principles of selection and composition, and we should be able to say whether he was a theologian as well as an artist. Did he create his intensely personal gods or merely inherit them? Was he the first to describe in detail the hair of Zeus and Poseidon and the eyes of Athena and Aphrodite?

Homer seems to have inherited a psychology according to which any exceptional human performance is explained by the intervention of external superhuman power, and any ordinary human performance may be so explained. Homeric man less often acts than reacts. Not only does Zeus thunder, lighten and rain, but Athena prompts Odysseus or Telemakhos, and the (undifferentiated) Muse prompts Homer himself. The self-awareness of the individual and his conviction of his power of self-determination developed slowly. In Homer the greatest successes are achieved by heroes who are well-endowed because they are descended from a god and who are lucky because they receive the help of an appropriate god.

This may appear a more deterministic account of human performance than our ascription of, say, an athlete's success or failure to his being or not being 'in form', but it is compatible with the ascription of responsibility. (Indeed, there could not be a society which did not regard some exceptional performances as praiseworthy and others as punishable.) The Homeric gods do not so much overrule the passions of the heroes as work through them.

In the notion of men receiving the help of an appropriate god we may discern the means whereby poets were able to build up the personalities of their gods. Characters in Homer's *Odyssey* very often ascribe an exceptional event to an unspecified god or *daimon*, but, on the whole, good writing or story-telling is specific. It is more interesting to say 'Athena prompted' than 'Some god prompted'. Yet there can be little doubt that the anonymous idiom came first. Any primitive man might feel that a sudden thought came to him from without; it might take a poet to identify the god who sent it. It was the poet's interpretation of the successes and failures of his human heroes in terms of interventions by particular gods that built up the personalities of those gods. One source of difficulty for the student of Greek religion is the fact that Homer's Zeus and Athena and the rest are entertaining characters in his story, and have to an unknown extent diverged from the Zeus and Athena of cult.

Once gods with proper names, super-human forms and distinctive personalities had emerged, it was natural to build them houses in appropriate places and to ensure their presence therein by making, as we should say, images of them. This is the origin of the most familiar aspect of Greek religion – the rectangular temple containing the image, together with any dedications made to the god, and the priest looking after the temple and its contents and supervising the sacrificial and other rites due to the god.

What made a place appropriate was an established association with deity, most simply expressed by the erection of an altar in a precinct or temenos (Iliad 8.48). The Telesterion or Hall of Initiation at Eleusis was built over a Mycenaean palace: the Mysteries no doubt began as a palace-cult. The cult of Athena Polias on the Athenian Akropolis no doubt derived from the cult of a Mycenaean palace-goddess. The Sounion promontory was naturally associated with Poseidon. There are few clear signs of Mycenaean temples, which suggests that, though the names of most of the Classical gods are to be found in the Linear B tablets, those gods had not by then acquired complete personalities.

The holiest object in Athens, eventually housed in the west end of the Erekhtheion, was an olive-wood stump. How that stump became a fetish and how the fetish became Athena will never be known, but the veneration of such an aniconic object should not surprise us. Like the images that succeeded them, they were regarded as divine and not just as symbols of the divine.

The god, present in his image, required honour from his human worshippers, if he was to help rather than hinder their purposes. Sacrifices would be made to him at regular intervals and dedications at irregular intervals, as worshippers who had sought his assistance came to believe that they had received it. Sacrifice was an institution as central to Greek culture as marriage, but if it was mysterious to the Greeks themselves, it is still more so to us.

In front of the temple there would be an altar. The gods did not live solely on ambrosia and nectar, and they were believed somehow to be able and indeed eager to participate in human eating and drinking. Hence the prevalence of animal, vegetable and drink offerings. They were believed also to enjoy singing, dancing, processions and games.

The tops of hills, if not of mountains, were eminently suitable sites for the worship of Olympian gods, but the same could not be said of caves. The rites practised in inaccessible caves since Palaeolithic times had not lapsed by Archaic times, although Homer turns his back on the 'chthonic' aspect of early Greek religion. Among the features of that religion more or less ignored by Homer are: possession, magic, pollution and purification, human sacrifice, local cults of the dead. Demeter was later counted as one of the Twelve Olympians, but her subterranean connections were too marked, and Homer rarely mentions her. He is no less reticent about the mad god Dionysos, and he omits all mention of Hestia.

If, as is commonly believed, the *Iliad* and *Odyssey* were composed in Ionia or on an offshore island, for the edification and enjoyment of the local aristocracy and their guests, we should not be surprised to find much that was thought vitally important in Old Greece being allowed far less importance on the other side of the Aegean. Homer does, however, preserve memories of earlier stages of belief. 'Owl-eyed' Athena and 'cow-faced' Hera were once as close to owl and cow as shaman to familiar. The elaborate funeral which Achilles provided for Patroklos, including the sacrifice of a dozen Trojans, was at variance with what Homer himself thought proper.

The account of early Greek religion so far given has represented it as something man-made, as a, largely unconscious, human construction. In opposition to this account, it might be asked how such a construction could have lasted so long without a divine foundation. The answer is complex.

First, as we have already seen, the general intent of Greek mythology, its affirmation of the virtual indifference of the universe to human purposes, matches much of the experience of humanity. For a while some men enjoy a success that seems inexplicable except in terms of divine intervention, but both individuals and their houses rise only to fall sooner or later.

Second, once a religion has formed in a traditional society (that is, an illiterate society more or less secluded from the influence of other societies), the whole process of education, in the widest sense of the word, tends to induce acceptance. Even when men become aware of other, structurally different, religious traditions, they will not easily cut completely adrift from the one in which they were brought up, nor will they be looking for contradictions within it. Only a catastrophic reverse in war or a disastrous earthquake, famine or plague could produce sudden rejection.

Third, in so far as religion retains a magical element, it says 'If you do so-and-so at such-and-such a time, something-or-other desirable will follow, unless something else untoward has happened.' Because primitive man is well aware of the cycle of seasons, he does so-and-so (performs a rite) at just the season when something-or-other (say, the germination of sown seeds) will normally happen anyhow, for other reasons, and, if it does not, it is not difficult to find something else which may have prevented it from happening. And again, those who have been brought up on such lines are no more looking for falsifying counter-examples than are believers in astrology today.

Fourth, in addition to such foreseeable 'confirmations' of supernatural activity, there are such unforeseeable 'confirmations' as admonitory or oracular dreams, voices and visions, to all of which divine origins may be ascribed. To a large extent dreams conform to the expectations of the dreamer and his culture. It was not uncommon for Greeks to receive in dreams advice or orders from supposedly supernatural beings. 'The fair and beautiful woman in white' (Plato, *Kriton* 44a) who appeared to Sokrates in a dream shortly before his death spoke to him clearly enough for him to be confident of her supernatural veracity. It was Sokrates also who heard, when awake, the dissuasive voice that he called his 'daimonic sign', a much rarer phenomenon than an admonitory dream (*Republic* 496c). On the eve of the battle of Marathon, the Athenian generals despatched the professional runner Philippides to Sparta with vital news, and, according to the story that he told on his return, the pastoral god Pan had met him on a mountain above Tegea, addressed him by name, and told him to ask the Athenians why they neglected him, well disposed as he was (Herodotos 6.105). The Athenians accepted the courier's story, and gave Pan a cave-shrine on the north side of the Akropolis.

Fifth, as foreseeable as the germination of sown seeds and as supernatural-seeming as unforeseeable dreams and voices were induced dreams, trances and voices. In Aristophanes' *Wasps* (123f.), Bdelykleon is said to have taken his father to Aigina, where the nearest temple of Asklepios then was. There the old man spent the night. The practice of incubation was based on the expectation that invalids would dream of the god of healing, who would tell them what remedial action to take. The most famous induced trances were those into which the Pythia, Apollo's priestess at Delphi, went when she sat on the god's tripod. No Greek copied the example supposedly set by Kroisos, King of Lydia (Herodotos 1.47), and tested the reliability of her utterances. It was generally assumed that when the Pythia was, as we should say, in one of her trances, she was *entheos*, had the voice of the god in her. Apart from the officially induced trances of the Pythiai and of the priestesses at Dodona (Plato, *Phaidros* 244ab), there were also those of private mediums. Aristophanes mentions (*Wasps* 1019) an Athenian medium called Eurykles. So does Plato, who also mentions oracle-chanters several times (*Apology* 22c, *Menon* 99c, *Ion* 534c), and they perhaps chanted in self-induced trances.

Finally, whenever old religion comes into conflict with new science or new philosophy, attempts will be made to reinterpret the old and reconcile it with the new, once the new has started to gain acceptance. These attempts will be the more likely to succeed if there is no holy book, and Homer, for all his prestige and influence, was never regarded as verbally inerrant. Even the more intellectual Athenians will have been slow to reject mythology root and branch – to dismiss it all as simply false; they will rather have continued to accept most of it, with reservations that they did not work out fully. The emphasis in Greek religion fell on the correct performance of customary rites rather than on belief in carefully formulated doctrines.

For all these reasons, it should occasion no surprise that atheists, meaning by that term people who deny the existence of any supernatural being, were rare in fifth-century Athens. As we shall see, Protagoras gave memorable expression to agnosticism, and Alkibiades probably parodied the Eleusinian Mysteries, and others mutilated the Hermai, but evidence of atheism is hard to find. Thucydides may have been an atheist, but it is impossible to be sure. Athenian society was diverse, and there was no uniformity of belief or practice, but most Athenians believed more or less whole-heartedly in:

  (i)   the existence of the personal gods of mythology, both Olym-
         pian and chthonic
  (ii)   the potency of divine images
  (iii) the appropriateness of prayers, sacrifices, dedications, festivals
  (iv)   the possibility of divination
  (v)   the importance of each man's *daimon* for his own life
  (vi)   the danger of pollution and the efficacy of purification
  (vii) the survival of death by ghosts in Hades
  (viii) the importance of the burial and tendance of one's dead
  (ix)   the potency of heroes in their tombs
  (x)   the value of initiation into the Eleusinian Mysteries.

We have seen that, barring some catastrophic reverse, loss of belief in the traditional religion could proceed only very slowly. Few Athenians, we may suppose, had experiences like that of Philippides on the mountain above Tegea, and most Athenians were as ready to talk of it raining as of Zeus raining, but it would not have occurred to most Athenians to take seriously the deistic speculations of thinkers like Anaxagoras, as these were mediated to them in the plays of Euripides and Aristophanes. The divine genealogy, as it was ultimately worked out, was, for all its complexity, a fair representation in personal terms of the main features of life.

Not only had the gods human personality, they normally had human form too. (It should, however, be remembered that confronted by Zeus as he really was, emitting lightning, mortal Semele shrivelled. When in the Homeric *Hymn to Demeter* (188–190) the goddess appeared as she really was, her height and radiance filled Metaneira with reverence, awe and fear. Later (276–280), Metaneira was struck dumb by a combination of factors, including the goddess's height and beauty, the fragrance of her clothing, and the radiance of her body, which filled the house like lightning.) It was therefore possible to make images of them, as we should put it. Originally, however, such an image was not just an image of a god, it was a manifestation of him, to be treated as something animated and potent, as a Mediterranean peasant woman will treat a holy image or icon to this day. It was not a mere absurdity for Aristophanes in *Clouds* (1478) to represent Strepsiades as talking to the Hermes outside his front-door, and it was a very grave matter when the Hermai all over Athens were systematically mutilated in 415.

Being personal and sharing the feelings of human aristocrats, the gods could be swayed by prayers, if the necessary conditions were satisfied. Few Athenians undertook a venture of any importance without a prayer to an appropriate deity. Everywhere altars and statues reminded the Athenians of their gods, and on countless occasions each day individuals, households and representatives of the community gave expression to their recognition of the gods.

In uttering a solemn prayer to an Olympian god, the worshipper stood, stretched out his hands with palms upturned, addressed the god by his full titles, and, if the prayer was petitionary, reminded the god of his (the worshipper's) past acts of piety, perhaps promised further acts of piety, and, finally, made his petition, which was not necessarily for anything that we should regard as a worthy object of prayer.

The acts of piety would consist of giving the god things he needed or wanted – gifts of food (vegetable or animal: only the smoke and savour of a partially or wholly burnt sacrifice could actually reach the gods above), or drink (libations), the smell of incense, or, if there was a temple, treasure (tripods or armour, for example) to adorn it.

In Sophokles' *Elektra* (637–659), after a maid-servant has presented a vegetable offering to Apollo, who stands before the palace door, Klytaimnestra, who has been frightened by an ambiguous dream, prays to the god. She cannot speak entirely plainly because her hostile daughter Elektra is present, but she asks quietly for the fulfilment of her dream if it is favourable; if it is unfavourable, reflecting the malice of her enemies, she asks that it be made to backfire on them. She asks also to be allowed to go on enjoying her present prosperity. The unspoken part of her prayer (that Orestes may die) she expects the god to understand.

Animals were sacrificed to the gods of Athens almost daily and on some days on a large scale. Perhaps because the decision to march out to Marathon was taken on a day sacred to her, the Athenians vowed to sacrifice a she-goat to Artemis for every Persian they killed. When to their surprise, they killed some 6,400 Persians, they were obliged to commute the sentence to 500 she-goats a year, a practice that still continued in Xenophon's time (*Anabasis* 3.2.12). Some hundreds of bulls were sacrificed to Dionysos at the end of the procession that opened the City Dionysia. Athena probably claimed at least as many cows at the end of the Panathenaic procession. It cannot have been easy to find so many large animals in Attike, and it is not surprising that Athens required each of her colonies and numerous allies to provide a cow for the Great Panathenaia.

What was originally the hunter's rite of animal sacrifice is described in some detail in Homer and in Attic drama. An unblemished domesticated animal was adorned and induced to walk to the altar, seemingly of its own volition. The congregation was enjoined to be silent. Barley grains, a myrtle garland for the sacrifice and his sacrificial knife were put in a basket, which was carried round the altar from left to right. The sacrificer then took a brand from the altar-fire, dipped it in a bowl of lustral water and sprinkled altar, victim and congregation. The water sprinkled on the victim would make it shake its head and so seem to assent to its fate. The sacrificer washed his hands, scattered barley grains on the altar fire and on the victim's head, and cut a lock of the victim's hair and threw it on the fire. It was now time for him to pray to the god. Finally, he cut the victim's throat to an *aulos* accompaniment, whereupon the women shrieked. The blood was caught in a special bowl. The victim's tongue was cut out and the carcase flayed and cut up. Certain portions were reserved for the god and burnt on the altar, as wine was poured into the flames; most of the meat was distributed among the congregation. Few of us would enjoy attending such a blood-sacrifice, let alone the sacrifice of hundreds of beasts.

Belief in the efficacy of public sacrifice is illustrated by this extract from a speech of Lysias (30.18):

> By performing the prescribed sacrifices, our ancestors left the community the most powerful and prosperous in Greece. It is therefore right that we offer the same sacrifices as they did, if only for the sake of the fortune which has resulted from those rites.

In popular belief, the bigger the gift the better the god was pleased; it took a Sokrates (Xenophon, *Reminiscences* 1.3.3) to recognise the propriety of Hesiod's injunction in his *Works and Days* (336):

> Render sacrifice to the immortal gods according to your capacity.

The building of a temple presupposed the appointment of a priest to tend it and to supervise the cult of the resident god. An Athenian inscription (ML 44) records a decision of the Assembly to select by lot, from those Athenian women who were willing to serve, a priestess of Athena Nike before the building of her temple. Just as Homer was not regarded as verbally inerrant, so priests did not form a caste apart. If there was no Bible, there was no church either. There were no theological seminaries and no rites of ordination. If the gods were morally no better than ordinary men, neither were their priests. According to Isokrates (2.6): 'Any man is considered capable of being a priest.' The priestly function might be performed by the head of a household or by a magistrate as one part of his duties. The clan of the Eumolpidai always provided the Hierophant or High Priest of the cult of Demeter at Eleusis, no doubt because what the Athenians were glad to see turning into a Panhellenic cult had begun as the religion of the royal family of Eleusis, and the Eumolpidai were their descendants. Likewise, the clan of the Eteoboutadai provided both the priestess of Athena Polias and the priest of Poseidon in the Erekhtheion, and they were perhaps the descendants of the Athenian royal house. Under democracy, as we have seen, it was possible for a priestess to be appointed by lot from the volunteers who came forward.

Priests might be paid: Athena Nike's priestess got 50 *drakhmai* a year for discharging her not very exacting duties. There were also perquisites, such as the legs and hides from public sacrifices, for Athena Nike's priestess, and, reasonably enough, a front seat in the theatre for the priest of Dionysos Eleuthereus, as well as many other priests.

The public religion of Athens consisted essentially of the honouring, usually annual, of gods by human groups, ranging in size from deme to community, with sacrifices and sometimes processions and contests as well. (The Greek word *thysia*, which originally meant a burnt offering, came by a natural transition to mean a festival.) The Athenian religious year, as opposed to the conciliar year of ten *prytaneiai*, consisted of twelve lunar months, each twenty-nine or thirty days long: Hekatombaion, Metageitnion, Boedromion, Pyanopsion, Maimakterion, Posideion, Gamelion, Anthesterion, Elaphebolion, Mounikhion, Thargelion, Skirophorion. They were so named after festivals falling within them, some of them obscure even to most fifth-century Athenians. The Arkhons and the generals took office on 1 Hekatombaion, some financial magistrates on 28 Hekatombaion. Athenian chronology is made complicated by the fact, apparent from inscriptions, that the religious year might begin on the first new moon before the summer solstice (about 21 June) or the first or second after it. If the start of the new year could vary by sixty days in the fifth century, this must have weakened the link between the religious calendar and practical activities – agricultural or military – of a seasonal kind.

Between 403 and 399 an official calendar of community sacrifices, assigning to each its correct day in the month, was drawn up by Nikomakhos and others. Unfortunately, only fragments of this work, inscribed on the walls of the Stoa Basileios, have been preserved, but it is nevertheless possible to reconstruct at least the main features of the calendar of community festivals.

The first eight days of each month differed from the rest in being mostly devoted to monthly festivals honouring gods born on the days in question. The first day of the month, the holy day of the new moon, was a day for putting incense on one's altars (Aristophanes, *Wasps* 96) and also for buying and selling (*Knights* 43f., *Wasps* 169ff.); no annual festival fell on it. The second day was the day of the Good Daimon, to whom libations were poured at the end of dinner (Aristophanes, *Wasps* 525). The third day was Athena's birthday. The fourth day was the birthday of Aphrodite, Hermes and Herakles. The sixth day was Artemis' birthday. The seventh day was her brother Apollo's birthday; the rites of no other deity fell on it. The eighth day belonged to Poseidon and his son Theseus.

Such annual festivals as fell within the first eight days of the month mostly honoured gods born on the days in question. On 6 Boedromion was celebrated the annual festival of Artemis Agrotera, the Huntress, which included a procession to her temple at Agrai by the Ilisos; it was on this day too that Marathon was commemorated. On 6 Mounikhion young girls went in procession to the Delphinion, the temple that Artemis shared with her brother. On 7 Pyanopsion was celebrated Apollo's Pyanopsia, and on 7 Thargelion his Thargelia. On 8 Pyanopsion was celebrated the Theseia.

It seems that the Assembly rarely met on any of the first eight days of the month, whereas the Council avoided only the annual festival days among them. In the course of the year Athens celebrated more festivals than any other Greek city. (Thucydides (2.15.2) describes the Synoikia as a festival 'paid for out of public funds'. Total community expenditure on festivals can hardly be guessed.) How many of them should be regarded as national festivals comparable in their effect on secular business with our Sundays or Christmas and Good Friday is a difficult question. A sacrifice listed by Nikomakhos might have been held at some distance from the city or might have fallen out of fashion. Festivals restricted to women or girls – Stenia and Thesmophoria (five days in all), Delphinia, Arrephoria, Skira – would not perhaps have prevented men from conducting secular business, though we are told (Aristophanes, *Women at the Thesmophoria* 78–80) that the Council did not meet on the second day of the Thesmophoria. The question may be taken as equivalent to the question on how many days in the year did neither Council nor Assembly meet. If the Council was excused from meeting on all the days on which annual community festivals seem to have fallen, that would amount to some ninety days, to which would have to be added the days on which the Assembly met – not more than fifty and possibly fewer. It may, however, be that the Council worked on some of the less important of the ninety or so annual community festival days. There was no equivalent of the Lord's Day Observance Society.

As measured by number of days of annual community festival, the most prominent deities in Athenian thinking were Demeter (with her daughter Kore) and Dionysos, followed by Athena, followed by Zeus, followed by Artemis and Apollo. The pre-eminence of the deities of corn and vegetation is not surprising. Examination of the sequence of festivals reveals the agrarian origin of very many of them, but on the evidence of inscriptions it is certain that in the second half of the fifth century festivals often fell a month or more away from the corresponding agricultural activity.

Aristotle (*Nikomakhean Ethics* 1160a) noted that the older sacrifices and assemblies seemed to fall after the gathering of the crops, because the people had leisure then. This applies to the Panathenaia and Greater Mysteries and if we ask why the dramatic festivals of Athens – Rural Dionysia, Lenaia and City Dionysia – took place in the chilly, if not wet, months of December, January and March, part of the answer must be that there was little agricultural activity then. (As we have seen, an equation between, say, Athenian Posideion and our own December is only approximate.)

The Kronia, dedicated to the father of Zeus, was a harvest festival, at which masters and slaves feasted together. (The old name of the first month of the year was taken from this festival, but the month was later re-named Hekatombaion from the sacrifices offered to Apollo at his Hekatombaia, probably on the 7th.) The Greater Mysteries, held in Boedromion, originally anticipated the bringing up of the seed-corn from underground granaries for sowing. The Pyanopsia (so called from *pyanos*, a bean boiled, with other vegetables, for Apollo) both celebrated the fruit harvest, as the Kronia celebrated the grain harvest, and anticipated the sowing of vegetables. It was the occasion on which an olive-branch wreathed with wool and hung with figs, loaves and pots of honey, oil and wine, the *eiresione* (from *eiros*, wool), was carried around. Each householder would set one up outside his front door, where it would hang for the ensuing year (Aristophanes, *Knights* 729, *Wasps* 399, *Wealth* 1054).

The Thesmophoria, held shortly after the Pyanopsia, was a three-day festival, celebrated by married women in honour of Demeter Thesmophoros, on the second day of which they fasted, and on the third day of which (Kalligeneia, Fair Birth) they hauled up the putrefied remains of sacrificed piglets that they had thrown into pits, probably at the Skira in June. The earthy pig was Demeter's animal, and the exhuming of its remains, the placing of them on altars in the Thesmophoreion and the mingling of them with the seed-corn by women, was no doubt originally intended to promote both their own fertility and the germination of the corn.

The Oskhophoria, so called because two noble youths carried vine branches (*oskhoi*) laden with grapes, was a vintage festival. The nature of the Haloa, honouring Demeter and Dionysos at Eleusis, is not entirely clear, but it was certainly a fertility festival for women as well as men, taking its name from a word meaning either threshing-floor (surely irrelevant in December) or any cultivated ground (work was still going on in field and vineyard). The Rural Dionysia, celebrated by demes, in the same month as the Haloa, had as its central feature a procession escorting a phallos held aloft (Aristophanes, *Akharnians* 237ff.). The original intention was no doubt to stimulate the corn shoots.

The first two days of the Anthesteria, the Flower Festival, were concerned with wine. The first day, 11 Anthesterion, was called Pitho-igia, because on it were broached *pithoi* or jars containing wine made from the grapes that had been gathered the preceding September. Only when due honour had been paid to Dionysos was it right for the community to drink it. Then all alike, slaves and hired men included, took part. The second day, which strictly began on the evening of 11 Anthesterion, was called Khoes, because every one had his *khous* or jug, and was celebrated by drinking all over the city. The Basileus presided over a drinking-contest at the Thesmotheteion (the headquarters of the six Thesmothetai, near the Prytaneion), and at the Boukoleion (his original headquarters, also near the Prytaneion) his wife, the Basilinna, was in some way given in marriage to the god. The third day, which strictly began on the evening of 12 Anthesterion, was called Khytroi, because of the pots (*khytroi*) of porridge offered to the dead. It was a polluted day, on which ghosts walked and on which it was prudent to chew purgative buckthorn and smear one's doorway with pitch. It might seem unrelated to the first two days, but according to the Hippokratic *Regimen* (4.92): 'From the dead come nourishment, growth and seeds.'

The Khloia was celebrated at Eleusis to mark the return of greenery (*khloe*), and at Athens Athena was invited at the Prokharisteria to show the crops her preliminary favour (*kharis*).

Though the City Dionysia became the most important urban festival after the Great Panathenaia, a magical element remained prominent. The decree of the Assembly (ML 49) authorising the foundation of the colony at Brea required the colonists to send a cow and a panoply to the Great Panathenaia and a phallos to the Dionysia. As at the Rural Dionysia, so at the City Dionysia a phallic procession was central, but the national procession was much more magnificent and numerous phalloi were carried.

The Thargelia took its name from *thargelos*, a pot of boiled vegetables, first fruits offered to Apollo on 7 Thargelion. As the Pyanopsia anticipated their sowing, so the Thargelia anticipated the harvesting of the vegetables. On 6 Thargelion two ugly men, chosen as scapegoats or *pharmakoi*, one for men and one for women, were led through the streets, beaten with green branches and finally driven out. Apollo was the god chiefly concerned with purification, and the hope was that, by loading the *pharmakoi* with all kinds of pollution, the crops might be preserved.

The last month of the year, Skirophorion, took its name from the Skira. Like the Stenia and the Thesmophoria, it was restricted to women. It appears to have honoured the gods of the Erekhtheion, Athena and Poseidon, and also Demeter. Demeter, it seems, was honoured by the throwing of sacrificed piglets into caverns. Thrown in at the start of the summer drought, they, or rather their putrefied remains, were to be hauled up at its end, on the last day of the Thesmophoria. It is likely that on the third day of Skirophorion occurred the mysterious rite of the Arrephoria. Four noble young girls were chosen each year by the Basileus and approved by the Assembly. They were called Arrephoroi because it was the business of two of them to carry down from the Erekhtheion things probably associated with the dew (*erse*) which they were given by the Priestess of Athena Polias. Under cover of darkness they carried them down on their heads by a concealed staircase in the north cliff of the Akropolis to the sanctuary of Aphrodite in the Gardens, and then carried something up. It is hard to doubt that the Arrephoroi were doing something analogous to what the women were shortly to do at the Skira – trying to ensure that the earth did not lose its fertility in the ensuing drought.

It is clear that many festivals had originally reflected the hopes, fears and joys that accompanied the successive stages of the farmer's year. It is no surprise to find this in the case of festivals honouring Demeter and Dionysos. It may be more surprising in the case of festivals honouring Apollo and Athena. Apollo was more commonly associated with flocks and herds than with agriculture, but his general function of purifier would have made it appropriate to call on him to avert pests and diseases from the crops. The Arrephoria no doubt reflects a time when Athena as palace-goddess of the Mycenaean kings of Athens performed a more complete range of functions than she did in the Classical Age.

The Panathenaia, honouring Athena on and around 28 Hekatombaion, was a festival of great antiquity, consisting of an all-night vigil (*pannykhis*) with singing and dancing on the Akropolis, an early morning procession to the Akropolis, a sacrifice and a feast. By the late fifth century the Panathenaia involved also contests in dithyramb and pyrrhic dancing. In the 560s every fourth festival was made a Great Panathenaia by the addition of equestrian and athletic contests between individuals from anywhere in Greece. The Olympic Games provided the model. The winners were awarded sets of Panathenaic amphorae – two-handled pots with narrow necks, standing two feet high – filled with oil from the sacred olives. Each amphora was decorated on the front with a black-figure Athena brandishing a spear, and on the back was depicted the athletic event in question. The front bore the legend 'One of the prizes from Athens'. The number of pots awarded depended on the standing of the event and the place obtained. Coming second in the boys' foot-race – the most prestigious athletic event – earned ten pots; coming first earned fifty pots. The winner of the same event among the beardless youths earned sixty pots.

Perhaps it was at the same time as the games were introduced that contests were introduced between musicians of three or four kinds – kitharodes (singers to the lyre), aulodes (singers to the playing of an aulete), auletes and possibly kitharists. Not later than the time of Hipparkhos, son of Peisistratos, an official contest between rhapsodes was introduced in Athens, probably as part of the Great Panathenaia. It too was open to individual contestants from anywhere in Greece. The prizes for *mousike* may have taken the form of gold wreaths and silver coins from the first. Itinerant virtuosi would have found coins more portable and more useful, and gold wreaths more eye-catching, than pots of oil.

Other events were confined to citizens. The contest in manliness (*euandria*), the torch-race and the boat-race were tribally organised and liturgically financed. The contest in *euandria* between tribal teams was a matter of size and strength (Xenophon, *Reminiscences* 3.3.12f.). In the torch-race, which perhaps preceded the *pannykhis*, each contestant had to run as fast as he could from an altar in the Akademy to the altar of Athena on the Akropolis without letting his torch go out (Aristophanes, *Frogs* 13, 1087ff.). The boat-race at Sounion (Lysias 21.5) was a contest between tribally manned triremes.

Though this rich variety of contests was unmatched by any other festival, the Great Panathenaia did not attain Panhellenic status, perhaps because, unlike the Olympic, Nemean and Pythian games, it was very obviously under the direct control of a powerful *polis*. Nevertheless by the fifth century it had become the most important festival in the calendar of Athens. The board of ten Athlothetai selected to manage all the contests undertook four years of increasingly hard work, and for the last twenty-four days of their term they dined at public expense in the Prytaneion. In addition to the contests there was also the procession to delight spectators, local and foreign. In the fifth century it was only the quadrennial Great Panathenaic procession that brought the embroidered *peplos* to the olive-wood image of Athena on the Akropolis (Plato, *Euthyphron* 6bc).

On the last day of Pyanopsion was held the Khalkeia, a festival in which craftsmen and especially bronze-workers honoured their patrons Athena and Hephaistos. This was also the day on which the Priestess of Athena Polias and the Arrephoroi set up the loom on which the woollen *peplos* was to be woven. This gave the Ergastinai, aristocratic girls assigned to the task, nearly nine months in which to complete their work. They had to depict in embroidery the Olympians' defeat of the Giants and in particular Athena's defeat of Enkelados. To judge from the east face of the Parthenon frieze, the *peplos* was about four feet long and seven wide. How it was conveyed to the Akropolis is uncertain. The procession included the Ergastinai, the Kanephoroi (aristocratic girls carrying on their heads baskets of grain for scattering on the sacrificial victims), metics wearing purple and carrying trays of offerings, handsome old men carrying olive branches, colonists and allies bringing cows and panoplies (as required in a number of surviving decrees (ML 46, 49, 69)), Athenian hoplites, chariots with *apobatai* (hoplites trained to jump off and back onto them), cavalry, marshals and somewhere the magistrates of Athens, including those responsible for the festival.

After the presentation of the *peplos* to the goddess, a huge number of cows and sheep were slaughtered, and some of the meat was burnt for the goddess. Then after fixed portions had been assigned to various boards of magistrates and to the rest of the Athenian participants in the procession, the remaining meat was distributed among the congregation of citizens. This was apparently done by demes in the Kerameikos. The dietary excesses that might follow are alluded to by Aristophanes (*Clouds* 386ff.).

The great majority of the ninety or so days of annual community festival honoured the half-dozen gods already mentioned. Another ten or so gods enjoyed a day or two each. The hero Theseus had had his own festival, the Theseia, on 8 Pyanopsion since Kimon's recovery of his bones from Skyros. He also had a share in the Synoikia, Panathenaia, Pyanopsia, Oskhophoria and Delphinia. Finally, there were the Genesia, a kind of Remembrance Day, and the Apatouria, the three-day phratry-festival.

It is not always easy to decide whether a festival figured in the community's calendar and was supported by public funds or whether it was merely a popular festival put on by a rich deme situated not far from Athens. Urban Halimous held its own Thesmophoria immediately before the city's Thesmophoria, and upper-class women from Athens took part. The Mysteries of Coastal Eleusis had come under Athenian control and been incorporated in the religious life of the city by the middle of the sixth century. The calendar of festivals of Inland Erkhia partly reflects the community calendar and partly reminds us that local religion honoured many divinities and heroes unknown to the community calendar.

The calendar of community festivals was originally, as we have seen, closely tied to the farmer's year. Gradually, as the city grew, its festivals developed in new directions, appropriate to an increasingly urban society. This process must have been accelerated by the Peloponnesian invasions in the Arkhidamian War and still more by the Peloponnesian occupation of Dekeleia. When the elderly and eminently urban Chorus-leader of *Wasps* (264f.) predicts rain and adds that the late crops need it and then a drying north wind, we are not to suppose that he had any crops of his own or even that he has more experience of the fields than had Sokrates (Plato, *Phaidros* 230d).

Greek religion in general was something of very great age and complexity, and so was the calendar of Athenian festivals. The festivals are full of anthropological interest. Even when we are quite well informed about what happened at a festival, we must remain uncertain what it meant to its participants. How much of the enthusiasm of respectable women for the Stenia, Thesmophoria and Skira derived from their normally being confined at home? How many members of the audience in the theatre thought they were honouring the presiding god? How many of those who drank on the occasion of Khoes were engaged in the production of wine?

By the fifth century the prevailing mood of the festivals seems to have been cheerful. Because Greek religion did not include the notion of a morally perfect creator, it did not include the notions of sin, repentance or redemption. On the day after their arrival at Eleusis, those to be initiated seem at least partially to have fasted, and the women celebrating the Thesmophoria certainly fasted on the second day of that festival. The third day of the Anthesteria, Khytroi, was a polluted day, as was the Plynteria, the day on which the olive-wood statue of Athena was cleaned by being taken for a bathe at Phaleron. On both days it may have been thought that unclean powers were abroad. According to Xenophon (*Greek History* 1.4.12), 'No Athenian would dare to touch any serious business' on the day of the Plynteria. The principal festival honouring Zeus Meilikhios, the Gracious, was the Diasia (Thucydides 1.126.6). It was held at Agrai and everyone was there, including the men of Erkhia, who offered a ram, although, according to Thucydides, the numerous offerings were not animal but vegetable and local in character. In fact, families burnt cakes in the shape of animals if they could not afford animals. We are told that on this occasion the Athenians sacrificed in sullen gloom, and a holocaust or wholly burnt offering was an attempt to propitiate an angry god.

With these exceptions and a few others, the prevailing mood appears cheerful, and Thucydides (2.38.1), allowing Perikles to make just one reference to community religion in the Funeral Speech, has him do so in these terms: 'Furthermore, we provide the mind with the most relax-ation from business, by holding contests and festivals all the year round.' If Perikles said this, or something like it, he was expressing a very pragmatic view of community religion but a quite different one from that of Lysias.

Just as the gods were much more powerful than men, so they knew much more. Because he was the Sky-father, Zeus saw all, and because he saw all, he knew all about human affairs, and might intervene to punish wrong-doers. But Zeus' knowledge was not confined to the present and past. An especially valuable kind of knowledge is foreknowledge. Just as there were degrees of power among the gods, so there were degrees of foreknowledge. In the *Iliad* (8.470ff., 15.49ff.) Zeus tells Hera things that she does not know about the future course of the Trojan War. There is an obvious connection between power and foreknowledge, and in the case of Zeus what he intends is what happens. Apollo is his mouthpiece (Aiskhylos, *Eumenides* 19, 616–618).

Since gods have foreknowledge, they may wish or be willing, if the appropriate conditions are satisfied, to impart it to men. The art of interpreting signs sent by gods or of inducing them to impart some of their foreknowledge is that of the diviner or *mantis*. The *mantis* was one of the heirs of the shaman, who had combined the roles of musician, poet, doctor, and diviner. The word *mantis* may well be cognate with *mainomai*, I am mad, and so serve as a reminder of the ecstatic origins of divination.

The author of *Prometheus Bound* (442–506) makes Prometheus describe how he raised men from the condition of ignorant troglodytes. He told them about astronomy, arithmetic, writing, the yoking of beasts and the harnessing of horses, navigation, medicine, and finally, divination, including the recognition of oracular dreams, augury, and the inspection of entrails.

In *Phaidros* (244) Plato distinguishes between two sorts of divination – one inspired and the other rational. The Pythia in her ecstasy exemplified the former, and augury exemplified the latter. Originally, however, the bird-shaman had not only been the licensed visionary of his human following but had also known how to control the flight and cries of birds; his distant heirs, like Teiresias of Thebes, had to content themselves with observation.

Dreams and trances provided the basis of inspired divination. Herodotos (7.16.β2) was familiar with the theory that dreams were only extensions of daytime thinking, and even by the conventionally pious not all dreams were regarded as significant. Of those that were, some, as we have seen, took the form of clear admonitions from superior persons. Others were symbolic and needed interpretation by a professional *oneirokrites*. In *Wasps* (53f.), Aristophanes makes one slave say to another who has just interpreted a dream of his: 'Then shall I not pay two obols to one who interprets dreams so clearly?'

Originally, the shaman had been the master of ecstasy in the literal sense of the word, and had made psychic trips. After the rise of the Olympian gods, his heirs, whether attached, like the Pythia, to an institution, or private persons, like Eurykles and the oracle-chanters or oracle-utterers, had to content themselves with being mouthpieces of the god who possessed and spoke through them.

Supposedly rational divination reaches back, as we have seen, to the time of the bird-shaman. Eventually, shaman and familiar gave place to god and avian embodiment – Zeus and his eagle, Athena and her owl, and many more. By systematic observation of the behaviour of birds, it was supposed that the intentions of the gods above could be divined. So prevalent had this method of divination once been that the Greek equivalent of 'bird' could be used for omens of any kind – involuntary bodily movements, like sneezes, or chance words or encounters.

More important in the Classical Age than augury was a derivative of animal sacrifice – the observation of entrails, and especially the liver, which was believed to be the source of blood and life. The practice originated in the wish of the worshipper to assure himself that his sacrifice was acceptable.

Those who consulted either an official oracle like that at Delphi or a private medium or any other kind of diviner sought practical guidance on matters not covered by any other *tekhne* or, very often, endorsement of decisions already taken more or less firmly.

Sokrates held that one should not ask a god the answer to an obvious question or one that could be answered by counting, measuring or weighing (Xenophon, *Reminiscences* 1.1.9). The difficulty was to decide where the obvious ended and uncertainty began.

In Sophokles' *Elektra* (33f.) Orestes says that he asked Apollo how he should exact vengeance for his father from those who had murdered him – rather than whether he should. In 401, when Xenophon was invited to join the expedition of Kyros, the younger brother of the Persian king, he asked the aged Sokrates if he should accept (*Anabasis* 3.1.5). Sokrates advised him to consult Delphi. The question that Xenophon actually put asked to which god he should sacrifice and pray in order best to accomplish the journey he had in mind and return safe and successful. Sokrates reproved Xenophon for not having asked whether it was better for him to go or to stay.

On the other hand, generalship, or at any rate tactics, was a *tekhne*. While his fleet was still at Aulis, delayed by contrary winds, Agamemnon might well hesitate to defy the diviner Kalkhas, who had called for the sacrifice of his daughter, Iphigeneia, but the Platonic Sokrates knew that Lakhes and Nikias, both of them generals, would agree with him that in warfare the general gives orders to the diviner and not *vice versa*, because the general knows more about what will happen than does the diviner (*Lakhes* 198e). (This was not a novel point of view: Homer's Hektor had said (*Iliad* 12.243): 'The one best omen is to fight for your country.' It was unfortunate for Athens that in Sicily Nikias' practice did not conform with the theory that Plato makes him accept in the dialogue.) Unless generals consulting diviners on campaign or cities consulting oracles had been reasonably confident of securing the endorsement of plans carefully considered, intolerable tension between secular and sacred would have resulted. The Sicilian expedition sailed despite the fact that those responsible for the ill omen (Thucydides 6.27.3) of the mutilated Hermai had not been identified. In the dialogue that Plato named after him, the diviner Euthyphron (3b) says that whenever he speaks in the Assembly about religion and makes predictions, they laugh at him as though he were mad. He claims that all his predictions have been fulfilled, and comforts himself by attributing the Assembly's laughter to its envy of all diviners. Divination is attacked in half-a-dozen of Euripides' plays.

Situated as it was, Delphi, when consulted on questions of international politics, was bound to espouse the Peloponnesian cause during the latter part of the fifth century. According to Sparta's 'hawks', when the Spartans had consulted the oracle in 432 on their chances of success if they went to war with Athens, Apollo had said not only that they would win if they exerted themselves, but also that he would help them, whether invoked or not (Thucydides 1.118.3), and when the plague fell on Athens in 430, those who knew of the oracle to the Spartans believed that Apollo, the lethal archer, had indeed intervened on the Peloponnesian side (2.54.4).

Thucydides says nothing about the consultation of oracles before the launching of the Sicilian expedition in 415, though he does mention (8.1.1) the incitement of oracle-utterers and diviners, and, despite a story twice told by Plutarch, it is not likely that the Assembly at any stage gave Delphi a chance to condemn the expedition before it set out. It could still, however, consult Delphi on purely religious matters, such as the purification of the holy island of Delos, birthplace of the god.

On 27 August 413, an eclipse of the moon was visible at Syracuse, when the Athenian force was just about to sail away to safety (Thucydides 7.50.4). Most of the Athenians took the phenomenon to heart, and Nikias, who 'was somewhat over-addicted to divination and similar practices', and whose regular diviner Stilbides had recently died, accepted the findings of the remaining diviners that they should not move for 'thrice nine days', that is, another sidereal month. Plutarch (*Nikias* 23.5) reports that Stilbides had been able to set Nikias free from most of his superstition (*deisidaimonia*). Thucydides, who has been taken for an atheist and was certainly interested in the bearing of astronomy on chronology, perhaps implies that Nikias, as an educated man, should have paid no more attention to diviners than was necessary to reassure his men.

In the Melian Dialogue (5.103.2) Thucydides appears to make a direct attack on divination. The Athenian embassy says that in adversity most people have recourse to invisible hopes, divination, oracles and the like, and are thereby ruined. The generalisation is hardly relevant, since it does not apply to the Melians; so presumably the view is Thucydides'

own. It is no doubt true that in adversity most Athenians did have
recourse to divination and oracles. Inscriptions recording decrees of the
Assembly include respectful references to oracles. Aristophanes might
sometimes make fun of oracles, oracle-utterers, diviners and priests, but
a great comedian does not usually make fun of what is powerless; he
asserts himself against power, in at any rate some of its forms. The
servants of the gods might be greedy and parasitic upon productive
labour, but their position in the community was strong.

If most people were superstitious, by the standards of Thucydides, the
opportunity for the 'clergy' to magnify their office was ever present,
though increasingly circumscribed by the growth of organised knowledge, in the shape of the various *tekhnai* (Plato, *Greater Hippias* 281d).
Divination itself was a *tekhne* of a kind, and laymen might know something about it. Xenophon was able to use his knowledge of it to limit
the scope of Kyros's Ambrakiot diviner, Silanos (*Anabasis* 5.6.29): 'The
answer of Silanos the diviner assured me of the main point, that the
victims were favourable; for he knew that through constant attendance
at sacrifices I too was not unversed in his art.'

Xenophon elsewhere (*Reminiscences* 1.4.2) put divination on a level
with prayer and sacrifice. Is it possible for us to distinguish superstition
from religion in Athens? Looking at Athenian religious belief from
outside, one might say that it was all false and that all Athenians, apart
from the few atheists and agnostics, were superstitious, but it would
perhaps be unhelpful to brand as superstitious a farmer from Erkhia
who believed what he had been brought up to believe and practised
what he had been brought up to practise and who saw no reason not
to. It may be more helpful to relate superstition to the norms of the
culture in question. Superstition is then believing in things that most
members of the stratum of the society in question do not believe in,
especially when believing in those things obstructs effective action.
Nikias' reaction to the lunar eclipse was not typical of his social stratum,
had disastrous consequences and put him on much the same level as
those who believed that Thessalian witches could pull down the moon,
that is, cause lunar eclipses (Aristophanes, *Clouds* 749f.).

The distinction between god and *daimon* is not easy to draw, but one
important sense of *daimon* is preserved in the Greek words *eudaimon*
(happy or fortunate) and *kakodaimon* and *dysdaimon* (unhappy or
unfortunate). Homer spoke of a man's *moira* or lot. Hesiod and the
Megarian poet Theognis preferred to speak of a man's *daimon*. Though
Herakleitos proclaimed that character was *daimon*, most people agreed
with Theognis (161–166) that *daimon* was stronger than native endow-
ment, and the way was left open for one kind of superstition. 'Alas,
kakodaimon am I!' exclaims Xanthias in *Frogs* (196). 'What did I meet
when I was setting out?' 'What *daimon* was it,' cries the Chorus-leader

as Oidipous emerges self-blinded from his palace (Sophokles, *King Oidipous* 1299–1302), 'that leapt further than furthest upon your *dysdaimon moira?*'

Belief in the danger of pollution (*miasma*) and the efficacy of purification (*katharsis*) was widespread in Athens. The prime source of pollution was homicide. Unless the homicide was lawful or the dying man had absolved him, pollution would immediately infect a killer and, to a lesser extent, anyone with whom he came in contact and indeed the whole community. If the killer was brought to trial and convicted, his execution or exile would disinfect the community. If an exiled killer was pardoned by his victim's relatives, he might return to Athens, but he would then have to purify himself by making an appropriate animal sacrifice. Other sources of pollution were incest, childbirth and death from natural causes. In the winter of 426/5, the Athenians purified Delos, birthplace of Apollo and the original headquarters of their alliance, by exhuming the dead who had been buried on the island, and by forbidding any more births or deaths to take place there. They hoped perhaps to control the second visitation of the plague (Thucydides 3.104,87). In 422 they went further and expelled all the live Delians, though they subsequently brought them back (Thucydides 5.1,32). They brought them back partly because they had suffered military reverses; so no doubt they had removed them in the hope of gaining military successes.

Homer distinguished a dead man's ghost from his corpse, and he realised that a corpse could not benefit from the attentions of the living. The ghosts of all those who had been duly buried he located in the subterranean realm of Hades and Persephone, where, apart from a few notorious sinners, they endured a painless but bleak and insubstantial existence. These ghosts needed nothing and were not to be feared.

It was perhaps easier for Ionians to think like that, sundered as they were from the tombs of their ancestors in Old Greece. There the tendance of the dead in their tombs, presupposing the identity of ghost and corpse, went on, even after the introduction of cremation. The third day of the Athenian Anthesteria was, as we have seen, one on which the dead were supposed to walk abroad.

Athenians attached enormous importance to being buried by their own family in their own country (hence in part the furore over the performance of the generals after Arginousai), and after burial came regular tendance. Aristophanes never even mentions rites honouring the dead. Prospective Arkhons were asked at their *dokimasia* or preliminary vetting if they had family tombs and where they were.

In the case of an inhabitant of Athens these tombs would be in a family plot in a cemetery beside a road leading out of the city – beside a road and only just outside the city, for publicity and ease of access, but outside the city all the same, for fear of pollution and fear that the dead might walk. There may also have been a wish to save precious space inside the walls. Intra-mural burial became a great honour to be conferred by the community, as it honoured the bones of the hero Theseus. Most of the intra-mural graves of the Classical Age that have been found are those of children.

Both inhumation and cremation were practised, but the offerings made to the dead were the same in both cases. Most characteristic of the ceramic offerings are the beautiful white-ground *lekythoi*, some of which depict funerary scenes, either mythological or taken from real life. Little trace remains of the food and drink offered.

The fact that such offerings were made and that over some graves round mounds or walled tombs were raised and on them were erected columns or slabs, either plain or decorated with reliefs depicting the deceased as he had been in life, may have been as much a matter of convention and family pride as of conviction about the fate of the dead. In default of evidence to the contrary, it should be assumed that in the mind of bereaved Athenians there was both a reluctance to face the fact of death and separation and also an acceptance of the Homeric theory.

Epic poetry, local tradition and the mighty monuments of the Mycenaeans, including their 'beehive' or *tholos* tombs, kept alive through the Dark Age the idea of an age of heroes, men with some divine blood in their veins (the offspring of a god and goddess was another god and not a hero) who had performed great exploits, above all, the sacking of Troy. In some cases, where continuity was unbroken by invasion, local tradition might correctly link hero and tomb; in other cases epic poetry would supply names unknown to local tradition. None of the architecture of the Archaic Age could match that of the *tholos* tombs for precision of craftsmanship, and the emergence of hero cults, resembling the cults of chthonic deities and going far beyond the ordinary tendance of dead ancestors, is not surprising. With the formation of the *polis* in the eighth century, an increasing need was felt for foci of community sentiment. Ideally, the hero was indigenous, but if Oidipous of Thebes had died at Kolonos Hippios, north of Athens, so much the better for Athens. Possession of the hero's bones was highly desirable, and the recovery of the supposed bones of Theseus and their interment in the Theseion was an event of national importance. Operating from their tombs, local heroes could render the community powerful assistance in time of war. Plutarch (*Theseus* 35.5) records that many who fought at Marathon thought they saw Theseus, whose bones were not then supposed to lie in Attike, leading the attack on the Persians. According to Herodotos (8.109.3), Themistokles told the Athenian contingent at Andros in 479 that the defeat of Persia had been due to gods and heroes. Whether he himself believed it or not, he must have supposed that most of his hearers would believe it. Unlike Herakles, Theseus was not ridiculed in comedy.

The Classical Greeks did not suppose that the age of heroes was quite over. The founders of new *poleis* had commonly been worshipped after their deaths (Herodotos 6.38), and Hagnon, the founder of Amphipolis, was honoured there in his lifetime, even though he was back in Athens at the start of the Peloponnesian War. In 424 Brasidas captured the city for Sparta, and after his death in 422 he superseded Hagnon in popular esteem and was buried inside the city and honoured as hero, second founder and saviour (Thucydides 5.11.1). The Greeks who had fallen at Plataiai in 479 were honoured as heroes well before 427 (Thucydides 3.58.4), and Pausanias (1.32.4) tells us that in his day the Marathonians still worshipped as heroes those who had fallen in the battle in 490. As we shall see, it is likely that the Athenians were thinking of their 192 dead as heroes within forty years of the battle.

Of all the Athenian festivals the Eleusinian Mysteries, honouring Demeter and her daughter Kore, perhaps come closest to what a Christian would regard as religious rites. All Greek-speakers, adults or children, male or female, slave or free, were eligible for initiation, provided that they were not polluted. It appears that most Athenians were initiated. At any rate, Andokides (1.12) describes the Prytaneis as clearing a meeting of the Assembly of those who were not initiated, without implying that any Prytanis had to leave or that the Assembly was much reduced in numbers. The Platonic Sokrates never alludes to his own initiation, but he uses the language of the Mysteries.

The first stage of initiation took place at the Lesser Mysteries, celebrated in honour of Kore beside the Ilisos at Agrai in the month of Anthesterion, roughly our February. Each candidate was purified and then perhaps admitted to the grade of *mystes*. The transitive verb *myeo*, I initiate, is cognate with the intransitive verb *myo*, I close, of eyes or mouth. The *mystes* kept his mouth shut, and to this day it is impossible to be sure just how one became a *mystes* or what was involved in the two stages of the Greater Mysteries – the *telete* and the *epopteia*.

The rites of Agrai and Eleusis had once been independent of each other, but after the incorporation of Eleusis into Attike in the sixth century, the rites of Agrai were made preliminary to those at Eleusis. The Basileus in Athens was in administrative charge of the Eleusinian festival, but the chief priest, the Hierophantes or Revealer of Sacred Objects, was always drawn from the Eleusinian clan of the Eumolpidai, who were supposedly descended from the old kings of Eleusis. He held office for life. The second most important Eleusinian priest, the Daidoukhos or Torch-holder, was, in the fifth century, drawn from the Athenian clan of the Kerykes. Unlike other priests, both Hierophantes and Daidoukhos wore elaborate vestments when officiating.

The Greater Mysteries took place in Boedromion, roughly our September, and constituted an event of international importance. The Hierophantes had earlier sent out messengers, chosen from the Eumolpidai and Kerykes, to all the Greek communities that respected Eleusis, proclaiming a 55-day truce, asking for tithes of first fruits and inviting the sending of delegations. The purpose of the truce was to secure safe travel to and from Eleusis, and a similar truce was proclaimed for the Lesser Mysteries. Perhaps in about 422, when the Peloponnesian invasions of Attike had stopped but while the Arkhidamian War was still on, a decree of the Assembly (ML 73) called upon the farmers of Attike 'according to ancestral custom and the oracle from Delphi' to offer small fractions of their wheat and barley harvests to the Two Goddesses. The demarchs were to collect these first fruits by demes and to deliver them to the board of Eleusinian officials. The allies were to offer first fruits likewise. Finally, the Hierophantes and Daidoukhos were to call upon the Greeks in general to offer first fruits of their corn 'according to ancestral custom and the oracle from Delphi'. No large amount of corn seems to have been expected from this third source.

On 14 Boedromion Demeter's sacred objects were taken from the Anaktoron, their repository in the middle of the Telesterion or Hall of Initiation, and brought in procession to the Eleusinion in Athens. Priestesses, who travelled at least part of the fourteen miles by carriage, carried the sacred objects in small round boxes.

The 15th, the first day of the festival proper, was known as 'Agyrmos', because the Basileus called a gathering (*agyrmos*) of the people at the Painted Stoa. In the presence of the Hierophantes and Daidoukhos, the Sacred Herald read out their proclamation, inviting candidates to come forward, but banning barbarians and those who were polluted. (Barbarians were excluded because they would be unable to understand the sacred words and perhaps also because of the sacrilegious deeds of the Persians in 480 and 479.) There may have been some checking of such qualifications as previous participation in the Lesser Mysteries, and it may have been necessary to ensure that not more candidates were registered than the Telesterion could hold. Each *mystes* needed to find a *mystagogos* to take him through the various rites. This may also have been the time when the *mystai* paid their fees – perhaps 10 *drakhmai* each.

The 16th was known as 'Halade (seawards). Mystai', because candidates for the next grade, the *telete*, drove down to the sea at Phaleron or Peiraieus to purify themselves and also the piglets that they had to sacrifice to Demeter on their return.

The 17th was probably the day known as 'Hither the Victims', the day on which the Basileus and his assistants offered the official community sacrifice to the Two Goddesses at the Eleusinion. On the

18th the *mystai* stayed quietly indoors, which was an unusual thing for a Greek citizen to do.

It was on the 19th that the sacred objects were returned to Eleusis in a great procession from the Eleusinion, through the Agora along the Panathenaic Way, and out of the city by the Sacred Gate and along the Sacred Way. At the head of the procession rode the wooden statue of Iakkhos, holding a torch. Iakkhos derived his name from the cry (*iakhe*) of the *mystai* on the journey. Then came the priests, the priestesses carrying the sacred objects, the magistrates and Council, the foreign delegations, and finally the *mystai* and their *mystagogoi*. The participants wore garlands of myrtle and carried branches of the same shrub tied with strands of wool. It was prudent also to carry a staff, with a bundle of provisions or new clothes hanging from the end.

When the procession eventually reached the bridge over the Eleusinian Kephisos, apotropaic insults, intended to avert bad luck, were hurled by hooded men at the dignitaries at the front. It was evening when the *mystai* finally reached the end of the Sacred Way with torches blazing. The night was devoted to singing and dancing in honour of the goddesses. Mounting fervour lent the *mystai* the necessary strength.

Daylight on the 20th was devoted to resting, fasting and sacrificing. In the evening the *mystai* drank the Eleusinian potion of meal, water and pennyroyal (a kind of mint), the *kykeon*. Once more the Basileus and his assistants offered official community sacrifice to the goddesses. Then the *mystai* entered the *temenos*, wearing their new clothes: the secret part of the festival had begun. The ensuing *telete* involved things done, things shown and things said. It seems that the story of Demeter's loss and recovery of Persephone was somehow enacted outside the Telesterion, partly perhaps by means of dancing with torches. The Periklean Telesterion (*Clouds* 303) was a square building some fifty-five yards by fifty-five. Its roof rested on forty-two columns, six by seven. Round the walls ran eight steps, giving standing-room for some 3,000 people.

What was said, or possibly chanted, by the Eumolpid Hierophantes inside the Telesterion was perhaps a set of ritual formulae. What he showed, in radiant light, must have been at least some of the sacred objects taken from the Anaktoron to the Athenian Eleusinion on the 14th and returned to it on the evening of the 19th. (The Anaktoron was the walled-off Holy of Holies, which only the Hierophantes might enter.)

Those who had been through the *telete* might return a year later for the final stage, the *epopteia*. The *epoptes* must have seen something. Perhaps after the completion of the *telete* he was shown other sacred objects.

Daylight on the 21st was devoted to rest and to preparation for the second and final night in the Telesterion. The 22nd was the day called 'Plemokhoai', after the vessels from which libations for the dead were poured into a chasm. On the 23rd everyone started to make his own way home.

Demeter of Eleusis may once have been the counterpart of Athena of Athens and Hera of Argos – the palace goddess of Mycenaean kings. In the course of time her Mysteries evolved to promote the continuity of the corn crop and therewith of human life. When the continuity of human life seemed less in doubt, emphasis began to fall on the lot of the individual after death.

In the seventh-century Homeric *Hymn to Demeter* those who had seen what was to be seen at the Mysteries were promised a happy lot after death and those who had not were promised a worse one (480–2). Earlier (365–9) Hades had told Persephone that she would rule over all that lived and moved on earth and that eternal punishment awaited those who did wrong, by not propitiating (alternatively, if they did not propitiate) her power by sacrifices, proper performance of rites and making due gifts. Whichever way one takes the reference to propitiation – either that wrong-doing consisted of not propitiating Kore or that the normal consequences of wrong-doing could be avoided by propitiating her – there is no suggestion that just dealings with one's fellow-men would lead to a happier lot after death, or unjust dealings to an unhappy lot. Yet by the time that Aristophanes wrote *Frogs* that suggestion was current. (What had made it current was perhaps the recognition of the civilising effect of agriculture, the techniques of which had been revealed by Demeter to the Eleusinian prince Triptolemos and by Triptolemos to the world.)

In *Frogs* we find reward in the next world for Initiates who habitually showed respect in this one for *xenoi* and private persons. Their reward was to go on celebrating the Mysteries, by taking part in the Iakkhos procession, ribaldry and dancing. (Aristophanes does not, of course, allude to anything that happened within the *temenos* at Eleusis, but it does appear that in one respect participation in the Eleusinian Mysteries was more like the Christian Communion than Confirmation: one could go through it more than once.) By contrast, Herakles warns (145–50) Dionysos and Xanthias that they will see lying in mud those who on earth had wronged a *xenos* or struck mother or father or perjured themselves. In due course (273–5), they do see the father-beaters and perjurers – in the audience.

The exemption of the Mysteries from mockery in comedy and the uproar in 415, followed shortly afterwards by the outlawing of Diagoras, show how highly the Athenians valued this link of theirs with the divine.

We have considered so far the genesis and main components of Athenian religion and the way in which it gained and maintained its hold on most Athenians. It remains to consider the extent to which that hold was weakening.

It is necessary to emphasise again the intellectual diversity of Athenian society. The views of Perikles, Anaxagoras, Protagoras, Euripides, Prodikos and Thucydides were not identical, but the views of each member of that group resembled those of the other members much more closely than they did those of, say, the inhabitants of Erkhia. Somewhere between the two lay the views of Sophokles and Sokrates.

We know little about the beliefs of Perikles, but something may be inferred from the record of his public speeches and from his choice of associates. In his Funeral Speech of 431/0, in the course of explaining how Athens managed to combine freedom and order (*eunomia*), he referred to the 'nomoi, which, though unwritten, bring admitted disgrace' upon those who break them (Thucydides 2.37.3). Perikles was presumably thinking of social rather than divine sanctions upholding – in Athens, as no doubt in the rest of Greece, if not in barbarian parts as well – such principles as reverence towards the gods (already brought partially within the scope of the written law by the introduction of the prosecution for irreverence, *graphe asebeias*, but probably without a definition of 'irreverence'), respect for parents (already brought partially within the scope of the written law by Solon's prosecution for maltreatment of parents, *graphe goneon kakoseos*) and for the old generally, burial of deceased kinsmen (partially within the scope of the written law), hospitality towards strangers and the rendering of good for good. In another speech, itself quoted in a speech that may have been written by Lysias (6.10), Perikles referred to the unwritten *nomoi*, advising a jury that in cases of irreverence they should 'invoke not only the written laws dealing with it, but also the unwritten laws, in the light of which the Eumolpidai give their decisions – laws which no one has ever been in a position to annul or dared to gainsay, and whose very author is unknown.' (The Eumolpid clan enjoyed the sole right of deciding questions that related to the cult of the Eleusinian goddesses.) Aiskhylos and Sophokles believed that the source of the unwritten laws was divine, but it is doubtful whether Perikles did. In the whole of the Funeral Speech he made no reference to the gods, and his reference to them in an earlier speech of the same kind was hardly an expression of conventional piety. On that occasion he said that those who had died in putting down the Samian revolt had become immortal like the gods: 'for though we cannot see the gods, from the honours they receive and the blessings they bestow, we infer that they are immortal.' In his Last Speech (Thucydides 2.64.2), he referred to unforeseeable disasters like the plague, which killed his sister and his two legitimate sons, as 'acts of God' (*daimonia*), which is no evidence of religious conviction.

On the other hand, if he was an associate of Anaxagoras and Protagoras, he was also an associate of the diviner Lampon. According to Plutarch (*Perikles* 6), the head of a one-horned ram was once brought to Perikles from his estate. Lampon, on seeing the strength of the horn, interpreted what had happened as a sign to Perikles that he would triumph over his political rival Thoukydides, son of Melesias. Anaxagoras had the skull split open and gave an anatomical explanation of the phenomenon. At the time, the by-standers were more impressed by Anaxagoras, but when, shortly afterwards, Thoukydides was ostracised, they were more impressed by Lampon.

If Lampon clashed with Anaxagoras over the explanation of the horn, he probably shared with Protagoras in the establishment of the Athenian colony at Thourioi in 443: Lampon was joint founder and Protagoras apparently drew up the constitution.

The fact that Lampon was assailed by Aristophanes in *Birds* (521, 988) is no evidence that he was not a man of influence. In the Assembly he carried a rider to a motion about offerings to the Eleusinian goddesses (ML 73), and he was the first Athenian to sign the Peace of Nikias, which ended the first stage of the Peloponnesian War in 421.

It is hard to believe either that Lampon was a mere pawn in the hand of Perikles or that he thought that Perikles was an atheist. According to Plutarch (*Perikles* 8.4), Perikles always prayed to the gods before making a public speech, but we are not told which gods.

Anaxagoras, who brought Ionian natural philosophy to Athens, where he spent some time, seems to have influenced Perikles more than anyone else did. No one who had reflected on the meteorite that fell at Aigospotamoi in 467 could easily regard the heavenly bodies as divine. Anaxagoras called the sun an incandescent stone, and he knew that the moon circled the earth and shone by the reflected light of the sun. His dispute with Lampon over the horn must be dated to about 444. Plutarch (*Perikles* 32.1), alone of our sources, mentions a decree carried in the Assembly by the diviner Diopeithes. It authorised the use of the process of *eisangelia* against those who rejected religion or who taught doctrines about the heavens. It was aimed immediately at Anaxagoras and ultimately at Perikles. Now Diopeithes would have been quite right to suppose that the teaching of Anaxagoras undermined belief in personal gods, but did he in fact carry such a decree in the Assembly? That Plutarch is our only source is not decisive against the story, but his word for 'heavens' is not Attic and, as it stands, the wording would have applied to Meton and Euktemon (see chapter 8), to whose activities even Diopeithes would surely not have objected. Because he was a religious fanatic, Diopeithes, unlike Anaxagoras, was named by Aristophanes – *Knights* 1085, *Wasps* 380, *Birds* 988 – and by other comic poets. The possibility that the story of his decree originated from later misunderstanding of a comic poet's joke cannot be excluded: such misunderstandings were common enough. How much truth there is in the less precise story transmitted by the fourth-century historian Ephoros, that the enemies of Perikles prosecuted Anaxagoras for impiety, is impossible to tell. Plato (*Apology* 18c) makes Sokrates say that astronomers (and geologists) were commonly believed not to worship the gods, but clear evidence that anyone before Sokrates was prosecuted for not worshipping the gods is lacking. (Sacrilege or blasphemy was another matter.) Actually, though the distinction would not have been appreciated by a jury-court, Anaxagoras was, as we shall see, a deist rather than an atheist.

Protagoras began his essay *On the Gods*, the first reading of which was perhaps given in the house of Euripides, with the declaration: 'About the gods I cannot know either that they exist or that they do not, or what they look like; for many things prevent knowledge, such as the obscurity of the matter and the brevity of human life.' No one knows how the essay went on, but something can be made of its opening sentence. Protagoras doubtless stressed 'know'. If he had had an experience like Philippides', he would have known; as it was, he could only study the evidence afforded by mythology-cum-history and anthropology, and opine. Protagoras believed that the conditions of human life had improved greatly and were still improving but he was probably struck by the fact that all communities known to him had a religion of some sort. Such an anthropological constant could not be dismissed.

In Aristophanes' *Women at the Thesmophoria* (450ff.) a seller of the myrtle-wreaths worn on sacred occasions complains that her trade has fallen by half because Euripides, by writing his tragedies, has persuaded the men (*andras*, as opposed to women) that there are no gods. The words of an aggrieved stall-holder in a comedy need not always be believed, but at least it is clear that in 411 it made sense to charge Euripides with atheism, as we understand it. He was certainly interested in the latest speculations, and his characters give powerful expression to almost every point of view. Some of them reproach gods on moral grounds. Kadmos, for example, says to Dionysos (*Bakkhai* 1348): 'It is not fitting that gods should become like men in temper.' But such reproaches were not new – Theognis (743–6) had reproached Zeus for injustice – and certainly they were no evidence of atheism. Euripides was not, of course, a traditional believer. Neither his Medeia nor his Phaidra attributes her feelings, thoughts, or actions to the prompting of a particular god. But Phaidra does refer to her beguilement by *a* god (*Hippolytos* 241), and Aphrodite, the Cyprian, is a character in *Hippolytos*, perhaps best understood by the Nurse (359f.): 'So the Cyprian is no god, but rather something greater than a god.' That is to say, proper consideration of the power of sexual attraction in the universe results in a rejection of the Homeric portrait of Aphrodite as quite inadequate but also in an awe that may be called religious.

Aphrodite is brought in by Helen in *Trojan Women* (946–950) to excuse her flight from Sparta with Paris. She asks a rhetorical question:

'What on earth was I thinking of when I left with a stranger, and so betrayed my country and my house? Reprove the goddess and be stronger than Zeus, who exercises power over the other gods but is slave to her; yet pardon me.' (This line of defence had been anticipated by Penelope in *Odyssey* 23.222.) Hekabe rejects the whole story of the beauty contest as unworthy of the goddesses concerned. Paris was extremely handsome – 'As soon as you saw him, your own thoughts became your Cyprian.'

By Homeric, and perhaps Euripidean, standards, both parties in this *agon* or rhetorical contest are right and both are wrong. Helen was indeed powerless to resist the attractions of Paris, but that did not excuse her, because Aphrodite worked through Helen's own inclinations. (This topic will be considered further in chapter 8.)

Euripides knew, as Xenophanes and Pindar had known, that the tales of the poets who had written or dictated late in the eighth century or early in the seventh could not entirely satisfy later and more reflective generations, but that does not make him, any more than it made either of them, an atheist. His numerous references to the divine *aither* or fiery upper air of Diogenes of Apollonia suggest rather that he was a kind of pantheist. Belief in the divinity of the *aither* was at least as old as Hesiod (*Theogony* 124f.).

Prodikos was an earnest if unexciting moralist, as his fable of *The Choice of Herakles* shows: the youthful hero had to choose between the way of Virtue and the way of Vice (Xenophon, *Reminiscences* 2.1.21ff.). His account of the origin of religion seems to have been that men started to treat as divine the things, natural or artificial, that contributed to human life – sun, moon and rivers, bread and wine. We perhaps hear an echo of this view in a speech made to Pentheus by the diviner Teiresias in Euripides' *Bakkhai* (274 ff.): 'Two things are primary in human life: the goddess Demeter – she is Earth, but use which name you like; she it is who gives mortals solid food; then came Semele's son who discovered its counterpart, the fluid liquor of the grape . . . god though he is, he is poured out for gods.' Prodikos was, as we have seen, quite right about the agrarian basis of much of Greek religion. His own attitude to that religion as he found it is not clear (although Aristophanes (*Clouds* 360f., *Birds* 692) refers to him as a natural philosopher, Plato presents him as primarily a linguistic philosopher), but Euripides certainly presents Teiresias as a 'modern churchman' rather than a covert atheist.

Thucydides evinces some interest in enigmatic oracles, but 5.103.2 seems to show that he rejected divination in general, and the gods play no overt part in human affairs as he records them. Quite certainly, he did not draw the line between natural event and supernatural act where most Athenians drew it, and it has been thought that he made no allowance at all for supernatural acts (see chapter 8). Perhaps it is not important that in his account of grasping political *hetaireiai* (3.82.6) he appears to contrast human law with divine. But his *History* as a whole may properly be described as the tragedy of imperial Athens. The Assembly's decision to launch the Sicilian expedition was just such a *hamartia* or error as brought down the heads of heroic houses in tragedy. Prosperity had bred *hybris* – a *hybris* that destroyed both Melians and the judgment of those who authorised that destruction. His meticulous accuracy made his work useful (human nature being constant, similar behaviour would recur when similar circumstances recurred) but did not prevent it from being more deeply edifying than the fable of Prodikos.

Even among the leading talkers and writers of Athens there was more diversity of view than we have so far met. Sophokles and Sokrates were men not less able than the half-dozen intellectuals we have just considered.

Enough stories are told about Sophokles to make it probable that he was a, no doubt sophisticated, believer in traditional religion. He was the priest of a healing hero, and in 420, when the cult of Asklepios reached Athens, Sophokles was authorised to house the divine snake from Epidauros until his permanent home on the southern side of the Akropolis was ready. He also wrote a hymn in honour of the god. After his death he himself was honoured as the hero Dexion, the Receiver.

The famous words of the Chorus of old men in *Antigone* (332–375) may express Sophokles' own views. Man is formidable (*deinos*). His achievements include even the conquest of disease. Only death is unconquered. But, for all his astonishing skills, 'he turns now to evil, now to good. He who carries out his country's laws and the gods' justice to which he is sworn stands high in the community; outcast from the community is he who dares to live with what is not good. May he who so acts share neither my hearth nor my mind.'

Sophokles believed in a divinely governed world-order or *kosmos*, and he almost certainly believed in the possibility of divination. But, being a man of the world as well as a poet, he knew about the possibilities of human error and venality. In *King Oidipous* (497–501) he makes the pious Chorus of old men sing: 'Zeus and Apollo are wise and acquainted with human affairs, but there is no certainty that a human diviner knows more than I do.' It was possible for communities or individuals to bribe or otherwise sway the Pythia, and it was possible to ask her loaded questions, as Orestes did, but complete rejection of Apollonian prophecy would, like the failure of the gods to punish offences against themselves or against parents or against strangers, entail the collapse of religion (910).

Of course, the dramatic value of oracles was very great, and the heavier the emphasis on divine knowledge, the heavier the emphasis on human ignorance: brilliantly clever though Oidipous was, even about himself he made numerous disastrous mistakes. If *King Oidipous* has a moral, it resembles closely the thinking of the Chorus in *Antigone*.

Sokrates, as we have seen, believed in consulting Delphi on practical questions that were beyond the scope of any *tekhne*. Although Apollo might riddle, he could not lie (Plato, *Apology* 21b). He believed also that some dreams were veridical (*Apology* 33c, *Kriton* 44ab). Again, 'like other men', he recognised the divinity of the sun and moon (*Apology* 26d). Their behaviour was too highly predictable for Athenians to credit them with much personality (Aristophanes, *Peace* 406ff.), but belief in the all-seeing eye and all-hearing ear of Helios was not dead, and Nikias' troops at Syracuse certainly revered the moon. (It is important to note that all these three beliefs are attributed to Sokrates in Plato's *Apology*, which is unlikely to have departed very far in substance from what some hundreds of men had heard Sokrates say not many years earlier.) Finally, according to Xenophon (*Reminiscences* 4.3), Sokrates accepted, if he did not invent, a version of the argument from design, which seeks to establish the existence of a Designer from the evidence of design in the world about us.

The leading talkers and writers of Athens did not share a common scepticism, but even had they done so, it would have been slow to spread, partly because the only audiences that it would have been safe to subject to sustained and serious scepticism were small ones. Few Athenians read books, and few could afford regular instruction by Sophists. The story that the books of Protagoras were burnt in Athens is much less likely than the story that he was prosecuted there. Reflective reading was a politically insignificant activity, and private instruction was unlikely to arouse public feeling. It does, however, appear that, in 415/4 (Aristophanes, *Birds* 1073f.), Diagoras of Melos was outlawed for deriding the Mysteries. This foreigner had said disparaging things about the Mysteries. We do not know where or to whom he said them, but if he said them just after the revelations of profanation in 415, his timing was bad. The Athenians always required respect for the Mysteries, and they had been outraged by the revelations. Upper-class symposiasts could say almost what they liked in their own homes, though, as Alkibiades and his friends discovered, they could not do what they liked.

Playwrights addressed huge audiences in the theatre. Aristophanes and, perhaps to a lesser extent, his rivals exploited a tradition as old as Homer (*Iliad* 5.297–430, *Odyssey* 8.266–366), that within limits certain deities could be presented in a ludicrous light, but parodying the Mysteries was not tolerated, even in private houses. Because shamanic tricksters lay directly behind some Olympian deities and indirectly behind them all, there was a humorous aspect to many of them, which epic and comedy could exploit without risk of accusations of irreverence. Of course, comic poets wished to avoid not only conviction by juries but also defeat by their rivals. We must therefore assume that, pious though almost all Athenians were, Aristophanic ridicule of some gods was not found offensive by his audience or the judges, though it must be remembered that only the best educated third of the citizen body attended the theatre.

As for tragedy, an anecdote is told of hostile audience reaction to the opening line of Euripides' *Wise Melanippe*:

Zeus – whoever Zeus may be: I know but what men say . . .

This was no doubt arresting, particularly since the playwright had not had time to develop the speaker's character or situation, but the story that he was prosecuted by Kleon for irreverence is not well attested. Whatever the advantages of his following his younger rival Agathon to the court of Arkhelaos, King of Macedon, they are unlikely to have included greater freedom of expression. Euripides did not use the theatre to propagate atheism. The defiance and the doubts voiced by many of his characters were within the limits of what his audience would tolerate, though they might have been unacceptable to some of those who did not attend the theatre.

It was not only the talkers and writers who expressed and to some extent influenced the mind of Athens: so also did the sculptors. We know much too little of Pheidias, 'son of Kharmides, of Athens' (Pausanias 5.10.2), who stands for the visual art of Classical Athens as Sophokles does for its literary art. Before the conclusion of peace with Persia, he had been commissioned to cast in bronze the huge Athena Promakhos (the Champion) on the Akropolis as a monument to Marathon and also the so-called Lemnian Athena (Pausanias 1.28.2). Another huge commission had been the casting of a monument to Marathon at Delphi, which consisted of thirteen figures – Athena and Apollo, the victorious Miltiades and ten Attic heroes. Until the conclusion of peace in 449, few, if any, of the Athenian temples destroyed by the Persians had been properly rebuilt. The Periklean building-programme was primarily a rebuilding-programme – a new temple of Athena, a new gateway to the Akropolis, a new Hall of Initiation at Eleusis. The motivation behind the proposal, approval and execution of the programme was complex, but there is no reason to doubt that most Athenians believed that the astonishing success of Athenian arms, especially at Marathon and Salamis, was proof of the favour of the gods in general and of Athena, favourite daughter of Zeus, in particular. Which being so, it would have seemed foolish ingratitude not to restore, and more than restore, the temples destroyed by the Persians.

The heart of the building-programme was the double project of the Parthenon and the gold and ivory cult-image that it housed. Pheidias was appointed to design and make the image of Athena Parthenos. He was also given authority over the architects Iktinos and Kallikrates (Plutarch, *Perikles* 13.4). He was thus in a position to co-ordinate all aspects of the work. From a very early stage he must have been thinking about the iconography of the image, and of the ninety-two metopes (square panels, carved in relief, above the architrave that rested on the outer rectangle of columns), the 524 feet of frieze and the two gables or pediments. The Parthenon was to be adorned with more sculpture than any other Greek temple known to us. With whom he discussed the matter no one knows, but a good deal is known about what was decided. The image was of Athena Parthenos holding a six-foot Nike (Victory) in her out-stretched right hand. The nature of the victory was indicated by reference to three famous battles – Olympian gods, including of course Athena, versus Giants, painted on the inside of Athena's shield; Athenians versus the mounted female warriors from the edge of civilisation known as Amazons, in relief on the outside of her shield; human Lapiths versus the drunken hybrids – human to the waist, equine from the forelegs – known as Centaurs, in relief on the rims of her sandals. In other words, the victory was one of sober and civilised order over unrestrained and brutal aggression. Inside the shield was the snake of Erikhthonios, a mythical king of Athens, whom Athena had nursed as a child. The three battles recurred in the metopes – Olympians versus Giants on the east side, Athenians versus Amazons on the west, Lapiths versus Centaurs on the south (though there are no Centaurs in metopes 13 to 21, and it is not clear what is depicted). On the north side was apparently depicted another related episode – the fall of Troy. Despite the subject matter of most of the metopes, unusually much of the sculptural adornment of the Parthenon directly honoured the resident deity. The east pediment recalled her birth from the brain of Zeus, the west recalled her contest with Poseidon for the patronage of Athens, and the frieze showed the community honouring her in its grandest procession, the climax of which was the presentation to the olive-wood Athena of her new *peplos*. The design woven on the *peplos* was always the battle of the Olympians versus the Giants.

It is not easy to believe that Pheidias and his numerous associates attached as little religious value to their mythology as Aristotle was to in the next century, or that the ordinary Athenians who gazed up at the metopes or at the central scene in the frieze or who peered at Athena Parthenos and her accoutrements failed to receive their message.

Everything suggests that the mass of Athenians were credulous. In Sophokles' *King Oidipous* (977–979) Jokaste had good reason to say:

> Why should a man be afraid, when the turn of events rules his life
> and there is no true foreknowledge of anything?

but the author of *Prometheus Bound* would hardly have made Prometheus lay so much emphasis on the *tekhne* of divination had it been widely regarded as a pseudo-*tekhne*. Thucydides' references to the attention paid to oracles, Delphic and otherwise, and diviners, the references to oracles and diviners in inscriptions recording decrees of the Assembly, the introduction of the cult of Asklepios in 420, the furore about the mutilation of the Hermai and the profanation of the Mysteries, the effect of the lunar eclipse on the Athenians at Syracuse – all this evidence points in one direction.

It would be a mistake to think of all such manifestations of Athenian piety as springing simply from the personal devotion of thousands of individuals to Apollo, Asklepios, Demeter and the other gods. Skilful speakers might, especially in time of crisis, exploit popular credulity or work up the feelings of the mass against eccentrics and deviators from the norm. Perikles' proud claim in the Funeral Speech (Thucydides 2.37.2) about Athenian tolerance was justified by Greek, but not by modern standards. Speaking plainly for once, Herakleitos had said (fragment 44) that the people should fight for the norm (*nomos*) as for their city wall. Irreverence (*asebeia*) – especially in deed but also in word – was not only an affront to the gods; it was also a prime instance of lawlessness (*anomia, paranomia*). If it came to public notice, it was likely to be repressed.

· 7 ·

Art and Patronage

Poetry in general

The phrase 'art for art's sake' conveys our idea of fine art as the production of objects for aesthetic contemplation and nothing more. The corresponding idea of history, unknown to Herodotos or Thucydides, is the telling of a true story of events of a certain magnitude solely to satisfy a certain sort of curiosity. How far the poets, musicians, painters and sculptors of Athens thought that they were engaged in the production of fine art is hard to say. In *Frogs* (762) Aristophanes makes a domestic slave of the king of Hades distinguish from other *tekhnai* 'those that are great and skilful'. What else qualified apart from tragedy we are not told, but the slave seems to have at least the notion of a hierarchy of arts.

Towards the end of a poem (13.49–62) Solon groups together the occupations of craftsman-cum-artist, poet, diviner and doctor as all being under the patronage of gods (Athena and Hephaistos, the Muses, Apollo, Paian) and all involving some kind of knowledge. Referring to the first two occupations, he says:

> One man, who knows the works of Athena and Hephaistos, master of many *tekhnai*, gets his living by his hands; another, who has been taught gifts that come from the Muses of Olympos, does so by his knowledge of the measure of much-desired *sophia*.

The direction of economic history was from the more or less self-sufficient household to more or less specialised groups of experts, on whose expertness households and community found it increasingly convenient to draw. Smiths, masons, potters, carpenters and cobblers, on the one hand, and poets and composers of music, on the other, were all proud of knowing something that most people did not know. What craftsmen, including in due course sculptors in marble and bronze, architects and painters, knew was commonly called a *tekhne*, and what poets and musicians knew was commonly called *sophia*. A distinction was drawn between those who made something tangible with their hands and those who made something intangible but performable. Understandably, the masters of the verbal arts were inclined to reserve for themselves the more laudatory *sophia*, which, as in Pindar, might imply prowess derived more from nature than nurture. But, as we have seen, *tekhne* could be applied to the composition of tragedies as well as to the making of pots. In Aristophanes' *Frogs* (939; compare 762–770, 1495), Euripides, talking of tragedy, says to Aiskhylos: ' "Now when I took over the *tekhne* from you . . .".'

It is reasonable to consider the composition of various kinds of verse separately from the composition of prose. Verse, often accompanied by music, and sometimes by dancing as well, appealed primarily to the emotions, prose primarily to the intellect. The prose manuals that came after Anaxagoras are lost, and the Old Oligarch's crude pamphlet, the earliest extant work of Attic prose, can hardly be compared with Euripides' *Medeia* or Sophokles' *King Oidipous*, works of about the same date.

The amazing efflorescence of tragedy overshadowed all other literary production. In a single year, nine new tragedies were staged at the City Dionysia and another four at the Lenaia. At both festivals the tragic choruses were produced by *khoregoi* – one indication of the importance attached by the community to performances of the kind in question. Epic – the *Iliad*, the *Odyssey* and the rest (known as the Epic Cycle) – had virtually ceased to be written, as had personal lyric and drinking songs. Elegiac poems – in which the hexameter line of epic alternated with the shorter pentameter, and which had originally been sung to the *aulos* – continued to be written, many of them being dedications, inscriptions or epitaphs. Euripides was commissioned to write an epigram on the Athenians who had died before Syracuse (Plutarch, *Nikias* 17). Choral hymns were written in honour of a variety of gods, paians originally in honour of Apollo. In Plato's *Ion* (534d) we are told that 'everyone is singing' a paian by Tynnikhos of Khalkis. It was Apollo too who was originally honoured by the solo nome (*nomos*), a genre of which we can gain some idea from the surviving two hundred lines of a late specimen – the *Persians* of Timotheos of Miletos, who was active in Athens from about 420. (The incomplete papyrus copy of his *Persians*, dating from the fourth century, is the oldest Greek book we have.) Apollo's nome was accompanied by his characteristic instrument, the lyre or *kithara*, and Timotheos was a kitharode, a singer of his own compositions to the *kithara*. Corresponding to the choral paian, originally honouring Apollo, was the choral dithyramb, originally honouring Dionysos, and accompanied by his characteristic instrument, the *aulos*. Both Apollonian paian and nome and Dionysiac dithyramb were primarily narrative compositions, and in that respect, as well as others, they were distinguishable from the three forms of exclusively dramatic composition – tragedy, satyr play and comedy. (Satyr plays were so called because their choruses were composed of Satyrs, wild followers of Dionysos.)

The link between elegiac poetry and the *aulos* was by now weakened, but not that between nome and lyre (*Frogs* 1282) or that between dithyramb and *aulos*. Poetry in general was still closely linked with song. Poets were more often than not also composers. Though there were Panathenaic prizes for solo auletes and possibly kitharists, most music accompanied poetry. This accompaniment was originally intended to reinforce and not to obscure the meaning of the words. Thus, for example, the rule of the one note per syllable prevailed until the time of the later plays of Euripides (*Frogs* 1314). The total loss of Athenian music is more complete and, because it was so pervasive a feature of life, more serious than the almost total loss of Athenian painting.

Choral song was still closely linked with the dance (*khoros*). The use of the word 'foot' reminds us that the origins of metre lie not only in the raising and lowering of the voice (not to mention other vocal variations, as of emphasis and duration) but also in the raising and lowering of the foot. All poets were working with words, most with words and music, many with words, music and dancing.

All artists work in some relation to tradition, though that relation may be one of the almost total conformity, of partial conformity and partial innovation, or almost total innovation. The Athenian poet of the latter part of the fifth century inherited traditions that included preference in certain circumstances for the use of a certain vocabulary (the alternatives given in the parentheses that follow are mutually exclusive but not always jointly exhaustive) (elevated or colloquial), of a certain dialect of Greek (Attic or Ionic or Doric), of a certain style of delivery (speech unaccompanied or speech accompanied or song), of a certain metre (dactylic hexameter or elegiac couplet or iambic), of a certain musical scale or mode (Dorian or Mixolydian or Phrygian), of a certain instrument (lyre or *aulos*), of a certain kind of dance (*emmeleia* or *kordax*), of a certain subject matter (the deeds of gods or heroes or rascals). In so far as Athenian poets conformed to tradition, it was, as we shall see, mainly because they chose to do so.

Kitharodes like Timotheos of Miletos competed in the Periklean Odeion; dramatic and, apparently, dithyrambic choruses competed in the theatre, in the *orkhestra* of which they danced as they sang. The dithyrambic chorus was not masked, but it was expensively costumed. The dramatic poet had at his disposal the additional resources of masks, for both chorus and actors, and also a simple set and some stage machinery.

A dithyrambic chorus was also called 'circular', because, by contrast with the rectangular formation of a dramatic chorus, its fifty members danced round the altar in the *orkhestra*. Dithyramb had long been an important part of the City Dionysia, and it was a part also of Apollo's Thargelia and of the Panathenaia. At all three festivals it was produced by *khoregoi*. As poetry, dithyramb could not in the latter part of the fifth century compete with tragedy – partly because of innovations that began with Melanippides of Melos (Xenophon, *Reminiscences* 1.4.3) and were taken further by Kinesias, son of the kitharode Meles (Plato, *Gorgias* 501e), and Timotheos, which reduced the text to the level of a mere libretto: the language became extravagant, solos were introduced and metrical structure was abandoned. (Kinesias was one of the few Athenian composers of dithyramb, whereas most tragic poets and all comic poets were Athenians.) Only fragments of dithyramb survive, but as we have seen, much time and trouble were devoted to the training of the tribal choruses that competed at the City Dionysia. Aristophanes, who gives Kinesias a scene in *Birds* (1373–1409), may have deplored, and Plato certainly did deplore, the innovations in dithyramb, but popular interest was intense.

Like dithyramb, comedy had long been an important part of the City Dionysia and it was the principal dramatic part of the Lenaia. At both festivals its choruses were produced by *khoregoi*. But in at least one respect it was subordinate to tragedy – it was parasitic upon it, in that it endlessly parodied or in some other way alluded to it. A striking proof of the prominence of tragedy in Athenian life is the extent of paratragedy in Aristophanic comedy. Large parts of *Women at the Thesmophoria* and of *Frogs* are devoted to Euripides.

Tragic poets had to write a light-hearted satyr play to complete each entry of three tragedies, but though Sokrates may have claimed (*Symposion* 223d) that a man who really *knew* how to write comedy would also know how to write tragedy, and *vice versa*, in fact no poet seems to have written successfully in both genres (*Republic* 395a). Despite *Birds* 787, there is no clear evidence of the audience in the theatre being divided between the partisans of comedy and those of tragedy. It is generally assumed that for most of the Peloponnesian War, each of three days of the City Dionysia was devoted to three tragedies and a satyr play followed by one comedy. (This would have amounted to fewer than 7,000 lines and taken less than seven hours to perform.) There would, it seems, have been little possibility of attending the comedy without having attended the tragedies.

Tragedy

The impact of tragedy was overwhelming: its language, elevated but not therefore frigid; its variety of dialect, delivery, metre, musical mode; its stately dancing; its harrowing plots, familiar perhaps in outline and yet novel in detail, ancient and yet topical; its imposing spectacle – all these factors combined to produce an impact even greater than that produced by Ion, the rhapsode after whom Plato's dialogue is named. If Ion could reduce his audience to tears, so could the actor Kallippides (Xenophon, *Symposion* 3.11). Tragic actors were heirs of the rhapsodes.

Early tragedians needed talent and training to enable them to combine the roles of poet, composer, choreographer, actor and director. Such men were understandably highly esteemed in the community: theirs was indeed a 'great and skilful' art. The introduction of second and third actors and Sophokles' decision to stop acting himself created the acting profession.

If one speaks of a profession of actors, auletes or rhapsodes, one means that a number of such people, for a number of years, earned their living by acting, piping or reciting. In the latter part of his career Aiskhylos employed an actor called Mynniskos, who came from Khalkis in Euboia. Apparently tragic actors did not have to be Athenians, and it may have been felt important to attract the best actors from all quarters. In 449 a prize was introduced at the City Dionysia for the best principal actor or protagonist in tragedy, who did not have to be the protagonist of the winning poet. The winning protagonist was entitled to compete the next year. 449 may have been the date from which the three tragic poets were relieved, presumably by the Arkhon, of the task of finding their three actors. Thenceforth the protagonists selected were assigned to the poets by lot. (It is not known how the second and third actors were selected.) Professionalism and competition bred jealousy or envy. Mynniskos called the young Kallippides an ape (Aristotle, *Poetics* 26) – a mere imitator. As the century proceeded, the prestige of actors rose, and in the fourth century they surpassed the poets in importance.

Not by facial expression, but by gesture and movement and, above all, by voice actors had to communicate with an audience of 13,000 or 14,000. (According to Plato (*Republic* 395a), no one acted in both tragedy and comedy.) Few men had the vocal resources needed, and Sophokles was apparently not one of them. Our word 'audience' is etymologically more apt than the Greek *theatai* (spectators). Though they were mostly literate, Athenians mostly communicated orally. Their ears were as well trained as our eyes; six hours of listening in the theatre would have been no more testing for them than six hours of televiewing today. The achievements of rhapsodes, actors, choruses and political speakers have all to be set in a predominantly oral context. On the stage, spectacle (*opsis*) – chiefly masks and costumes – counted for something, but not for as much as the eloquence of the actors and the diction of the chorus. Attic tragedies were not composed to be perused in the study but to be heard in the theatre, and heard with close attention. Aristophanes (*Frogs* 303) was not the only comic poet to treasure a small but unfortunate mispronunciation by the protagonist in Euripides' *Orestes*, produced three years earlier.

Auletes were an unimportant profession in Athens until Melanippides began to subordinate form in dithyramb to expression. Despite their remarkable powers of memory and voice, rhapsodes were regarded as stupid by the educated (Xenophon, *Reminiscences* 4.2.10), but they had probably competed for a prize at the Great Panathenaia (Lykourgos, *Against Leokrates* 102) since at least the time of Hipparkhos. Tragic protagonists at the City Dionysia competed for a prize from 449, comic protagonists at the Lenaia from about 442. Prizes for rhapsodes and actors are proof of some standing, but the standing of such performing artists still remained lower than that of the poets.

As we shall see, accurate portraiture, chiefly of generals and statesmen, was only beginning in the fifth century and, apart from the poet Ion of Khios, hardly anyone was recording personal information about the dramatic poets of the day. Consequently, very little is now known about the lives of the great poets of Athens. Much of what is presented as knowledge is only inference from their own writings or from misinterpreted jokes in comedy.

The fathers of Aiskhylos, Sophokles and Euripides were, it seems, an Eleusinian noble, an owner of industrial slaves from Kolonos and a native of the Inland village of Phlya. The great tragedians did not apparently learn their *tekhne* from their fathers, though descendants of theirs made their mark in drama. It is hard to say much about how the three great tragedians equipped themselves to write their tragedies. They must have had instruction in music and dancing (as Sophokles did from Lampros) and in metre (such as Sokrates attempts to give Strepsiades in Aristophanes' *Clouds*), and presumably they read all the epic poetry they could, as well as attending, from an early age, all the poetical performances they could.

When a young poet felt ready to face the ordeal of public performance at the City Dionysia, he had to ask the Arkhon for a chorus. In granting a chorus, the Arkhon was dispensing public patronage. (There was no private theatre.) How he chose his three poets, or from how large a field, is not known, but once a poet had come first or second he was no doubt likely to be preferred to any rival who had not.

Sophokles was granted a chorus for the first time in 469/8, when he was about twenty-eight, and for the last known time in 410/9. During that span of sixty years he wrote some 123 plays, of which we have seven tragedies and most of one satyr play. He was victorious with eighty plays – twenty trilogies, or sets of three tragedies, and twenty satyr plays – and he may also have been victorious at the Lenaia with eight plays – four sets of two tragedies only. He never came third. To have competed at the City Dionysia every year he would have had to

write 240 plays. In fact, it looks as though he competed, at one festival
or the other, roughly every other year. After his initial victory in 468,
he is not likely often to have been refused a chorus, but on one occasion
the comic poet Kratinos attacked an Arkhon for refusing a chorus to
Sophokles while granting one to an unworthy rival.

Euripides was granted his first chorus in 456/5, but did not win his
first victory until 441. He won three more victories, making a total of
only four. Between 456/5 and 409/8 he was granted twenty-two choruses.
If they were all granted for the City Dionysia, he would have had to
write eighty-eight plays. He is said to have written ninety-two plays in
all, of which we have nineteen, including one satyr play and one that
took the place of a satyr play. How often after 456/5 he was refused a
chorus is not known, but he competed on nearly half the possible
occasions, often against Sophokles. In 431, for example, the year in
which his *Medeia* and *Philoktetes* were produced, Aiskhylos's son
Euphorion came first, Sophokles second, and Euripides third. In 428,
the year in which his (second) *Hippolytos* was produced, Euripides came
first, Sophokles' son Iophon second, and Ion of Khios third.

Immediately after assuming office, the Arkhon appointed three tragic
khoregoi. How much later he granted choruses to three tragic poets is
not known. Nor is it known how he paired *khoregos* and poet. Themistokles was once *khoregos* for Phrynikhos (Plutarch, *Themistokles* 5.5),
and Perikles was *khoregos* for Aiskhylos in 472, and in both cases poet
and *khoregos* may have held similar political views. But we have no
such information about Sophokles or Euripides. There is no sign of the
tragic poets' freedom of expression having been curbed by a need to
humour the prejudices of Arkhon or *khoregos*. Plato (*Gorgias* 502b)
thought that tragedies were written to give pleasure to the audience, and
we may suppose that both Arkhon and *khoregos* were as eager as the
poets to hear their plays applauded by the best educated third of the
citizen body which attended the theatre. (The question whether the
poets' freedom of expression was curbed by a need to humour the
prejudices of the audience will be considered later.) If the Arkhon had
obviously chosen his poets ineptly, he would in the fourth century, and
perhaps in the fifth, have been liable to be called to account at an
Assembly held in the theatre on the last day of the City Dionysia to
review the management of the festival. He would certainly, as we have
seen, have been liable to face the mockery of comic poets.

It might seem that Athenian tragedians were hampered by numerous
conventions. Quite apart from the limitations of the open-air theatre
itself, there was a convention restricting the number of actors and
another requiring them all to be men. But in view of the extent to which
theatrical conventions were modified in the fifth century – the addition
of a second actor and then (between 468 and 458) a third, Sophokles'

declining to act himself, the enlargement of the chorus from twelve members to fifteen, the diminishing of its part in the action, the introduction and dropping of plots taken from recent history, the introduction and dropping of the connected trilogy with all three tragedies devoted to the affairs of the same household – we must suppose that by, say, the 430s both playwrights and audiences liked the conventions the way they were. The conventions that survived did not in fact hamper but were accepted. Athenian acceptance of the three-actor rule, inconvenient though it must have been at times, may partly be explained by reference to the intensity achieved by restricting the number of possible speakers at any one time to three, or at most four, if the leader of the chorus joined in. Indeed the tragedians showed a marked preference for duologue. The huge paintings of Polygnotos were composed of small groups of figures. The all-men rule, somewhat more stringent than the all-male rule prevailing in Elizabethan England, may perhaps be explained by reference to the arduous, honourable and public nature of the work: it would have been thought too arduous for any woman or boy, too honourable for any woman who was not free, and too public for any woman who was respectable. The fact that the heroines of tragedy were impersonated by men was not incongruous with the 'public' roles and 'masculine' characters that they were given.

It is natural for a modern student to wonder whether the presence of the chorus throughout the larger part of a tragedy was felt to be a nuisance by Sophokles and Euripides, if not by Aiskhylos. Its presence virtually required the action to take place out of doors, usually outside a palace or temple; but a large part of Greek life, including theatre-going, did take place out of doors. Its presence also made changes of scene difficult. On the other hand, the chorus was an impressive and versatile part of the playwright's resources. It served as a social bridge between the heroic figures on stage and the ordinary people in the audience. It related the action on stage to the thinking of the community and especially its moral and religious thinking. Only when Euripides began to give tragedy a melodramatic twist did the chorus become more of a hindrance than a help. Then its odes became no more than musical interludes.

A more important question is whether the tragedians were or felt themselves to be hampered by the convention that plots were taken from the network of Greek myth. Tragedy seems to have originated in dramatic reenactments of the limited number of stories about the doings and sufferings of Dionysos on earth. When tragedians first took plots from elsewhere in mythology, there was conservative resistance. At the City Dionysia that resistance was overcome by a rule requiring tragedians to supply a satyric after-piece, that is, one with a chorus of Satyrs, mainly human but partly equine followers of Dionysos. Thereafter, tragic plots could be taken freely from anywhere in mythology.

It is impossible to understand the place of tragedy in Athenian life without understanding the relationship of Athenians to the mythology from which most tragic plots were taken. As we have seen most Athenians did not make a sharp distinction between history with its datable events and myth with its timeless paradigms. Historical events might well serve as paradigms. Xerxes' invasion of Greece was a paradigm of *hybris*, arrogant aggression. Mythical deeds might not be datable, but almost no one doubted that the Trojan War, for example, had taken place much as described in epic.

When we examine the complex network of Greek myth, we see that it is mostly composed of stories about heroes. A few of the stories are exclusively about gods, but most are mainly about heroes with only intermittent reference to the gods. Even when the gods do play a part, the earthly manifestations of their power are not usually fantastic. There is nothing fantastic about sudden storms sinking ships or oracles coming true. The spheres of man and animal are usually distinct: animals rarely talk, heroes rarely turn into animals. Most of the actions of the heroes of Greek mythology are possible and intelligible. (That the mythology of the Greeks is more intelligible to us than that of North or South American Indians should, for several reasons, not surprise us.) Greek mythology is something of great antiquity, complexity and diversity, but it is possible to generalise about it. As we have it, it consists of those stories, originating in most cases in events of the Bronze Age, which were thought worth telling and retelling, with constant adjustments to the circumstances of teller and audience, through the early Iron Age until they were written down and eventually widely read. The stories were thought worth telling and retelling partly because they were good stories but partly also because they upheld the political or social or moral or religious order, or because they gave expression to tensions within that order. Thoughtful Athenians are unlikely to have believed in the Cyclops Polyphemos, but the story of Odysseus' encounter with him is a good one and it helps to define the Greek idea of civilisation.

Of course, some of the facts of politics had changed greatly since the heyday of Mycenae. Mycenae itself and many other once famous Greek cities had sunk into obscurity if not oblivion. In 468 Mycenae had been destroyed by Argos (which is where Aiskhylos located Agamemnon's capital); other places mentioned in the Catalogue of Greek contingents in *Iliad* 2 were now names and nothing more. On the other hand, for a surviving city to be mentioned in the Catalogue was a source of prestige. According to Herodotos (7.161.3), the Athenian member of the Greek delegation that in 481 appealed to Gelon, tyrant of Syracuse, for help against Persia, justified the refusal of Athens to cede the command at sea to Syracuse by reference to what the Catalogue (2.552f.) said about the generalship of the Athenian king, Menestheus, though by historical times he was little more than a name.

If political geography had changed, so had political structure. There were still kings in Sparta, but the only king in Athens was an annual magistrate. Nevertheless Homeric kings were very much less autocratic than the kings in the almost oriental world revealed by the decipherment of the Linear B tablets are likely to have been. But though kings had come down and down in the world, their aristocratic descendants were still proud to trace their line back through them to the gods. An even more important constant was the consciousness of Greek unity, albeit in diversity. Thucydides knew his Homer well enough to be able to say (1.3.3) that Homer never used the word *barbaroi*, but he does use the words 'Argeioi', 'Danaoi', and especially 'Akhaioi' (sometimes even 'Panakhaioi') to cover all the Greeks from Thessaly to Crete and from Kephallenia to Rhodes. And if he does not assert their cultural unity – linguistic, social, religious – that must surely be because he takes it for granted.

From Homeric to historical times Greek society remained founded on the *oikos* or household, with the father's power therein almost unfettered. (With the coming of more or less settled agricultural life, a feeling of local community emerged, but the community was mainly concerned with defence.) It was the business of the father to pass on the *oikos* to his son at least as strong as he had inherited it. It was the business of the mother to bear him that son and to manage the house. She enjoyed somewhat more freedom in the Homeric world than in fifth-century Athens, but not very much more.

The *oikos* and the father's position therein being the foundation of society, the most heinous offences were parricide (matricide was somewhat less serious, and other killings within the family somewhat less serious again) and incest, with direct ascendants or descendants, or with siblings. Other serious offences within the *oikos* were adultery by the wife and fornication by a daughter. Any form of disrespect of parents was prohibited. Offences against other *oikoi* included homicide and rape, as well as adultery and fornication. The most heinous offence against the community was betrayal in time of war, especially betrayal for personal gain. Also prohibited were: disrespect of the old, of benefactors, of hosts, guests, strangers and suppliants; needless savagery; perjury and, to a lesser extent, other forms of deception (the gods were no strangers to deception, nor was the hero Odysseus, but his anti-type, Achilles, upheld the ideal of truthfulness (*Iliad* 9.312f.)); all forms of irreverence to the gods. Many myths are, in part at least, cautionary tales, warning of the evil consequences that sooner or later overtake those who violate these prohibitions. In various aspects of his complex nature, Zeus himself, the king of kings or father (not in the biological sense) of gods and men, was believed to punish both disrespect of hosts, guests, strangers (Zeus Xenios) and suppliants (Zeus Hikesios) and also perjury (Zeus Horkios).

In communities that have no signed documents or only a few, great importance must attach to oaths. The making of oaths may be reinforced by the shaking of right hands or by the invoking of gods. If the latter, stronger, course is taken (Euripides, *Medeia* 735–739), perjury becomes an offence not only against Zeus but also against any other gods invoked. Such disrespect of divine *time* is irreverence (*asebeia*). Other kinds of irreverence include disobedience to divine commands, failure to fulfil vows to gods, neglect of cult, attempting to blur the distinction between mortal and immortal, blasphemy, sacrilege, and disrespect of a god's priests or ordinary worshippers, Many myths are, in part at least, cautionary tales warning of the evil consequences that sooner or later overtake those who commit irreverence.

Iron Age Greece was no doubt very different in many ways from Bronze Age Greece. A great gulf separated the absolute monarchy of Mycenae, in which writing was the preserve of a tiny minority, from the democratic community of Athens, in which most free men were literate. Iron, the *polis* or community, the alphabet, coined money, written laws, democracy – all these things were new and of great importance. But Athenians were unaware how different the past had been. No doubt the heroes had been bigger and stronger, braver and more forceful, richer and closer to the gods than any Greeks of their own day, but it did not occur to them that the conditions of life might have changed radically. And, as we have seen, there was much that had not changed. Men still lived in families. The twin societies of gods and men were still related as they always had been. (Zeus, Hera, Poseidon, Hermes, Artemis and Athena are all known to have received worship in Mycenaean times, and they continued to do so in historical times.) The stories that men preserved were those that retained their interest despite economic, political and legal changes. Somewhere in that corpus could be found almost all human life.

It is not possible for us to list and compare the plots of the 1,000 or more tragedies produced at the City Dionysia and (from about 440) the Lenaia in the fifth century with the total range of epic poetry then current, and so to generalise about the sort of plot the poets and their audiences preferred. In the first place, the fewer than three hundred tragedies that we have or at least know something about are not a random selection: they reflect the selectors' interests. (As we shall see, it is possible to generalise about the areas of mythology from which the plots of these plays were taken.) Secondly, when we have the titles of tragedies but no more, they may not be very informative. Thirdly, all but some 120 lines of the so-called Epic Cycle are lost. (We do, however, know that the *Iliad* and to a lesser extent the *Odyssey* rejected much lurid material that the Cycle admitted, including horrors in the household.) It is therefore prudent to turn to Aristotle, who says in his *Poetics* (13):

> Originally the poets used to work through the stories as they came to hand, but now the finest tragedies are composed round a few households, like that of Alkmeon, Oidipous, Orestes, Meleagros, Thyestes, Telephos, or any others whom it befell to suffer or do fearful deeds [*deina*].

Aristotle further holds that it is best if the doer or sufferer of the fearful deed fails to recognise a kinsman. Alkmeon killed his mother to avenge his father. His story was written about by Sophokles, Euripides and, in the fourth century, Astydamas, who represented Alkmeon as not recognising his mother. Oidipous killed his father and married his mother, in neither case recognising his own parent. Aiskhylos, Sophokles and Euripides all wrote about him, and so did at least nine lesser dramatists. After returning unrecognised to his country, Orestes, like Alkmeon, killed his mother to avenge his father. The three great tragedians all wrote about him. After killing his maternal uncles, perhaps unintentionally, Meleagros was killed by his mother. Phrynikhos, Sophokles and Euripides wrote about him. Thyestes committed adultery with the wife of his brother Atreus. Atreus first banished him and then, at a supposedly reconciliatory banquet, served Thyestes with the flesh of his own sons, which, not surprisingly, he failed to recognise. By committing incest with his own daughter, without recognising her, Thyestes begot another son, Aigisthos. Sophokles wrote a play about this last episode. Telephos was exposed in infancy, and later would have married his mother but for a last-minute recognition. He did kill his uncles without recognising them. The three great tragedians all wrote about him.

Earlier in his *Poetics* (11), Aristotle has described a fearful deed (*pathos*) as: 'destructive or painful, such as deaths in public, agonies, woundings and so on', and later (14) he says that the most tragic *pathe* are those that occur 'within the family, as when brother kills brother, or son kills father, or mother kills son, or son kills mother, or intends to do so, or does something else of the sort.'

What survives of Aristotle's *Poetics* is chiefly his analysis of what makes a good tragedy. It does not purport to examine systematically the tragedies of greatest interest to us or to generalise about the practice of the authors of those tragedies. Nevertheless, what it says about horrors in the household is important, as is what it says (13) about tragedy arousing pity for someone who comes to grief without deserving it and fear for someone psychologically like ourselves. The tragic hero – to use a phrase not used by Aristotle – is 'one who is not pre-eminent in moral virtue, who passes to misfortune not through vice or wickedness, but because of some piece of ignorance, and who is of high repute and great good fortune, like Oidipous. . . .' Though the adult Oidipous was not a saintly figure like, say, Sokrates, he was a good king and obviously did not deserve the fate that was his from conception onwards (Aristophanes, *Frogs* 1183ff.), but because he failed to recognise his parents, he did things that were absolutely prohibited. His self-blinding – less painful than his newfound knowledge – might be likened to a man's burning the car with which he has, not through his fault but theirs, killed his parents. Tragedy is concerned not only with horrid deeds but also with intentions beforehand and reactions afterwards. We might question the need for 'high repute and great good fortune', but to Greek ways of thinking tragedy could hardly be written about people without resources or ambition.

In his *Defence of Helen* (9), Gorgias had already written, in his elaborate fashion: 'Those who hear poetry are overcome by a shuddering fear, a tearful pity and a longing for lamentation. Through the words, the soul undergoes its own reaction to successes and misfortunes in the lives of other people.' Aristotle's mention of pity shows that he accepts that the complex feelings of the audience are at least partly altruistic: the character on the stage is remote from the audience in time and status and yet evokes pity. Euripides' royalty in rags had that effect on the audience (*Frogs* 1063f.). On the other hand, the fear that both Aristotle and Gorgias also mention may result from reflection on the precariousness of all human fortune, including the audience's, as well as from identification with the character on stage. Somehow, Gorgias knows, these feelings of pity and fear are pleasant. (A different but related source of tragic pleasure was suggested by Aristotle's contemporary, the comic poet Timokles: whatever your trouble, some tragic hero had it worse (*Athenaios* 223).) Both Gorgias and Aristotle are clear that, like myth, tragedy is mainly about the affairs of men.

Aristotle's requirements of a tragic plot are exacting, and it may well be that out of all the stories in the network of Greek myth those of only a few houses met them, but the requirements of the fifth-century tragedians and their audiences were less exacting. As the tragedians read and reflected on the mass of epic poetry then current, many stories struck them as suitable for dramatic treatment. The plots of half the plays that we know something about concerned either the Trojan War, the royal house of Thebes from Kadmos onwards, the house of Tantalos from Pelops onwards or the voyage of the Argo, but the other half concerned many different stories. Aristotle attached great importance to failures of recognition, but Euripides' *Medeia* is a fine play, even though Jason, Medeia and their children never fail to recognise one another. Some fine tragedies were not concerned with horrors in the household. For example, the three great tragedians all wrote about Philoktetes, marooned on Lemnos. (Only Sophokles' play survives, but we know something about the other two from *Oration* 52 of Dion Khrysostomos.)

As at the oral stage, so at the literary: there was no standard version of any of the myths. Aristotle says (*Poetics* 14) that Orestes must kill Klytaimnestra, but that is not what Aiskhylos learnt from Homer's *Odyssey*, where the emphasis falls on the crime and punishment of Aigisthos. If the Homeric version was not definitive, none was.

Aristotle wrote in a fully literate society, and myth was dying. According to him (*Poetics* 9), even the well-known stories were well-known only to a few, but this can hardly have been so in the fifth century. Athenian schooling, followed by regular attendance at poetical contests, both dramatic and narrative, must have ensured that knowledge of the main myths was widespread among theatre-goers. In Euripides' *Hippolytos* (451ff.) the Nurse says that 'those who have the writings of the ancients and are themselves always immersed in poetry know that once upon a time' Zeus loved Semele and Eos loved Kephalos. The emphasis on written sources is surprising: the Nurse is a slave, and slaves had no first-hand knowledge of written poetry or, come to that, of oral performances either. The numerous incidental allusions to mythology in the surviving plays of Sophokles may have been picked up only by a bookish minority in the audience, but regular theatre-goers, who surely formed the majority of the audience, cannot have been ignorant of the outlines of the story of Oidipous. Part of the audience's pleasure lay in discovering how the poet of the day would reshape old stories to his own dramatic ends. Just where would he start? (The prologue would make clear to both learned and ignorant members of the audience what the scene was and what previous events were to be assumed.) What would he emphasise? What merely allude to? What ignore? (What the poet ignored learned members of the audience had to try to forget.) Very little had been decided when the poet had decided which stories to treat. The curious could discover which stories were to be treated by attending the Proagon held in the Odeion before both City Dionysia and Lenaia (Plato, *Symposion* 194b). At the Proagon each poet, accompanied by his cast in ordinary clothes, announced the subjects of his plays.

It was open to playwrights to take their plots from recent history: Phrynikhos and Aiskhylos had done so, but in the fifth century they were not followed in this. Eventually, plays were written, like Agathon's *Antheus*, in which both characters and incidents were the author's own invention, but such plays were few. It is hard to believe that Euripides, who finished, if he did not begin his highly conventional *Bakkhai* in Macedon, felt oppressed by such conventions of Attic tragedy as he observed. From 412 his plays were often more like complicated melodramas than tragedies of the kind favoured by Aristotle. By introducing narrow escapes from disaster and also domestic details (Aristophanes, *Frogs* 959, 980–988) previously ignored by tragedy, he narrowed the gap between tragedy and satyr play and prepared the way for the New Comedy of the fourth century.

Tragic treatment of the old stories was bound to be different from epic treatment. Epic celebrated the exploits of heroes. The advent of written laws and of democracy was bound to lead to the asking of new questions about heroic behaviour in relation to the values of the community. The heroes were, as we have seen, still vivid in Athenian imagination, but because nothing was known about their Bronze Age milieu, many features of the tales long told about their births, deeds and deaths had ceased to be data and became instead problematic. The lonely heroes in the tragedies of Sophokles are magnificent, but they are not held up for unqualified admiration.

If we ask about the intentions of Sophokles or Euripides in repeatedly asking Arkhons for choruses, the answer is not likely to be simple.

It appears from Aristophanes' *Frogs* (367) that the poets selected were paid sums determined by the Assembly, and in addition there was a prize for the winner. It is not known what sum was paid to each competing poet or what the winner received beyond his ivy crown. None of the three great tragedians is likely to have been a professional who needed the money. Even Euripides may have been a rich man, despite Aristophanes' references to his mother's having been a greengrocer.

Though the subjects of tragedy, like those of dithyramb, had once been exclusively Dionysiac, they were so no longer, and it is hardly credible that Sophokles and Euripides wrote their plays primarily to honour Dionysos. Did they, however, see themselves as the heirs of a long didactic tradition, stretching from Homer to Solon, and the theatre as the pulpit of their modern churchmanship? The Sophist Gorgias and the philosophers Plato and Aristotle ('Everyone enjoys imitations') thought that the purpose of tragedy was to give pleasure. But if we may judge from *Frogs* (1008ff., 1030ff., 1054f.), Aristophanes thought that poets from Orpheus down to Aiskhylos had been teachers of morals and useful arts. No doubt there *had* been some decline in status here – from ecstatic shaman through Muse-inspired singer towards mere teacher (1054f.), but this view of the poet fits Hesiod and Theognis better than it fits Aiskhylos, and it is just possible that Aristophanes is playfully ascribing to tragedy what was really the function of the comic *parabasis* – the part of a comedy where the chorus 'comes forward' and addresses the audience. Included in the address might be reproach or advice. In the *parabasis* of *Akharnians* (649f.), the Chorus-leader claims in jest that the King of Persia believes that the Athenians have been improved by the constant abuse of Aristophanes.

The social function of epic in the early Iron Age had been a dual one:

the celebration, mainly by narrative, of the exploits of Greek heroes and also of Greek ways of doing things. (We need not suppose that performance of the latter function was accompanied by conscious intention.) According to Hesiod (*Theogony* 99ff.), the bard, the servant of the Muses, assuages grief in his audience by singing of the glorious deeds of men of old and the blessed gods who inhabit Olympos. In the Homeric *Hymn to Apollo* (189–193) the Muses delight the Olympian gods by singing of the immortality of the gods and the god-given miseries of men.

One function of choral song had long been the celebration, mainly by narrative but occasionally by impersonation, of the exploits of such gods as Dionysos and Apollo. It had very likely begun as the ritual reenactment of divine exploits, but the narrative element, perhaps inherited from epic, became predominant. Tragedy began in the same ritual setting as such choral song, but the tragic chorus, unlike the dithyrambic, did not lose its dramatic role. By the time of Aiskhylos, however, tragedy's only remaining obvious link with Dionysos was the Satyr chorus of the satyr play.

Though tragedians now took their plots freely from epic, they could hardly have claimed, as did the epic poets and rhapsodes, to be telling the truth about what had happened long ago. The facts of dramatic performances imposed conditions on poets far more stringent than those imposed by the dactylic hexameter. For the first time in Greek history, had the question of their veracity been raised by, say, Sokrates, the poets would have had to admit that veracity was by no means their main concern. But though Plato was to denounce them for untruthfulness, ordinary theatre-goers were content if their plays enthralled them, without departing too far from traditional form or traditional story. The Muses, daughters of Memory, were no longer the handmaidens of history or religion or warfare or athletics or education. (Homer had been thought an authority on all these subjects.) The play was the thing in itself.

Nobody who thought about it could have supposed that Achilles and Agamemnon had spoken in Homeric hexameters, and still less that Hektor and Andromakhe had. But hexameters spoken by someone who did not pretend to have been present, though his rendering of the speeches was as dramatic as he could make it, were much closer to reality than choral odes, *stikhomythia* (dialogue in alternate lines), rhetorical duels, maxims (still something of a novelty in an age without preachers and almost without lecturers), messenger speeches (relating fearful things that had happened off stage) and the rest of the verbal patterning of tragedy. That patterning combined with music and dancing and masks and rudimentary set to produce what Gorgias might well call 'illusion'. Epic preserved a lost world; tragedy reshaped and dramatised epic stories chosen for their unchanging emotional impact, and so created a new world – a world that was both Mycenaean and Classical, and yet neither.

In a characteristic but all too brief fragment that certainly concerned tragedy Gorgias said:

> The deceiver is more just than the non-deceiver, and the deceived is wiser than the un-deceived.

We may guess from this what he meant by tragic illusion or deception. A tragedy did not purport to be, as it were, a mere re-play of some interesting episode in the Greek past. Rather, by using a huge range of effects, aural and visual, the successful poet or deceiver created a short-lived but concrete new world, which was no more than suggested by epic. This new world took the members of the audience out of themselves, which is what they went to the theatre for. Any member of the audience who had sat through the performance applying historical or scientific or theological or moral standards to what was said and done instead of losing himself in its complex artistry would simply have missed the mark.

In order to create the illusion and maximise the emotional impact, tragedians had to ignore many considerations that we should call historical. And whatever didactic function or purpose it is right to ascribe to their predecessors in poetry, Aiskhylos and Sophokles, pious and morally serious though they no doubt were, were not, as perhaps Bernard Shaw was, writing plays primarily to propagate their religious or moral or political opinions. Nor should it be assumed that their opinions were the opinions they gave to their choruses. Aristotle (*Poetics* 18) thought that the chorus should be, as it were, a fourth actor. Its members were the heirs of the anonymous mass in the *Iliad*. They should not be expected to provide, and certainly do not provide, shrewd commentary on the course of events, such as the authors could no doubt have provided.

The tragedians were exhibiting men (human beings) in action in extreme situations, or, as Plato put it more fully in *Republic* (603c):

> men acting under compulsion or voluntarily, thinking that in the event they have done well or ill, and throughout either grieving or rejoicing.

(There was not necessarily a hero in the modern sense of 'hero'. Though tragedies were often named after single characters (*Antigone* or *Medeia*), they were often named after the chorus too (*Women of Trakhis* or *Bakkhai*). Even when they were named after single characters, the character named might not be the most important. Euripides' Medeia enjoys the same prominence as Sophokles' Oidipous, but his Hippolytos hardly dominates the play that bears his name. We may assume that the protagonist took the part of Medeia, but it is much less obvious what parts he took in *Hippolytos*.) Because the human beings were heroes in the Greek sense, their fortunes often involved those of many lesser men. Because they fell from such a height – from being Queen of Troy, for example, to slavery – their falls naturally occasioned reflections about the nature of the gods, that is, about the nature of the world in which men had to live. But it is an unprofitable exercise to search the extant tragedies, or the choral odes in particular, for systematic theology.

Far removed though they may have been from the actual deliverances of Delphi, oracular predictions of doom have obvious literary attractions. These attractions were not resisted by the Epic Cycle as they were by the *Iliad*, in which the will of Zeus was largely left in decent obscurity. Under scrutiny the will of Zeus would be hard to distinguish from the plot of the author. In Aristotle's favourite tragedy, *King Oipidous*, which is not typical of the surviving tragedies of Sophokles, Oidipous is doomed to disaster before he is born. Logically speaking, if anyone knows that a new-born baby is going to kill his father, he is bound to do so. Consequently, Sophokles' play has been taken for a study in predestination, but Sophokles had never heard of the theories of predestination or determinism. When disaster lays a great man low, it is natural for those involved in the disaster to attribute it to malignant or punitive divinity, but nothing in Sophokles suggests that he thought of Oidipous as a puppet manipulated by Apollo and having only the illusion of free choice, or that he wished to propagate the view that such was the condition of every man. Tragedy presupposes men who do not just suffer but who also act. Aristotle (*Poetics* 6) attributes tragic action to the agent's disposition (*ethos*) and thought (*dianoia*, chiefly manifest in his arguments) and not to external influences. We may add that it presupposes also that the concern that the gods show for the righteous on earth is strictly limited and that the lot of all men alike is death and after that a joyless survival in Hades.

The world created by the tragedian was both remote and contemporary. He made no obvious allusions to persons or problems of the day. We have plays about such topical questions as whether to legalise euthanasia, but for Athenians such questions as whether to sacrifice one's daughter, like Agamemnon, or to murder one's mother, like Orestes, were not topical. No Athenian entertained the possibility of human sacrifice or of proceeding against the killer of a kinsman otherwise than before the appropriate magistrate and court. Nevertheless, it was not hard to discern the essentials of the human condition in tragedy.

Tragedy, released from anything more than nominal service to Dionysos, was an end in itself. Neither Plato nor Aristotle takes the tragedians seriously as philosophers, and there is no reason why we should do so either. In his *Republic* Plato attacks both epic (the dramatic element in which he is careful to stress (394c)) and tragedy as being untrue. Both epic and tragedy tell lies about gods and heroes. Plato, who admired the stoicism of Sokrates, assumes that the heroes, descended as they were from gods, must have been stoical, and he is convinced that the description by rhapsodes, or the exhibition by tragedians, of heroes bewailing their lot is not only false but also morally harmful to their audiences, who will find it harder to be stoical themselves. Statements by poets that many unjust men are fortunate and that many just men are wretched are likewise false and harmful. Aristotle, by contrast, is so little concerned with the question of truth in poetry that, while he may agree with Xenophanes that poets' stories about the gods are neither true nor edifying, it is enough for him that they are believed (*Poetics* 25).

We may conclude that the tragedians of Athens were not using the theatre to propagate their own opinions, nor were they doing for Athens quite what Homer and his predecessors had done for the Greek settlements in Asia Minor and the offshore islands. But did they nevertheless aspire to the prestige of Homer?

In Plato's *Apology* (22ab) the poets, tragic and dithyrambic, appear to have been rated in popular esteem second only to the politicians in *sophia*. The politicians were expected to know how to preserve the community physically. The poets had once been expected to know how to preserve it morally, that is, to preserve its *mores*. But what of the tragedians? Meeting Sokrates' demand for translation into prose of the choral odes in tragedy (or of dithyrambs) would not, as we have seen, have yielded enlightening systems of morals, politics or religion. To receive the ivy crown in the theatre from the Arkhon before the admiring eyes of one-third of one's fellow citizens must have been an exhilarating experience for any tragedian, however aristocratic, even on the twentieth occasion. But what did the votes of the five judges signify?

The five judges of tragedy – whether they also judged the other three contests is not known – seem to have been average members of the audience. Before the contest the Council had drawn up a list of names from each of the ten tribes, though the dramatic contests were not organised tribally. How the names were chosen is not known, but presumably they were those of regular theatre-goers. The names were put in ten urns, which were then sealed and lodged on the Akropolis. At the beginning of the contest the urns were brought to the theatre and unsealed. The Arkhon drew one name from each. The ten men thus selected swore to vote honestly. At the end of the contest each judge wrote his order of merit on a tablet. The tablets were put in an urn. From it the Arkhon drew five at random, and thus the issue was decided.

Despite their oath, it can hardly be doubted that the voting of the judges was largely determined by the applause of the audience. It would have taken judges as courageous as Sokrates to ignore the manifest preference of ten thousand fellow citizens. Plato despised the mass audience as ignorant, and, of course, by his standards it was. It is hard to be sure how fairly, by our standards, the prizes were awarded. In order to be sure of the fairness of the voting in any one year we should need to have, but never do have, at least the texts of all nine tragedies, to say nothing of the three satyr plays, and we should also need to know how generously and efficiently the *khoregoi* had produced, and how convincingly the actors had acted. (Sophokles is said to have written with the talents of his actors in mind, presumably before protagonists were assigned to poets by lot.) Aiskhylos and Sophokles won the prize with more than half their plays, and it is not easy to believe that they often asked for choruses for inferior plays. On the other hand, the ill success of Euripides needs to be explained. It may be enough to say that some of his characters advance novel, if not shocking opinions, that some of his technical innovations may not have been well received at first, and that he was often competing with Sophokles, who had won his first victory a dozen years before Euripides was granted his first chorus.

There is much evidence of good relations between Sophokles and the Athenian community (he was, for example, elected Treasurer of the Greeks in 443 and general in 441), but no evidence of his writing for the gallery, the most obvious forms of which would be irrelevant praises of Athens or attacks on Athens' enemies in time of war. There is some evidence of writing for the gallery in Euripides, although, or perhaps because, his relations with the community were somewhat less good.

It seems reasonable to conclude that the award of the prize signified, and was understood by both poet and audience to signify, that the plays of the poet in question had enthralled the audience more than those of his two rivals. Among the many, many factors impressing audience and judges must have been: the bringing out of new aspects of old stories, the reanimation of great figures of the past, the exploitation of various traditional forms of speaking and singing, the vigour of the dialogue, the reassertion of the community's values in maxims, the perfection of the singing of the chorus.

Victorious poets must have been among the very best-known people in Athens: twice as many people attended the theatre as ever attended the Pnyx. In Aristophanes' *Women at the Thesmophoria* (189) Euripides claims to be known by sight even to women. Because the tragic poet's material, epic, was the original poetic formulation of Greek values, and because he was treating it seriously and to some extent adjusting it to current conditions, he was bound to teach *en passant*, as it were, and his work could be used for educational purposes as Homer's had long been used. But though he may have aspired to something like Homer's prestige, in that he longed to rivet the audience's attention for five hours or more, then to win the prize, then to have his plays discussed from every point of view for weeks afterwards, and after that to have them remembered and quoted (as Euripides was remembered and quoted by Aristophanes and also by some Athenian prisoners in Sicily (Plutarch, *Nikias* 29.2f.), including perhaps some former members of his choruses), he was surely not seeking to improve his fellow-citizens. In words used of Perikles in Plutarch's *Life* (11.4), he was 'entertaining the community with not uncouth delights'.

What, finally, of relations between tragic poet and patron? The community, or the Arkhon and *khoregos* who were its agents, provided the poet with occasion and opportunity, the theatre, the *personnel* and *matériel* (such as it was), an honorarium and the prospect of a prize and all that went therewith. The conditions it imposed in return do not seem to have been oppressive, though the audience was perhaps intolerant of anything that it took for the advocacy of novel and disturbing ideas in the fields of morals, politics or religion.

Attic tragedy needs much explanation today – explanation of its social setting and of its artistic assumptions. To reconstruct the plays, we have to reconstruct the audience for whom they were written or, rather, before whom they were performed. We understand the plays in so far as we understand the audience, and the audience in so far as we understand the plays that so enthralled them.

Comedy

The surviving fifth-century plays of Aristophanes are most of what remains of what is called Old Comedy. That comedy, remarkably different from all later comedy, is perhaps best understood by contrast with tragedy. Some huge contrasts are obvious. In the first place, though mythological plots were known, the surviving Aristophanic plots are all topical, and their leading characters are not great men in decline but, rather, little men in the ascendant. Aristotle (*Poetics* 2) describes the characters in tragedy as *spoudaios* or serious, the characters in comedy as *phaulos* or ordinary, insignificant or inferior. The *spoudaios* man is concerned about his honour, the *phaulos* man is not wicked but lacks the resources to pursue honour. Tragedy is concerned with good men doing unexpectedly ill, comedy with insignificant men doing unexpectedly well.

The public importance of comedy had been recognised since 486 when a prize was instituted for the best comedy at the City Dionysia. Very little is known about the development of Attic comedy between 486 and the first victory of Kratinos, which he perhaps gained in 454, and not much more is known about its development between then and the start of the career of Aristophanes in 427. A prize was instituted for the best comedy at the Lenaia in the late 440s.

The number of comic choruses granted in a year was five at each festival – a total of ten a year. It may have been easier to obtain a comic chorus than a tragic one: there were twice as many of them. If, as some think, ten comedies a year were produced throughout the Peloponnesian War until its last year (431–405), that would give a total of 270, of which only nine survive, all by Aristophanes. We have only fragments of his rivals, and no specimen of an important kind of comedy, the mythological burlesque. The greatness of Aristophanes was recognised by Alexandrian scholars in the third century, and a higher proportion of his work – eleven plays altogether out of a total of forty or more – happens to survive than of most other Greek poets. We may hope that in his nine surviving fifth-century plays we have a fair proportion of the best of Old Comedy.

Nothing is known of the circumstances in which Aristophanes came to write comedies. How much there was to be learnt by writer and producer he later declared in the *parabasis* of *Knights* (516, 542–544): the progress of the comic poet resembled that of the sailor, from oarsman to look-out man to helmsman. His father's name was Philippos and his deme was Urban – Kydathenaion. He was in his early twenties when his first play, *Banqueters*, was produced in 427 by Kallistratos. It is not known at which festival it was performed or where it was placed. His second play, *Babylonians*, was produced by Kallistratos, and probably won the prize, at the City Dionysia in 426.

The festival of the Lenaia occurred in winter, when it cannot have been easy to keep warm in the theatre and when it must often have rained. The City Dionysia occurred two months later, when the weather was more favourable and the sailing season had begun. One consequence was that the audience at the City Dionysia, unlike that at the Lenaia, was Panhellenic.

A consequence of the content of *Babylonians* was that Aristophanes' fellow-demesman, Kleon, then the most powerful man in Athens (Thucydides 3.36.6), prosecuted the young poet before the Council for 'wronging the community', in that he had made fun of the boards of Athenian magistrates 'in the presence of the Allies'. Nothing seems to have come of the prosecution, but thereafter it looks as though Aristophanes' plays known to have been produced at the Lenaia (*Akharnians, Knights, Wasps, Lysistrate, Frogs*) were somewhat more political than those produced at the City Dionysia (*Clouds, Peace, Birds, Women at the Thesmophoria*), which were perhaps more likely to interest Ionian allies.

At the next festival, the Lenaia of 425, Aristophanes' first extant play, *Akharnians*, was produced by Kallistratos, and it certainly won the prize.

It was named after its chorus, twenty-four elderly inhabitants of the largest rural deme, Akharnai. Though they have suffered severely from the Peloponnesian invasions, they are as keen to continue the war as the farmer hero, Dikaiopolis, is to end it. After failing to sway the Assembly, Dikaiopolis, whose name should mean 'Just City', succeeds in obtaining a private treaty with the enemy, to his great advantage. His bellicose opponent, Lamakhos, fares correspondingly ill. It is at first sight astonishing that a poet enjoying public patronage should have criticised Athens' entry into, and continued prosecution of, the war then raging, but no prosecution of Aristophanes followed. Indeed Arkhon and Basileus went on awarding him choruses. His career lasted forty years and he seems to have been awarded about the same number of choruses. He survived two oligarchic revolutions and two democratic restorations.

One satirical reference does not make an attack nor can an author's opinions normally be identified with those of one of his characters, but in *Akharnians* (377–382, 497–503), uniquely, the leading character identifies himself twice over with the poet and he also criticises the war consistently and repeatedly. We may therefore say that in *Akharnians* Aristophanes attacked the war. What he wanted instead was peace and, it seems, what Kimon had wanted: a dyarchy with Sparta (*Peace* 1082), strong enough to withstand Persia (*Lysistrate* 1133).

At the Lenaia of 424 Aristophanes produced *Knights* for himself, and it won the prize. It was named after its chorus, young men in the thousand-strong aristocratic cavalry of Athens. They are summoned to assist two domestic slaves (one of whom is probably to be identified with a general, Demosthenes) of Demos (People of Athens) in their efforts to replace a newly acquired slave called Paphlagon (Kleon) as their master's favourite with an even coarser fellow, albeit a citizen – a sausage-seller called Agorakritos or Market-haggler. Demosthenes describes his master (41ff.) as 'country-minded, bean-munching [beans were used in sortition], irascible Demos of Pnyx, an ill-tempered old man and a little deaf'. The play is a not very consistently sustained allegory on the style of political leadership embodied by Kleon.

Kleon, who had perhaps been a Councillor when he proposed the execution of the Mytileneans in 427 and when he prosecuted Aristophanes in 426, held no office in 425. Early that year, thanks to the initiative of Demosthenes, the Athenians first seized the promontory of Pylos on the west coast of Messenia and then trapped 420 Spartans and their Helot attendants on the adjacent island of Sphakteria. Sparta could not afford to lose even so few men, and she sued for peace, but in vain, thanks to Kleon. It was, however, impossible for Athens to blockade Sphakteria effectively, and her 14,000 men there (mostly sailors) would become harder and harder to supply as winter approached. In the Assembly it was proposed to send Kleon and another to inspect, but

Kleon replied that it was time for action. Pointing to Nikias, the senior general present, he said that if the generals were men, they would easily capture the Spartans, and that were he in command, he would do so. Thereupon Nikias, with extraordinary irresponsibility, offered to resign in his favour. Finding himself unable to decline Nikias' offer, Kleon said that with the sole additional help of some cleruch hoplites and some light-armed troops, he would do the job in twenty days. Demosthenes, who had probably been elected a general in the spring, would be his sole colleague. Within twenty days Kleon was back in Athens with an amazing exhibit – some 120 Spartan prisoners. This was the acme of Athenian achievement in the war.

It was against Kleon, made thus more powerful than ever, that Aristophanes launched a vicious attack in *Knights*. There is no doubt that the Paphlagonian slave is Kleon, and the charges brought against him and the style of leadership he embodied surely amount to a vicious attack: low origins, false accusations, manipulation of oracles, taking bribes, flattery and deception of the people, and sacrificing their long-term security for short-term gains (1350–1354). The dozen mentions of Pylos are never favourable to Kleon and usually unfavourable, and Kleon is twice (794–796, 1392f.) reproached with frustrating Sparta's efforts for peace in 425.

If we ask what Aristophanes wanted instead of Kleon and his style, we should bear in mind that, unlike Thucydides (2.65.10), he saw no great gulf, other than the social one, between Kleon and Perikles. From the start, radical democracy had required men who led by making speeches in the Assembly, and those speeches had to take account of the hopes and fears, wishes and needs of those who attended the Assembly. The good resolutions made by the newly enlightened Demos at the end of *Knights* involve no constitutional change, but, questioned in private, Aristophanes might have admitted to hankering after the moderate democracy that had prevailed until 462. He had not been alive then, but he inherited the pro-Kimonian thinking of Kratinos, who had.

Aristophanes may well have won three successive prizes with *Babylonians*, *Akharnians* and *Knights*, but he is not known to have won again until he won with *Frogs* in 405. Though he is unlikely often to have been refused a chorus after 424, he did not, it seems, enjoy a supremacy in comedy like that of Sophokles in tragedy. Certainly his next surviving play, *Clouds*, produced at the City Dionysia in 423, was placed third. Since we have neither the original version of *Clouds* nor the rival plays, we cannot explain this, but it was a bitter disappointment to Aristophanes: to Greek ways of thinking, winners came first, the rest nowhere. The version that we have is an incomplete revision of the original that failed.

The play is named after its chorus, who are among the unconventional deities worshipped by Sokrates. (Here, as with Lamakhos in *Akharnians* and with the Paphlagonian and First Slave in *Knights*, when they are translated into Kleon and Demosthenes – not to mention Perikles in the *History* of Thucydides – we should remember that a literary portrait, even a historian's portrait, is not a photograph; but it is too cumbersome always to say 'the Aristophanic Sokrates' or 'the Platonic Sokrates', as opposed to the real one.) Strepsiades, whose name suggests twisting, is a farmer with an expensive wife and an expensive son, Pheidippides. He hopes to escape his debts by enrolling Pheidippides among the students at the Thinkery run by Sokrates and Khairephon. There he can learn how to make the weaker argument appear the stronger and so lift the burden of family debt. Pheidippides refuses to enrol; so Strepsiades enrols himself, but he proves a poor student. Eventually Pheidippides is induced to enrol, and he proves all too apt a student. Realising that his son has been corrupted, Strepsiades proceeds, in our version, to set fire to the Thinkery.

Have we here an attack on Sokrates, comparable with the earlier attacks on the war and on Kleon? Aristophanes' portrait of Kleon might be regarded as a malignant caricature, exaggerating real traits rather than attributing alien ones. His 'portrait' of Sokrates is barely coherent. It represents him as both absurd and dangerous, as both ungodly scientific researcher and dishonest teacher of rhetoric. As we shall see there is no good reason to suppose that the real Sokrates pursued scientific research or taught rhetoric. Aristophanes attributes to him traits which were quite alien to him, and which the poet surely knew were alien to him. (It would be rash to conclude from Plato's *Symposion* that Sokrates and Aristophanes met socially, but by 424/3 Sokrates was a prominent Athenian and Aristophanes was a close student of current affairs. In *Birds* (1553ff.) and *Frogs* (1491ff.) he seems to know that Sokrates is a fascinating talker.) On the other hand, the audience of *Clouds* will for the most part not have known which traits were alien and which were not. In *Apology* (19c) Plato makes Sokrates say that the jurors have seen *Clouds* (twenty-four years earlier) with its portrait of a Sokrates who claimed to walk on air. Other comic poets, too, had contributed to the prevailing misrepresentation (18c). It is reasonable to suppose that comedy in general and *Clouds* in particular, although it came third, did damage the reputation of Sokrates and contribute to his conviction in 399, but if Sokrates had met Aristophanes at a *symposion* in the summer of 423, it is hard to guess how their conversation would have gone. It is no less hard to guess what, if anything, Aristophanes thought should be done about the real Sokrates. It might be said that his concern in *Clouds* was not so much to portray or to attack the real Sokrates as to draw attention to the dangerous effects of teaching like his – dangerous perhaps for teacher as well as taught.

At the next festival, the Lenaia of 422, Aristophanes' *Wasps* was produced by Philonides and placed second. It was named after its chorus of menacing elderly jurors. The hero is a passionately keen juror called Philokleon or Love-Kleon. His son Bdelykleon or Loathe-Kleon is determined to cure his father of his addiction to jury-service. He manages to do so, turning him instead into a disorderly party-goer.

Have we here an attack on the Periklean jury-courts of Athens? Part of Aristophanes' objection to Kleon and his like was their readiness to make accusations and bring prosecutions that he regarded as false or malicious. For them to succeed there had to be jurors like Philokleon. The unreformed Philokleon twice describes (322, 340) his role as doing harm, and he boasts (583–586) of awarding an orphan girl and her fortune without regard to the terms of her late father's sealed will. If this is funny, it resembles the humour in the negligent surgeon's amputating the sound limb – the humour in a functionary's performing the very opposite of his proper function. Outside *Wasps* it might be hard to find evidence of such unfairness in a property case (political cases, like that against Perikles in 430, were a different matter), but there are so many unfavourable references to jury-courts in Aristophanes that it is hard to doubt that he disapproved of the system, which had obtained throughout his lifetime, whereby large numbers of humble citizens were paid – not very much – to sit in judgment on their social superiors, safe in the knowledge that their findings could not be overturned and that unlike all magistrates and Councillors they were not subject to *euthyna* or final examination (587). We may take it that *Wasps* is an attack on the jury-courts of Athens, but if Aristophanes was hankering after the pre-Ephialtic supremacy of the Areopagos, he was wise enough not to publish the fact: he never mentioned the Areopagos in his extant plays.

Peace was produced at the City Dionysia of 421 and placed second. The war had entered its tenth year, but Kleon had been killed at Amphipolis the previous summer and peace was imminent. Trygaios, a vine-grower from an Inland deme, flies up to Olympos on a dung-beetle to see Zeus on behalf of war-torn Greece. Hermes the janitor tells him that the gods have just moved, in order to be out of earshot of the bedlam below. Furthermore, War has entombed Peace in a cave, and men may never see her again. Eventually, with the aid of a chorus who begin as Greek farmers, merchants, carpenters, craftsmen, immigrants, foreigners and islanders (292–298) but end as Athenian farmers, Peace is hauled out of the cave.

We are fortunate to have Aristophanic comedies from five consecutive years. They make it possible to consider one phase of his work from many angles and with some hope of achieving definite results.

For historians hoping to be able to use his plays as evidence, the question of Aristophanes' own political views is important. To the indi-

cations provided by the plots, we may add the indications provided by
the *parabaseis*, of which there are two in each of the five plays. The
earlier and fuller one comes at about the halfway mark. The *parabasis*
is the most striking feature of the verbal patterning of comedy. When
all the actors have left the stage, the chorus comes forward to address
the audience directly. In the first section, usually in the anapaestic metre
(ᴗᴗ-ᴗᴗ-), the leader, accompanied by the aulete, recites playful words,
usually praising the poet and disparaging his rivals. There follows an
ode, sung by the whole chorus, inviting suitable gods to join them at
the festival. In the third section, usually in the trochaic metre (-ᴗ-ᴗ) the
leader voices broadly political opinions, such as the chorus in question
might be expected to voice. The fourth section matches the second in
metre and may continue its theme. The fifth and last section matches
the third in metre and theme. In the third and fifth sections we may
have a chance of discovering the poet's political views.

In *Akharnians* the leader deplores the humiliation of the old, who
once fought at sea, by the young in the law-courts, and he expresses
sympathy for Thoukydides, son of Melesias, the old opponent of Perikles
and the last-known victim of ostracism but one. In the second *parabasis*
War is denounced as too uncouth a guest to invite to a *symposion*. In
Knights the leader praises the unmercenary fighting spirit of the Knights,
past and present, craving indulgence – should peace be restored – for
their long hair and their oiled and scraped bodies. He also praises the
conduct of their horses on a recent seaborne operation against Corinth
under Nikias. In the second *parabasis* the triremes of Athens are represented as declining to go on an expedition against Carthage proposed
by Hyperbolos. (We need not believe that just such an expedition had
been proposed by Hyperbolos.) In *Clouds* the leader reproaches the
audience with having elected Kleon a general and urges that he be caught
taking bribes and embezzling, and so removed from office. In *Wasps* the
leader praises Athenian fighting spirit in the Persian Wars and censures
jurors who draw their three obols without having earned them by service
on military expeditions. (In the fourth section the Wasps ascribe the continuing arrival of tribute in Athens to their former exertions with the
oar.) In the second *parabasis*, the poet declares that after a temporary
reconciliation with Kleon (perhaps the result of Kleon's reaction to
Knights) he has resumed hostilities. In the second *parabasis* of *Peace* the
leader describes how farmers like to spend rainy days in winter, and
he censures cowardly and corrupt taxiarchs, who discriminate against
country-folk.

The sentiments expressed in these *parabaseis* cohere to form an intelligible point of view, and they cohere with the political implications of
the plots. This point of view is sympathetic to farmers. It is more friendly
to the foibles of the very rich than to speech-making, especially forensic

speech-making. It is ambivalent about youth: the Knights are young, the Akharnians and Wasps are old; but though the Akharnians uphold the war and the Wasps delight in paid jury-service, both have done the state some service on land or at sea. It is not pacifist, but it is more favourable to defence and the maintenance of empire than to expansion. It is intensely hostile to politicians like Kleon and Hyperbolos, whose incomes were derived from manufacture and who are charged with corruption, though, as we have seen, incorruptibility in public men was unusual.

The use of the first person singular in four *parabaseis* (*Akharnians* 660, *Clouds* 518, *Wasps* 1284, *Peace* 754) indicates that the leader is for the moment simply the mouthpiece of the poet, who may be assailing Kleon or his comic rivals. At two points in *Akharnians*, as we have seen, the chief character becomes the mouthpiece of the poet. The second passage occurs at the beginning of Dikaiopolis' main speech, in which the serious claim is made that Sparta was not wholly responsible for the outbreak of the Peloponnesian War. There can be no reasonable doubt that this was Aristophanes' firm conviction. It is remotely conceivable that the views that emerge from his plays were not in fact his private views, but it is not at all likely. The theatre audience may not have contained many Thetes, and this might be thought to explain the right-wing bias of comedy: a predominantly hoplite audience wanted to hear praise of farming and Marathon and was not unwilling to hear dispraise of Perikles and Kleon and paid jury-service. But surely most of those who voted for Perikles and Kleon on the Pnyx also attended the theatre?

To attribute to Aristophanes a Kimonian political viewpoint is not to say that this is the most important fact about his plays or to say that he expected his plays to make much difference to the conduct of public affairs. Historians need to know his viewpoint in order to be able to allow for bias in his plays, but, biased or not, those plays are themselves an important part of the history of Athens and worthy of consideration from many different angles.

Since the Archaic Age, poets and public speakers had felt entitled to upbraid their audiences. Both Perikles and Kleon addressed the Assembly in blunt terms, and Aristophanes knew what sort of abuse would make his audience laugh at itself. Several passages resemble the one in which Trygaios on his return from Olympos says (*Peace* 821ff.): 'I thought you looked a pretty vicious lot from up there; but from here [the stage] you look much more vicious!' Aristophanes knew also what sort of abuse of the men for whom they had voted on the Pnyx would make his audience laugh. It was a feature of radical democracy that attacks on generals, ambassadors and successful speakers in the Assembly were indirectly attacks on the judgment of the people. In *Akharnians* 598, Lamakhos, who has been a general and who expects to be elected general again shortly, says: 'I was elected. . . .' 'Yes, by a couple of cuckoos,' replies Dikaiopolis, not altogether convincingly. Athens at war was surely not indifferent about the election of its generals and other military officers. To avoid suspicion of oligarchical leanings, Aristophanes had to say (*Knights* 1357) that Demos had been deceived by the Paphlagonian and his like, rather than that he was congenitally incapable of managing his own affairs. As the Platonic Sokrates, approaching from a very different starting-point, was to urge (*Apology* 30e), the community, that big thoroughbred horse, needed constant awakening.

The Chorus of Initiates in *Frogs* (381f.) sing of saying much that is funny and much that is serious. Much of what Aristophanes meant seriously his audience took less than seriously, but not all: *Frogs* was awarded a second performance because of its *parabasis*, which was unusually serious. On the other hand, in *Wasps* (650f.) Bdelykleon says that curing the community's chronic and congenital sickness (its addiction to paid jury-service) is difficult and takes formidable intelligence, exceeding that of comic poets. Comedy should of course be critical, but the province of the theatre was not that of the Pnyx.

Playful though it is, the first, and longest,' section of his *parabaseis* throws the most direct light on Aristophanes' relations with the community. In *Akharnians* the leader denies that the poet makes fun of the community. On the contrary, he is a benefactor because he has saved the community from being deceived by flattering speeches made by allied and other foreign delegations. In *Babylonians* he had shown how the allied communities were controlled by the community of Athens. The leader then (fancifully) suggests that the King of Persia expects the Peloponnesian War to be won by whichever side has the advantage of the upbraiding and advice of the poet. He for his part will not fail to go on giving Athens the best advice, 'without flattery, without offers of pay, and without deception' (unlike a politician, that is). In *Knights* the leader says that the poet has the same enemies as the Knights. The reason why he has not previously produced his own plays is the extreme difficulty of the task. The audience is fickle. Magnes and Kratinos are now neglected despite their earlier triumphs. The fortunes of Krates have fluctuated. The first section of the first *parabasis* of our *Clouds* has been revised, since it starts with the poet's referring to the failure of the first version. Such a clever audience should have appreciated such a clever play, into which he had put so much hard work. Unlike his rivals, he is constantly introducing new ideas (547) and does not repeat himself. (Professional jealousy was as old as Hesiod's *Works and Days*.) He struck Kleon once (in *Knights*) when he was at the height of his power, but his rivals go on trampling on Hyperbolos and his mother. Eupolis started the rot, inverting *Knights* and borrowing from another poet too. Hermippos and all the others followed.

In *Wasps* the leader recalls the triumph of *Knights*, but denies that it went to the poet's head. (It was not easy to achieve eminent success in Athens without also incurring envy.) Nor did he ever allow an aggrieved lover to influence his choice of subject matter. In *Knights* he had attacked not a man but a monster. A year later he was still fighting for the community, attacking (in a lost play, produced at the Lenaia) professional prosecutors who made life a nightmare for quiet people who could not cope with legal documents. Despite this service, *Clouds*, with its brand-new ideas, was placed third at the City Dionysia. The poet swears that no one ever heard better comic lines. In *Peace* the leader condemns the use of the opening section of the *parabasis* for self-praise, but his poet has stopped his rivals from making fun of rags and waging war on lice. He has got rid of the gluttony of Herakles and the sufferings of slaves. He has enlarged the comic *tekhne* and built it up. He does not make fun of insignificant private men or women. The leader then adapts half-a-dozen lines from *Wasps* about going for the big game, and finally he repeats a point about earlier successes not having gone to his head: he went straight home 'having done his full duty, by giving a little pain and much joy'.

One important question about the culture of Athens concerns the limits of toleration. It is evident from a number of passages in Euripides (*Hippolytos* 422, for example) that Athenians boasted of their *parrhesia*, right to say anything to anyone, but that right was not unlimited. According to Isokrates (8.14), writing in the middle of the next century, *parrhesia* was the privilege of the wildest speakers in the Assembly and the comic poets in the theatre. Obviously sensitive subjects were political principles, morals and religion, and there were limits to what might be said about individuals. Much depended on the context of utterance: to whom an utterance was made and how and when and where. In certain circumstances what we might regard as blasphemy was allowed and likewise slander. On the other hand, as we shall see, the prosecution of Sokrates for irreverence may be regarded as a move to check his freedom of expression.

It was not the function of comedy to advocate constitutional reform, nor was Aristophanes oligarchically inclined. Subversion of democracy was made illegal by a decree moved by Demophantos in 410, just after the collapse of the first oligarchic revolution. Before the revolution of 411 tyranny seems to have been more feared than oligarchy. Anyhow, in his plays of the 420s Aristophanes neither went, nor, we may believe, wanted to go, further in support of oligarchy than attacking one democratic institution, paid jury-service, without explaining what alternative he favoured.

Even if Kleon's prosecution of Aristophanes in 426 came to nothing, it is clear from passages in *Akharnians* (503, 515f., 631f.) that a charge of making fun of the community, at least at the City Dionysia, could be

dangerous. Some restriction had been imposed on comic freedom at the
time of the revolt of Samos in 440, but whatever restriction it was had
been lifted after three years. Even so, there remained at least some
justification for the Old Oligarch's claim (2.18):

> They do not allow the people to be made fun of or abused in
> comedy, so that their own reputation may not suffer; but they
> encourage mockery of individuals, because they are well aware that
> the victim of comedy does not usually come from the mass of the
> people, but is either rich or well-born or influential. A few poor or
> common persons are made fun of in comedy, but only because they
> are meddlesome and eager to rise above the people; so they do not
> mind if such persons are made fun of.

Had the Old Oligarch seen *Knights* when he wrote that? Whether he
had or not, it represented Demos as having allowed himself to be
deceived rather than as vicious, weak or stupid. The Old Oligarch was
no doubt right in thinking that it would have been dangerous to produce,
even if the Arkhon had granted it a chorus, a play that derided the very
idea of government by tens of thousands. Even if the audience had stood
it, how would a jury have taken it? But his suggestion that the comic
poets of Athens were a weapon in the hands of the anonymous mass
for use against the rich, well-born and influential is highly subjective.
Aristophanes' comedies of the 420s convey more or less clear political
messages (not the most important fact about them) and they also make
jokes about more or less prominent contemporaries. The contemporaries
brought on stage – Euripides, Lamakhos, Demosthenes, Kleon and
Sokrates certainly, and perhaps also the oracle-utterer Hierokles in *Peace*
– were among the best-known people in Athens; some of those merely
mentioned were less well-known. But any joke about a contemporary
would have failed unless he had somehow sufficiently distinguished
himself from the anonymous mass for most of the audience to have
heard of him. The political messages, naturally enough, are anything but
tributes to the wisdom of the Athenian *demos*.

Early in the fourth century a law allowed anyone said to have
committed murder, to have beaten a parent, or to have thrown away
his shield in battle to bring a private action for slander (*dike kakegorias*).
No doubt the list of forbidden slanders was longer, and it apparently
included the disparaging of business activity by citizens, male or female,
in the Agora. Such a case failed if the allegations could be shown to be
true. The terms of the law of slander in the 420s are not known, which
is one reason why we cannot fully appreciate such recurrent jokes in
Aristophanes as those that refer to Kleonymos' having thrown away his
shield and to Euripides' mother's having been a greengrocer. From 424
Aristophanes mentioned Kleonymos and his shield again and again –

three times in *Wasps* and three times in *Peace*. If Kleonymos had been cowardly enough to throw away his shield in battle, he would have been liable to a public prosecution and disfranchisement, but that does not seem to have happened. If he had not thrown away his shield, why did he not prosecute Aristophanes for slander? Perhaps the law of slander did not yet cover the allegation in question, or he might have made himself more ridiculous by prosecuting, or comic utterances were privileged. Again, Aristophanes often alleges that Euripides' mother, Kleito, was a greengrocer. As with Kleonymos, so with Kleito: we cannot say what (probably small) basis in fact the joke had or when disparaging citizens' business activity in the Agora became actionable. (That Aristophanes made jokes about a contemporary does not prove that he disliked him, but he paid strikingly different attention to the backgrounds of Euripides and of Sophokles, as he did those of Kleon and Nikias, despite the similarities.)

On the evidence of the surviving plays of Aristophanes, it is safe to conclude that in the 420s comic poets could say what they wanted about the living or lately dead without fear of legal consequences. At the City Dionysia they had to be careful not to make the imperial city look ridiculous in the eyes of the allies, and at neither festival would it have been prudent to ridicule the principle of democracy.

Among the crimes, vices or defects for which Aristophanes denounced or derided contemporaries were: embezzlement of public funds, taking bribes, blackmail (*sykophantia*); foreign birth, involvement in trade; passive homosexuality (assumed to be mercenary), effeminacy, cowardice in battle (the supreme effeminacy); ugliness, poor physique, disease. However well- or ill-deserved these charges may have been in particular cases, the list tells us something about what Athenians admired as well as what they despised. That many speakers, civilian magistrates and generals made money out of their positions we need not doubt; that Kleon did we cannot be sure. Aristophanes would perhaps have liked every political leader of Athens to be a landed aristocrat; Kleon was not that, but neither, of course, was there any reason to suppose that he was of Paphlagonian or servile origin. The high value set on manly prowess (*andreia*) ensured that the lack, or apparent lack of it in Kleonymos or Kleisthenes would be despised. The derision of physical deficiencies may strike us as inhumane, but the high value set on good looks, combined with the comparative indifference to the distinction between the failings that people can help and those they cannot, may explain it. If it is natural to praise beauty, to deride its lack is perhaps not unnatural.

Since comedy was concerned with the doings of inferior people, it was not shocking, as it might be in tragedy, if characters voiced immoral sentiments; indeed it was expected that they should.

Outside the thinking of a tiny intellectual minority of men like Xenophanes, the gods were not credited with moral perfection. They were
not bound by the rules of human morality, and they could not be
counted on to give help when help was needed. The anxiety that once
attended successive stages in the farmer's year had sometimes expressed
itself in assaults, verbal or physical, on the relevant god or his image.
Verbal abuse of the god was a challenge to him once more to do his
part for the crop. When anxiety about the crops had abated, the tradition
permitting abuse of gods in certain circumstances continued. The magic
rite gave place to the predominantly jolly festival, at which the patron
god and indeed other gods were thought to be able to take jokes against
themselves. 'The gods too love a joke,' according to the Platonic Sokrates
(*Kratylos* 406c). In the *Iliad* the gods are the chief source of comedy.
At one point in the epic (6.135) Dionysos is described as 'frightened'.
We should not suppose that Aristophanes' undignified portrait of Dionysos in *Frogs* was without antecedents or parallels. In Kratinos' mythological burlesque *Dionysalexandros* produced in 430, the god assumed
the part of Paris or Alexandros in the divine beauty contest on Mount
Ida. He was thus enabled to carry off Helen from Sparta to Troy. There
the real Paris married her and handed Dionysos over to the Greeks. (In
Dionysos and Helen the audience could easily recognise Perikles and
Aspasia, and, as in *Akharnians* five years later, Perikles was blamed for
the war.) In the *Taxiarchs* of Eupolis the god was subjected to military
discipline by a distinguished general, Phormion. Dionysos is no worse
treated in *Frogs* than is Hermes in *Peace* and *Wealth* or Poseidon in
Birds.

It seems that comic poets could make fun of most gods with impunity,
but as we have noted earlier, some immunities were recognised: the rites
of the dead, the Mysteries proper, the city's hero and the city's patron
– Theseus and Athena Polias – were spared. (It would be interesting to
know whether Hermippos' mythological burlesque, *The Birth of Athena*,
brought the goddess on to the stage.)

Gods who were not bound by human morality, who were not greatly
concerned about human welfare, to whom men were not often closely
attached (as Hippolytos was to Artemis) and about whom many curious
tales were told, were open to mockery by men, and we should not be
surprised if on certain occasions they were mocked by men.

The demands imposed on the citizen of the populous imperial city in
wartime were heavy. Part of the function of comedy was to provide
imaginary release from the demands of civil and military discipline and
from those of the contest for *arete*, which doomed almost all to failure.
Included in civil discipline was reverence for the gods, respect for the
magistrates, obedience to the laws, orderly behaviour in public, conserva-
tion of one's *oikos*. Military discipline included readiness to serve as

required and obedience to one's officers. The most impressive demonstrations of *arete* were successful political-cum-military leadership, courage in action, generosity in discharging liturgies. In the early plays of Aristophanes we find ordinary characters, like Dikaiopolis, Agorakritos, Strepsiades, Philokleon and Trygaios, crossing, at different points, the limits of everyday life. These five, and, still more remarkably, Peisthetairos in *Birds*, prove to be less tightly bound than other men by the familiar ties of custom, morality or law – human or even natural.

Dikaiopolis is a farmer from Kholleidai, Agorakritos is a sausage-seller with a pitch in the Kerameikos, Strepsiades is an elderly farmer from Kikynna, Philokleon is an elderly ex-sailor turned jury-man, Trygaios is an elderly farmer from Athmonon, and Peisthetairos is an elderly Athenian of apparently urban background. All six were ordinary Athenians, ranging from Agorakritos, worthless son of worthless parents (*poneros ek poneron*, *Knights* 181, 186, 336f.), to Strepsiades, who owns slaves, is able to borrow large sums of money and was once induced to marry a city girl, the niece of the grandly named Megakles (Greatfame), son of Megakles. The span from Agorakritos to Strepsiades is that from petty tradesman who sells what he makes and is accosted by slaves on equal terms to the fringe of society. Three of them are farmers from Inland demes, not very far from the city, and three of them have urban backgrounds.

In *Akharnians* Dikaiopolis, after obtaining his private peace, trades with the enemies of Athens and so obtains imported delicacies. Later he takes part in the drinking competition on the second day of the Anthesteria. He staggers off to claim the prize for drinking from the Basileus, supported by two girls whom he has picked up at a feast given by the Priest of Dionysos. (He does not seem to be giving any thought to his wife.) He is acclaimed by the Akharnians as gloriously triumphant.

In *Knights* Agorakritos stoops low enough to outbid the most powerful speaker in Athens for the favour of Demos, and he too is acclaimed as gloriously triumphant. Medeia-like, he rejuvenates Demos and turns into his wise adviser. In the revised version of *Clouds*, Strepsiades, who has earlier subjected one of his creditors to wanton assault (*hybris*), is finally cured of the delusion that sophistry is the way out of his debts, and he proceeds, with the encouragement of his Hermes (and without any thought of the Areopagos), to set fire to the Thinkery.

In *Wasps* Philokleon, cured of the delusion that the life of the convicting juror is not only happy but also divinely approved (158–160, 377f., 999–1002), is introduced by his son to the good life of dinners, *symposia* and the theatre (1005). He absconds from a dinner party with an *aulos*-girl. (Again, no thought of the hero's wife.) On his way home, his violent behaviour results in a threat of legal action from another reveller, in a summons by a bread-woman, whose stock he had damaged, to appear before the Agoranomoi, and in a summons by a citizen with a broken head to appear (before the Thesmothetai) on the serious charge of wanton assault. The play concludes with an exhibition of Philokleon's dancing.

In *Peace*, having ascended to heaven, Trygaios extracts from the cave not only Peace, a mere statue, but also her two beautiful handmaidens, Harvest and Festival. Festival belongs to the Council, seated in the front of the theatre, but Trygaios is to have Harvest as his wife. (Again, no thought of any existing wife.) Later, Trygaios and his slave drive the oracle-utterer Hierokles away from their sacrifice to Peace with blows.

In *Birds* Peisthetairos and his friend are looking for a community that is quiet (*apragmon*). They hope that the hoopoe that was Tereus may in the course of his flights have seen such a community. In conversation with him Peisthetairos conceives the idea of founding in the vault of heaven (*polos*) an avian city (*polis*) that will be in a position to starve out the gods by cutting them off from the sacrifices of men. The birds are persuaded to embark on the enterprise, and the work goes forward. Among a number of unwelcome visitors who are dismissed there are three from Athens – the astronomer Meton, an inspector, who summons Peisthetairos to appear in Athens on a charge of wanton assault in the month of Mounikhion, and a decree-monger. Later, Peisthetairos insults Iris, a messenger of Zeus, and drives her off. Eventually, a three-god delegation, consisting of Poseidon, Herakles and a barbarian Triballian, arrives and by a two-to-one majority agrees to hand over Sovereignty, Zeus' lovely stewardess and the keeper of his thunderbolts, to Peisthetairos for him to marry. (Once more, no reference to any existing wife.)

The plots of these six plays are in varying degrees stories of the success of ordinary, insignificant or inferior men (*phauloi*), who may, from the upper-class point of view, be regarded also as worthless (*poneroi*, *poneros* being nearly synonymous with *kakos*, the most general adjective of condemnation). In some cases the success is, literally, fantastic – obtaining a private peace, overthrowing the leading politician and rejuvenating Demos, ascending to heaven and marrying a goddess, overthrowing the gods and marrying a goddess. Such ordinary men would hardly have been competitors for *arete* in real life, but on stage once they have had an idea or have accepted a suggestion they go on to success. Sometimes they are, or pretend to be, frightened: Dikaiopolis hesitates to address the Akharnians and he cowers before Lamakhos, Agorakritos feels unable to face Kleon. But soon an enormously self-confident disregard for mere facts (*alazoneia*) asserts itself. (This is a characteristic which the comic hero is quick to attribute to rival talkers, as Trygaios to Hierokles (*Peace* 1120f.) and Peisthetairos to Meton (*Birds* 1016).) The comic hero has an answer to everything – often a deliberately shocking one. And not only is his language unbridled, but he is also quick to act in his own interest. With divine or heroic examples like those of Hermes and Odysseus before him, his *poneria* (roguery, knavery, villainy), the very opposite of *arete*, asserts itself triumphantly. Food, drink and women are the goods he is most eager to acquire and enjoy in peace. And not only is he acquisitive, but he is also aggressive. The comic heroes of Aristophanes – Strepsiades, Philokleon, Peisthetairos, in particular – are often violent towards other people. The threat of the *graphe hybreos* does not deter them, nor does it catch up with them afterwards.

Such behaviour – boastful, foul-mouthed, aggressive, gluttonous, bibulous, lecherous – was utterly at variance with democratic ideals. The evils of drinking, for example, were known to the unreformed Philokleon (*Wasps* 1253ff.). In Dikaiopolis' contempt for the Assembly, we find an almost Sokratic disregard for the thinking of the majority. In *Akharnians* 595 he claims to be a good citizen (*polites khrestos*), but the good citizen of democratic theory was most unlike the comic hero. In the Periklean Funeral Speech the good citizen is tolerant of his neighbour, he is respectful of the magistrates and the laws, he attends to public as well as private duties.

Perikles' Last Speech has not persuaded Dikaiopolis that the welfare of the private citizen depends upon the welfare of the community. In the words of the Funeral Speech (2.40.3), he is one of 'those who distinguish very clearly between the pains and pleasures of life' and he chooses to pursue the latter, with and for his family alone. And what of Philokleon's past? In *Wasps* (354f.) the Chorus-leader reminds him that at the capture of Naxos he stole some metal skewers. Philokleon agrees but adds that that was when he was young and fit and could get away with it. The most valorous exploit of his youth, so he tells Bdelykleon (1200f.), who wants to be sure that his father knows what counts as a suitable after-dinner story in educated circles, was not stealing spits from a Naxian but stealing vine-props from an Athenian farmer. (What actually counts is neither fable nor legend, but a true story of some athletic or military or political – in the wide sense – exploit, either performed or witnessed by the teller.)

A skilful funeral speech might for a while convince many of its hearers that all was for the best in the best of all possible cities, and for a few Athenians life did perhaps offer more than it had ever offered before. For those who had inherited estates large enough to free them from the need to steal or even to work and who had also inherited strength, looks and brains, life was good. Though war brought disadvantages, it brought also opportunities of command and fame. In peacetime, aggressive impulses could be channelled into a number of approved areas of competition. Sexual satisfaction of various kinds was not hard to find.

But for most Athenians, loyal as they were to the city and its laws, life was materially hard, obligations – to gods, to community, to tribe, to phratry, to deme, to *oikos* – numerous, and opportunities for self-expression and self-congratulation few. (Such opportunities might be sought in deme, phratry and tribe as well as in the community as a whole.) The right to address the Assembly and equality before the law were not to be despised, but to many quiet citizens they were of no practical value. For most of the year the unprosperous mass of theatre-goers doubtless endeavoured to be, or at least to be thought, as good citizens as was possible for them. But among the many things that the young Aristophanes gave them in his comedies was a chance to imagine a life with much more room for manoeuvre, as they identified with initially ordinary or inferior characters who managed to burst many of the bonds of *nomos* with impunity, to exploit their own kind of power and to achieve their own kind of success.

Visual art

Like Athenian drama, Athenian architecture, if not architects, depended on public patronage: domestic architecture scarcely existed. Of public constructions that which claimed the lion's share of available resources, financial and artistic, was the temple – essentially a rectangular house for a god. The all-stone Greek temple originated in north-east Pelopon-nese in about 700, and its development owed much to Egyptian exem-plars. Before the seventh century was out, the distinctive features of the Doric colonnade – stylobate, fluted columns, capitals, architrave, frieze, cornice – had emerged, and the Doric order of architecture remained dominant in Old Greece for at least half a millennium. The more graceful and elaborate Ionic order emerged on the other side of the Aegean about half a century later (see Figure 9). It is not certain that the terms 'Doric' and 'Ionic' were current in late fifth-century Athens, but they would have been useful. Sparta was the leading Dorian city, and Athens, her more or less overt antagonist from 461 onwards, claimed to be the mother city of Ionia (Solon 4a.2); so there may have been political as well as artistic reasons why even the major Periklean constructions – the Parthenon and Propylaia – contained Ionic elements.

Though not much can be said about the careers of the architects of Athens in the latter part of the fifth century – it is not even known that they were Athenians – something can be said about the conditions under which they worked. First of all, they inherited strong artistic traditions, which nevertheless left much scope for variations in design. That a god required a rectangular house, dignified in time with steps, porches and colonnades, was not questioned, but the proportions of the external

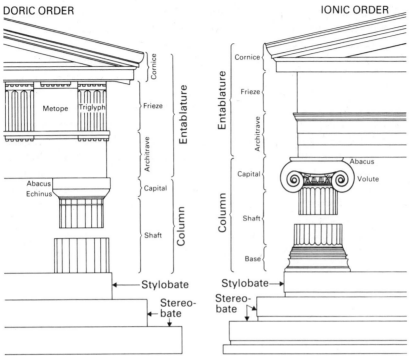

Figure 9   The Doric and Ionic orders

elements were for each architect to determine for himself on aesthetic-cum-mathematical grounds. Secondly, though the Greek word *arkhitekton* originally meant no more than 'master-builder', the architects of the Parthenon were not without theoretical knowledge. The earliest architectural treatises were written about Ionic temples built in the mid-sixth century – Theodoros on the third temple of Hera at Samos and Khersiphron and his son Metagenes on the temple of Artemis at Ephesos. Iktinos and Karpion, as we have seen, wrote on the Parthenon. Xenophon (*Reminiscences* 4.2.10) has Sokrates make several ironic suggestions to Euthydemos about the good that he hopes to derive from collecting books: 'Perhaps you wish to become an architect? That too requires a well-stocked mind.'

Thirdly, though the demand for tragedies and comedies at the City Dionysia had remained constant for many years, there had been no comparable demand for temple-building. After the return of the Athenians to their city in 479 essential public works had been carried out, from the rebuilding of the city wall and the repairing of the Akropolis wall to the development of the Agora as the civic centre and the building of the Long Walls. (The construction of seven or more miles of new wall was a considerable achievement, but we are told nothing about how it was done. In 479 everyone had been able and willing to join in the rebuilding of the city wall; circumstances were very different in the early 450s.) For some thirty years temple-building was largely, if not entirely, suspended.

So it seems that though Iktinos, Kallikrates, Koroibos and the architect of the Hephaisteion may have read and travelled and discussed, they cannot have had much practical experience. (If they did travel, the most instructive site in Old Greece would have been Olympia, where a local architect, Libon of Elis, had built at least the exterior of the limestone temple of Zeus between about 470 and 457.) It may, however, be that Iktinos had built the exterior of the limestone temple of Apollo at Bassai in Arkadia before he began to work for Athens. His first Athenian assignment was perhaps the new Telesterion at Eleusis, but he seems to have been taken off that project (his design being dropped in favour of that of his successor, Koroibos) and transferred to the Parthenon project.

Once an architect had made his mark in Athens at this time, he could expect further employment. Kallikrates, as well as working on the Parthenon, was responsible for the Middle Wall (*c.* 450), for strength-ening the security of the Akropolis (*c.* 447), and perhaps for the temple of Athena Nike (*c.* 425).

Finally, public patronage worked like this. A recommendation from the Council or, if the *probouleuma* was an open one, a motion from the floor, describing the project in general terms – 'to build a temple [of Athena Nike] according to the specifications of Kallikrates,' for example – would be put before the Assembly. If the motion was carried, with or without amendment, a decree resulted. Such a decree might well include reference to a building commission (*epistatai*) as well as to an architect. It might also instruct the Poletai about the placing of contracts and determine how the project was to be financed. Commissions were appointed annually for the Parthenon, for the Parthenos, for the Propy-laia and for the Erekhtheion, as they had been for Athena Promakhos. The decree would specify their duties, which would include obtaining materials, supervising the work, and administering the funds allocated. At the end of their term they were required to submit their accounts to the Assembly, which might publish them on stone.

It is likely that each project had its own architect or architects: there is no sign of a permanent state architect. It was the architect's business to produce written specifications (*syngraphai*). Whether he also produced scale-drawings is not known, but he certainly might produce models of particular features. A sanctuary would be expected to pay from its own treasury for any project undertaken within its precinct, if it could; if it could not, the Assembly would provide a subsidy from one source or another. The resources of the goddess Nemesis at Rhamnous, a flourishing if remote Coastal deme, did not exceed 10 talents (ML 53) – not enough to pay for the new temple built for her soon after 440.

If architects were educated gentlemen rather than master-builders, it might be thought surprising that architects supervising the later stages of the building of the Erekhtheion earned no more than a *drakhme* a day – the rate for a skilled artisan. But their payment should probably be thought of as a living allowance, comparable with the 4 obols, if that was the sum, paid to Councillors, rather than as a salary. A man with the requisite knowledge would undertake a building project chiefly in the hope of honour.

The heart of the Periklean building-programme consisted of the Parthenon and the Parthenos, together with the Propylaia and the Telesterion at Eleusis. (Though it was a rebuilding programme, there was no intention to preserve or copy Archaic buildings or sculpture destroyed by the Persians.) Thucydides has Perikles say in the Funeral Speech (2.40.1): 'We combine love of beauty with economy.' The 'we' may be taken as collective, but if we consider the quality of the Pentelic marble used, the precision of the masonry, the quantity and quality of the sculpture on the Parthenon, and the quantity of gold on the Parthenos, such a claim can hardly be allowed. The Parthenon was in part a demonstration of what Athenian naval power and the money it brought with it could do. It was so sited, on the highest part of the Akropolis, as to be as widely visible as possible from the town below. Those engaged in their own affairs were constantly being reminded of other things.

As we have seen, the alliance reserve of 5,000 talents or more was transferred to the Athenian Akropolis not later than 454 and apparently merged with the treasure of Athena. The Treasurers of Athena seem to have made most of the payments to the commissioners for the Parthenon and Parthenos. Thucydides (2.13.3) says that the greatest sum of coined silver on the Akropolis had been 9,700 talents, which had been reduced, by the building-programme and the siege of the rebel city of Poteidaia, to 6,000 in 431.

The evidence of Thucydides and inscriptions does not entitle us simply to say that it was the subject allies who paid for the Parthenon, and the relevant chapters of Plutarch's *Life of Perikles* are suspect. But if we assume that the three great works on the Akropolis together cost about 2,000 talents (a figure given by a late writer as the cost of the Propylaia, for which building alone it is certainly too high) and that the rest of the programme (chiefly the Odeion, the Middle Wall, the Alphitopolis in Peiraieus, the Telesterion at Eleusis, and four Doric temples in rural demes – those of Ares at Akharnai, Nemesis at Rhamnous, Poseidon at Sounion, and Demeter at Thorikos) cost another 1,000 talents, we may say that without the alliance reserve, Athens would not have felt it militarily safe to spend so much on civilian building. We may add that,

partly because the original programme of the alliance emphasised the
exaction of reparations from Persia for damage done, chiefly in Attike,
most Athenians would have thought it quite reasonable that the alliance
reserve, which included booty captured from Persia, should pay for the
Parthenon. This renders improbable Plutarch's claim (*Perikles* 12.1f.)
that the ground on which Thoukydides, son of Melesias, chose to oppose
Perikles in the 440s was that of extravagant use of allied money on
Athenian temples.

Pheidias had earlier cast in bronze the huge Athena Promakhos, the
point of whose spear and the crest of whose helmet could be seen –
presumably with the sun sparkling on them – by sailors rounding
Sounion. An inscription recorded that the work had taken nine years –
perhaps most of the 450s. He had also cast the beautiful Athena dedicated by cleruchs sent to Lemnos, and the thirteen figures at Delphi.
(His technique was hollow-casting, probably exploiting recent improve-
ments in the lost-wax process.)

His proven distinction as a sculptor made it entirely appropriate to
appoint him to design and make the gold and ivory Parthenos. Furthermore, since the dimensions of the image and its setting in the larger
room would in part determine the dimensions of the temple and the
temple was to be adorned with more external sculpture than any other
Greek temple, it was appropriate to put him in charge of the double
project of Parthenos and Parthenon. (The name that we give to the
whole temple was originally the name of the smaller room at the west
end of the temple: this room, the roof of which rested on four tall Ionic
columns, served as a treasury.) The Assembly recognised him as the man
for this enormous task. There was no competition of designs.

The Parthenon was dedicated at the Great Panathenaia of 438. Perikles
was a commissioner for the last year of work on the Parthenos, and it
may have been to embarrass him that Pheidias was prosecuted for embezzling precious materials. He was acquitted of that charge: the 44 talents
of gold, worth 616 talents of silver, needed for Athena's clothes and
accoutrements had been made into thin plates that could be removed
and weighed. But he was then accused of having represented himself
and Perikles on the outside of her shield. Whether he was exiled or fled
the country, he was soon working at Olympia on his gold and ivory
statue of Zeus, one of the wonders of the ancient world. (Of all the
greatest Athenians of the fifth century from Miltiades to Sokrates, only
Sophokles and Aristophanes seem to have lived out their lives in
unbroken harmony with their community.)

The iconography of Parthenos and Parthenon was coherent. To the
evidence already cited, we may add the framing of an event by the rising
sun and the setting moon (Helios and Selene) in the north metopes, the
east pediment and the front of the base of the Parthenos. The metopes

had to be ready first (and probably for that reason were the most variable in quality), followed by the frieze, followed by the sculpture in the pediments. Pheidias had left before the pediments were filled with their four dozen statues, but it is reasonable to assume that the entire iconography was worked out early, and that Pheidias had some say in what was decided. It is likely too that his opinions would have carried weight at the design stage, though it appears that much less precise instructions were given to the men who were to carve the west metopes and frieze than to those who were to carve their counterparts at the east.

Athena Promakhos, the Lemnian Athena and the Athena Parthenos have all vanished, the last two leaving some traces of themselves, the first leaving almost none. It is natural to ask where, if anywhere, the art of Pheidias may still be seen, and though there is no documentary proof or even evidence that his work on the Parthenos allowed him time to do more than advise on the design of the external sculpture, it has commonly and not unreasonably been supposed that one place to look is the frieze, and perhaps especially slab VIII in the west frieze. Stripped of its sky-blue background and bronze accessories and hideously damaged by an explosion in AD 1687, the frieze retains an extraordinary coherence, individuality and fascination. Its art is both realistic and ideal, restrained and suggestive rather than extravagant or even explicit. It is also possible that the Mediterranean has preserved for us two of Pheidias's bronze heroes of Delphi, and it is certain that it has preserved close marble copies of two scenes of Athenians versus Amazons from the outside of the shield of the Parthenos.

What was the frieze saying to the spectator of 432 BC? If it was difficult for him to make out the figures in the metopes (smaller and more distant than those at Olympia) and impossible for him to see more than a third of the surface of the figures in the pediments, was it not even harder for him to form a clear impression of this unique feature in a Doric temple – the Ionic frieze? To compensate for the steep angle of vision and the oblique lighting, the relief was higher at the top than the bottom, and the painting and bronze accessories will have helped too.

Standing at the south-west corner of the frieze, the spectator found himself at the back of a procession which divided to his left and right. Proceeding left, along the west side, he saw riders preparing for a cavalcade; turning right, along the north side, he saw some sixty riders and then some nine four-horse chariots with *apobatai* (hoplites trained to jump off and back onto speeding chariots), and ahead of them handsome old men carrying olive branches, four *kithara*-players and four *aulos*-players, four young men carrying water-pots, metics carrying trays of offerings, four sacrificial sheep and four sacrificial cows; turning right again, he saw girls, six Eponymous Heroes (or perhaps representative citizens), and six of the Olympian gods, facing away from the central scene. Returning to the south-west and proceeding right, along the south side, he saw another sixty or so riders and another nine or so chariots with *apobatai*, and ahead of them old men, men carrying tablets, and sacrificial cows; turning left, he saw, matching the north end of the east frieze, girls, the other four Eponymous Heroes, and another six Olympian gods, again facing away from the central scene.

It is hardly to be doubted that the frieze somehow represents the Great Panathenaic procession. The folded cloth in the central scene of the east frieze must be the *peplos*, in the hands of the Basileus and an Arrephoros, and the other adult figure must be the Priestess of Athena Polias. A representation of the Great Panathenaic procession would have provided a tactful link between the old worship of the olive-wood stump and the new cult of Athena Parthenos. Representation of the first procession of all might seem to have been appropriate, but that would make the indifference of the gods strange.

Representation of the procession as it was in the 440s – of contemporary Athenians going about their, admittedly religious, business – would hardly have seemed fitting (compare the second charge against Pheidias), and, furthermore, there is too much missing. There are no girls carrying baskets or water-pots on their heads, there are no hoplites appearing as hoplites, there are no colonists or allies.

The absence of colonists and allies would be correct, if the 'dramatic' date preceded the formation of the alliance, and it has been suggested that the frieze is, amongst other things, a tribute to the 192 Athenians who fell at Marathon. The number of human figures in the west frieze and in the north and south friezes up to the front of the lines of chariots, less the charioteers, has been computed as 192. Horsemen and *apobatai* in chariots had their place in the Great Panathenaic procession across the Agora, and *apobatai* competed there in the games. Furthermore, there was no sharp division between the Athenian cavalry and hoplites: the cavalry at any given time were simply 1,000 of the youngest, fittest and richest hoplites. Finally, horses and chariots were strongly suggestive of the heroic past. It is at least possible, then, that in the frieze of the new temple we have the hoplites who were to die at Marathon a month later honouring the goddess at the Great Panathenaia of 490 and being themselves honoured as heroes. It is perhaps their heroisation that the twelve Olympians are recognising.

We have also, it may be thought, a visual counterpart to the Funeral Speech of Perikles. Here is Athena's city (the people, not the buildings) on parade, showing how freedom may be combined with order and how unity may be preserved in diversity. The Funeral Speech is not very religious: there is only one reference to public religion (2.38.1), in which the calendar of sacrifices and contests is regarded as relaxation from toil, and the emphasis is on the self-sufficiency of the fallen – 'thinking it right to rely on themselves' (2.42.4). The frieze is naturally much more religious. If we have a portrayal of the Marathon dead, we should remember that by 450 the Marathon story had become part of Athenian mythology (which does not necessarily mean that it was told incorrectly). It would be a mistake to think of the frieze as self-glorification by the Athenians of the 440s. The gods had been kind to the Marathono-makhai, but the scene on the front of the base of the Parthenos warned against complacency. Twenty gods were attending the birth of Pandora, the gift of all the gods to men – given after Prometheus had stolen fire for them – and the source of all their woes.

Though it is easy enough to see why Pheidias was set over Iktinos and Kallikrates, the Parthenon's remarkable features were not all sculptural – the forty-foot gold and ivory Parthenos, the enormously long Ionic frieze with its almost contemporary subject matter, and the enormous amount of other external sculpture. The Parthenon was architecturally remark-able, too, and chiefly for its so-called 'refinements' – very small depart-ures from the straight, the horizontal and the vertical, intended, it seems, to improve the appearance of the building. Both the stylobate on which the columns rest and the entablature which they support curve gently upwards in the middle; the columns lean inwards and taper in a gentle curve (entasis); the corner columns are slightly thicker than the others. Just as there had been gold and ivory statues before the Parthenos, though never as large, so there had been refinements before the Parthenon, but never so many. It was unusual, though not unpreced-ented, in a Doric temple for the façade to contain eight columns (more than most people can take in at a glance), and this made it possible to give Athena Parthenos a more spacious and elaborate setting – with a two-storeyed Doric colonnade behind as well as beside her – than Zeus was to enjoy at Olympia.

That 20,000 tons of marble should have been quarried close to specifi-cations, transported, so precisely shaped by mason or sculptor, and put in position within the fifteen years from 447 to 432 shows that the Athenian building-programme attracted many highly skilled craftsmen from all over Greece and that the management of the Epistatai was highly competent.

With the dedication of the Parthenos in mid-438, the main structure of the Parthenon had been completed and it became possible to divert the mass of masons to the Propylaia of Mnesikles, which, like the Parthenon, was to be a mainly Doric building of Pentelic marble. It was under construction from 437 to 432, when the work was discontinued in the face of imminent war and never resumed. The evidence can still be seen that there were to be additional rooms to the north-east and south-east. Whereas Iktinos had built on, and northwards of, the founda-tions of the post-Marathonian Parthenon, Mnesikles gave his new gateway a new orientation. He was building on a slope and he had to respect the precincts of Athena Nike and Artemis of Brauron to the south. His was a task very different from that of the architect of a free-standing temple resting on a level platform. He could not achieve symmetry, but with the help of the later temple of Athena Nike, he could and did achieve balance. As the plural form '-aia' indicates, Mnesikles' building was much larger and more elaborate than its precedessor, a mere *propylon*. Elsewhere in Greece there were temples even larger than the Parthenon, but nowhere was there such a gateway. It could be built so much quicker than the Parthenon because it lacked sculptural decoration.

Passing the precinct of Athena Nike on his right and then the north-west room (perhaps a dining-room) on his left, the visitor went up through the middle of a row of six Doric columns, passed through three pairs of tall Ionic columns, supporting a coffered ceiling, and came to the main gate with two smaller ones on each side of it. As he passed finally through a second row of six Doric columns, he saw the Promakhos straight ahead and beyond it on the right the Parthenon.

The south-west bastion of the Akropolis, which had always threatened the exposed right side of anyone attacking the Akropolis, had long accommodated a cult of Athena Nike or Victory, and on it still stands her small Ionic temple. It is made of Pentelic marble and had four monolithic columns before and behind. An inscription (ML 44), probably to be dated before 445, records a decree of the Assembly calling, first, for the appointment of a priestess, with fixed remuneration; secondly, for a doorway to the sanctuary to be built according to the specifications of Kallikrates; thirdly, for a temple and marble altar to be built to the specifications of Kallikrates; finally (in an amendment), for three members of the Council to be appointed to co-operate with Kallikrates in submitting specifications for the doorway to the Council. The subject of the north and south friezes – Greeks fighting Persians – might have been thought appropriate after the conclusion of a not actually very glorious peace with Persia in 449, but the style is plainly later than that of the Parthenon frieze. Some years later still, for reasons of safety, a parapet was erected on three sides of the temple, and in relief on the outside were carved Victories or Nikai leading bulls to sacrifice and erecting trophies (enemy armour hung up to commemorate a victory), and on each side was a seated Athena. Enough of the parapet is preserved to show that the artist's chief interest lay in the carving of drapery. Why the temple was built so long after the decree was carried – probably after work on the Propylaia had been abandoned in 432 – is not known, but the decree does imply that the temple is not to be built until the doorway has been built.

The introduction of Ionic elements into the Doric Parthenon and

Propylaia, followed by the progressive adoption of Ionic in Athens and Attike, may reflect anti-Peloponnesian feeling or artistic inclination towards detail or both.

The last great work on the Akropolis was the Ionic temple-complex that we know as the Erekhtheion. It was at first known, more cumbersomely, as 'the temple on the Akropolis containing the old statue'. It was built of Pentelic marble, between 421 and 406. The original architect faced problems more severe than those that had been overcome in the building of the Propylaia. His task was to accommodate a number of primitive cults on a site that was far from level in a single structure that would balance the Parthenon on the other side of the Akropolis without diminishing its dominance. When the rebuilding of the Akropolis was begun in the early 440s, it is unlikely that anyone foresaw how it would end, but it is clear that each new architect related his own work to the whole site and indeed the city.

The main structure of the temple was divided by a cross wall. It seems likely that the smaller, eastern room accommodated altars of Poseidon, of Boutes – the brother of Erekhtheus, earth-born King of Athens (*Iliad* 2.547f.) – and of Hephaistos, and that the larger, western room accommodated: the salt well supposed to have been struck in the rock by Poseidon with his trident when he was competing with Athena for the patronage of Athens; a wooden Hermes; the olive-wood statue of Athena, illuminated by an ever-burning lamp; the grave of Erekhtheus and a pit for his sacred snake. The grander end of a Greek temple was normally the eastern, but in the case of the Erekhtheion we must notice that two remarkable porches lead into the western room. The lofty north porch has a magnificent doorway sixteen feet high. The south porch is much smaller, but when seen from the west, it appears to balance the north porch. Its roof is supported by six Karyatids – stone girls, who stand on a parapet. They look out over the foundations of the first temple of Athena towards the Parthenon. The folds of their dresses echo the fluting of its columns. They originally carried libation bowls, as do some ten of the girls near the front of the two wings of the procession in the Parthenon frieze. The only way into the porch from the outside is by a narrow breach in the parapet between the most north-easterly Karyatid and the main structure. It seems plausible to suggest that some ritual with the *peplos* was enacted in the porch. Both the main structure and the north porch carried friezes of grey Eleusinian stone, to which figures in white Pentelic marble were attached.

To the west of the temple an unroofed precinct contained: the grave of Kekrops, another early king of Athens; a temple of Pandrosos, his dutiful daughter; and the original olive-tree – Athena's riposte to Poseidon's salt well. The *moriai* or sacred olives of Attike were deemed to be offshoots of this tree. Herodotos (8.55) relates that although it was burnt by Xerxes along with the old temple, it had regenerated the next day.

The building-programme was not restricted to works on the Akropolis, although that was the most conspicuous site as well as the most sacred. The Akropolis works were the most elaborate and artistically the most remarkable, but important works were undertaken in Peiraieus, at Eleusis, and elsewhere in Attike. The development of the Agora as the civic centre of Athens came to a temporary end with the completion of the main structure of the Hephaisteion on Kolonos Agoraios in the early 440s. This, the best preserved Doric temple of the fifth century, had the conventional six columns in its façade and was made mainly of Pentelic marble. It was not until after the Arkhidamian War that the temple was finished and the cult statues of Hephaistos and Athena by Alkamenes were installed. The men who had worked on the first stage of the building were presumably diverted to the Akropolis.

Like the plays, the public buildings of Classical Athens have not survived for nearly two and a half millennia unscathed. Much has been lost and much that has not been lost has been damaged. As the plays have lost their music and their texts have been corrupted, so the buildings have been broken and stripped of their decorations and paint. It is hardly possible to contemplate this loss and damage with equanimity. Nevertheless, enough of the best survives in reasonable condition for us to be able to claim to know something of the mind and art of Athens, though not as much as we know of the Sokratic-Platonic style of philosophy.

Neither great plays nor great buildings can ever be understood fully – they are too complex and subtle, and they can be 'read' in too many ways. Even when all is known that can be known about the previous history of the literary genre or architectural order and about the beliefs and expectations of the patrons and artists, much will remain elusive, especially in drama, where it seems far easier to discredit theories than to establish them. But in architecture much may be understood. It does seem possible, when considering, for example, the temple of Athena Nike in relation to the Propylaia to say why the temple has the dimensions that it has and is aligned as it is.

In his *Life of Kimon* (4.6) Plutarch is anxious to acquit the painter Polygnotos of the charge of *banausia*, but in his *Life of Perikles* (1.4–2.1) he says that he (Plutarch) and people like him often enjoy the work and despise the worker, and he claims that no gifted youth, on seeing the Zeus of Pheidias at Olympia or the Hera of Polykleitos at Argos, wants to be Pheidias or Polykleitos, or, come to that, to be Anakreon of Teos or Arkhilokhos of Paros because he enjoys their poetry. It is by enjoying music and poetry that an aristocrat renders his due to the Muses (masters of the visual arts have no Muse – only Hephaistos); one is not called upon to admire the artists themselves or to understand their techniques (*tekhnai*).

The attitude of Plutarch is that of a Boiotian gentleman of the first century AD. It is the attitude, ultimately, of the self-sufficient warrior defending the territory of his household and tribe. To him the things that really matter are: inheriting and maintaining landed property; fighting, or preparing to fight, to defend it; taking part in politics, the peacetime replacement for fighting. The Muses may sweeten this life-style, but they do not transform or supersede it.

In the second half of the fifth century Athenian attitudes to visual art and artists were, like our own, diverse. Here and there traces may be found of an extreme view, according to which artisans, and with them artists, like slaves and metics (and even women), were necessary evils. In default of automata (Aristotle, *Politics* 1253b), the community could not survive without slaves, metics and artisans. Two confusing facts were these: first, though many artisans were metics or slaves – many were citizens, that is, full members of the community; secondly, much of what the artisans produced was indisputably fine (*kalos*) – not necessary for life, but necessary for the good life (Aristotle, *Politics* 1291a). 'We love the fine,' said Perikles, and the evidence is that, aristocrat though he was, he also liked Pheidias. It is hard to believe that his regard for a great artist was unique. It was not possible simply to say that the community concerned itself with landowning, defence and politics, leaving trade – the import of raw materials, the manufacture and sale of goods – to outsiders, that is, metics and slaves. Many citizens practised trades, often alongside slaves, and much of what they produced was fine. Most of these citizen artisans lived in Athens and thus, under normal circumstances, would find it easier to attend the Assembly than would the smallholders of Attike. Speakers in the Assembly had to speak respectfully of them. A striking testimony to the importance of craftsmanship in Athenian thinking is afforded by the interest shown in it by the far from democratic Sokratic-Platonic school of philosophy. Whether Sokrates was the son of a stonemason or not, both Plato and Xenophon show him as greatly interested in craftsmen and their works.

In its central sense, *tekhne* was knowing how to produce goods of a certain kind by working on materials of a certain kind. In Athens the variety of materials, skills (Old Oligarch 1.12) and products was wide. Into Peiraieus flowed the materials that Attike could not itself produce. As the population grew, so demand grew, and as demand grew, so specialisation grew. The vocabulary of Athenian trade is wide, though we need not assume that to each word of the '-maker' or '-monger' kind there corresponded a quite separate kind of tradesmen: specialisation had not gone that far.

The materials to be worked on ranged from guts and grain, through hides and wood, to clay, limestone and marble, and bronze, silver and gold. Aristophanes describes the hero of *Knights* as a sausage-*seller*. ('Poseidon, what a trade!' exclaims the Second Slave (144). But Agorakritos makes sausages as well as selling them. Comedy lays heavy emphasis on selling because that was a more contemptible activity than making. In Aristophanes' *Wealth* (903ff.) three methods of earning a living are recognised: farming, maritime trading and practising a *tekhne*. In theory farmers, small-scale as well as large-scale, were more or less self-sufficient and not therefore obliged to sell in order to buy in order to live. Marooned in Athens, Dikaiopolis (*Akharnians* 33ff.) yearns for his rural deme, which never heard the cry of anyone selling charcoal, vinegar, oil or anything else, because the deme was self-sufficient. (No doubt there was some exchange of necessities between villagers.) The artisan was obviously not self-sufficient and was obviously obliged to sell, and the more specialised he became, the more dependent on others he became.

More often than not the local seller sold goods that he himself had made. Bakers, shoemakers, cartwrights, potters, sculptors, smiths and armourers outnumbered middlemen, selling goods produced by others, and those who provided services, like barbers, landladies, doctors and teachers. The more pride that it was possible for sellers of their own products to take in their own *tekhne*, the less concerned they would be to maximise their profit. They would be at least as much concerned with quality as with profit. Sellers with little *tekhne* to boast of, like Agorakritos, or none, like the middlemen, would tend to have recourse to such tricks as giving short measure or passing off inferior goods as better than they were. Comedy is highly critical of the dishonesty of those who sell barley-groats, figs, fish, wool and other more or less untreated products of nature.

Craftsmanship, of whatever quality, tended to be associated in Athenian thinking with dependence on customers and with dishonesty, and there was a third unfavourable association – that with slavery. Slaves were engaged, either under the direction of their citizen or metic owners (or their slave foremen) or working on their own (*khoris oikountes*), in every sort of craft. Typical occupations of slaves might be regarded as 'servile' in the pejorative sense. Slaves certainly played a part in farming, small-scale as well as large-scale, but it was a less conspicuous part. And there was another contrast with farming: farmers led a vigorous out-of-door life; potters and smiths worked indoors and close to kilns, furnaces or forges. Furthermore, the work of the farmer was punctuated by two periods of leisure each year; the craftsman's work was never done.

It was not in general possible to distinguish -mongers from -makers, and the citizen craftsman's place of residence tended to include both a place of work and a place of sale. Many carpenters and masons would, however, need to go out to the dockyards or to building sites for their work. Although there were Thetic craftsmen who lived in lodgings and had no slaves, we should think of most Zeugite shoemakers, potters, sculptors and smiths as living 'over the shop' and training sons or apprentices or slaves in their *tekhne*. Any *tekhne* was knowledge that could be taught to others. Slaves so taught would assist, and perhaps eventually take the place of, their master. Some rich masters, like Kleon and Hyperbolos, who owned large *ergasteria* or workshops, entrusted their running to slave foremen in order to give themselves enough leisure for politics, but most workshops were managed by their owners.

The training imparted by potters and their painters, by sculptors and by smiths took a long time to acquire, though it could soon be lost through lack of practice. Those undergoing training by a skilled craftsman felt that they were being admitted to an honourable tradition. It was common for a craftsman son, trained by a successful father, to mention his father when he signed his own work.

Athenian industry consisted of craftsmen, their tools, and their stock-in-trade. As well as meaning a place of work, *ergasterion* could mean slave work force and stock. Since his place of work was not a well-equipped factory, the craftsman was not tied to it. If a potter or smith needed to move, he could build himself a new kiln, furnace or forge. (Our word 'factory' applies in the limiting case of the establishment of Kephalos, the metic shield-maker, but in not many others.) There are a few industrial scenes in Attic vase-painting and grave-reliefs, but they are idealised and simplified, hardly conveying any impression of bustle, noise, heat, smoke, dust or mess. The workshops of most interest to the historian of art seem to have been little larger than was necessary to produce work of high quality – perhaps a dozen men were engaged on fine work in most potteries. Technical innovation during the fifth century was negligible. The status of the metal worker had perhaps dropped since the start of the Iron Age. Processes that had once seemed awesome were now familiar, and he invented no new ones. Nor were administrative moves made in the direction of greater economic efficiency. Innovation was artistic, not technical.

There was a tendency for -makers and -mongers of a kind to work in the same area. In *Knights* (852ff.) the Sausage-seller says: 'You see the size of his phalanx of young leather-sellers; and round them live the honey-sellers and cheese-sellers.' Athenians spoke of going to the Wine or the Fish or the Olive Oil or the Pots. In an area overlooked by the temple of Hephaistos and Athena Ergane (the Worker), including the Urban demes of Kerameis (Potters, outside the Thriasian gate) and Melite (west of the Agora), lived most of the potters, metal-workers and marble-workers of Athens. The original Kerameikos, that is, the ceramic district or Potters' Quarter, stretched from the bed of the Eridanos, a useful source of water, to the slopes below the Akropolis and Areopagos. A hundred yards south-west of the Round-house, in the direction of the Pnyx, the American excavators have identified a street of marble-workers.

That shops and stalls of the same kind tended to be grouped together was convenient for customers in quest of quality and must have stimulated competition to satisfy them. Centuries before, Hesiod (*Works and Days* 25) had praised healthy competition and observed professional rivalry between potters. At the end of the sixth century the Athenian vase-painter Euthymides, presumably with the approval of his patron, had written, before firing, on a red-figure amphora, 'As Euphronios never did', taunting his rival, whom he judged less skilful at foreshortening.

When prospective patrons – private Athenians of all social classes, foreign tourists, *emporoi* – walked along the street of the marble-workers or compared the merits of rival potters and painters, they might be looking for an item already in stock or deciding where to place a special order. A poor man wanting a Herm or Apollo to stand outside his front door would be satisfied with a god already in stock, though the stock was unlikely to be large, but a rich man lately bereaved would commission a gravestone to be carved according to his specifications. There would be little attempt at individual portrayal, but he would want the deceased shown in some appropriate pose. (The series of Classical grave-reliefs begins in about 435, and resemblances can be traced between the early ones and the Parthenon frieze and pediments. Gravestones carved by men who had worked on the Parthenon would have been too expensive for most Athenians.) The potteries that produced fine painted ware also produced plain ware.

The Athenian pottery industry had been important since Geometric times. Long before the arrival of metics or of slaves in any number, there were enough native potters to give both deme (Kerameis) and district (Kerameikos) their names. In the sixth century some Athenian potters and their painters began to sign some of their work, and from the end of the same century they sometimes made dedications to Athena on the Akropolis that were substantial enough to merit an inscribed marble base. Whatever most aristocrats might think about banausic crafts, the emergence of artistic personalities like those of Euthymides and Euphronios is evidence enough of their self-respect.

Most of our knowledge of the Athenian pottery industry comes from the thousands of surviving pots and the few surviving inscriptions set up by potters. There is little to be learnt from contemporary literature, which never names a potter or a painter of pots. This may partly reflect upper-class indifference to banausic crafts, but it also reminds us that one reason for being interested in the painted pottery of Athens is that in the Classical Age it was overtaken by large-scale painting on wooden panels and now provides the best evidence we have of what that large-scale painting was like. That more than one red-figure vase-painter should have named his son Polygnotos after Polygnotos of Thasos, whose *Troy Taken* adorned the Painted Stoa, expresses the relationship between minor and major. Nevertheless Athenian painted pottery – black-figure, followed by red-figure and finally white-ground – was supreme of its kind for most of the sixth century and all of the fifth, and it was exported to the entire Greek world and beyond – from Skythia to Etruria.

Athens' largest export was silver, in bullion or coin. From the middle of the century, the Athenian mint was producing enormous numbers of silver coins – mainly 4-*drakhme* pieces but also some smaller denominations. Not all the silver need have come from Laureion: the foreign currencies in the alliance reserve, brought to Athens by 454, may have been reminted so that the building-programme could be paid for in Athenian coins. The design of these coins, called 'Laureion owls' by Aristophanes (*Birds* 1106), changed as little as the image of Athena on Panathenaic amphorae. On the obverse the head of Athena, wearing an Attic helmet, faces right; on the reverse her owl stares out between a spray of olive with a crescent moon and the Greek equivalent of ATHE, abbreviating 'OF THE ATHENIANS'. Though artistically undistinguished, these coins, constant in weight and purity, were of great economic importance. They paid for the building-programme and the navy; they returned in tribute and tolls. Unfortunately, although the American excavators have almost certainly identified the mint, almost all that is known about its operation is that it was managed by a board of Epistatai.

There is much more to say about the production of Athenian pottery. The painted pots of Athens are artistically valuable in themselves and valuable also for the light they throw on large-scale painting and on Athenian society; they, together with the inscriptions on potters' dedications, enable us to say something about the industry that produced them; they are remarkably durable, unlike textiles, and, unlike coins, have not been in danger of melting down; their durability has made the fact of their wide export certain.

We should not, however, imagine that there was any sort of Organisation for the Export of Athenian Pottery. We have rather to think of a number of small private enterprises owned and managed by citizens or metics, with slaves doing much of the rough work. Though little can be inferred from foreign-looking names like Lydos or Skythes, we may be sure that there were metic masters, and so the ceramic industry in Athens could not have been thought of as a national one. Furthermore, as we have seen, these small enterprises were competing in quality of workmanship as much as in quantity of sale. To sell a pot made in a somewhat original shape or decorated with a somewhat original drawing to a discerning customer, that was success. Widely exported as the fine pottery was, the complicated trade was in the hands of *emporoi* and not of the potters themselves. Some Attic pots were to pass through a number of hands before they reached Etruria.

Naturally, far less fine pottery was produced than plain stuff, such as tableware, cooking utensils, storage jars and lamps. Because so much fine pottery has been preserved – more than 30,000 black-figure and red-figure vases have been attributed to painters – there is a danger of exaggerating the scale of the fine pottery industry. Calculation suggests that at the height of activity in the late sixth and early fifth centuries not more than 200 painters and fifty potters were producing fine ware at the same time. Potters and their painters were a small minority of the minority that did not in one way or another live off the land.

It is not easy to establish prices for painted pottery, but there is some reason to think that a large painted water-pot (*hydria*) might cost 2 *drakhmai* (two days' wages for an Erekhtheion workman) and smaller pieces less than 1 *drakhme*. Clearly, poor Athenians did not buy pottery at 2 *drakhmai* a piece, but modest households may have had one or two fine pieces for decoration. The scenes depicted, whether taken from mythology or everyday life, might be thought most likely to appeal to those with a 'musical' and 'gymnastic' education. But scenes involving horses or *aulos*-girls might appeal to those who wished that such creatures played a part in their lives as well to those in whose lives they did play a part. Even artisans proud of their *tekhne* might not wish to be reminded of it out of hours. It is no surprise that barely a score of surviving vase-paintings depict potters at work.

It might be rash to say that the supersession of the black-figure technique of decorating pottery by the red-figure, to be considered shortly in connection with the development of painting in general, represented progress. What can be said is that change in Attic painted pottery was continuous – change in shape and style and even in the subject matter of the pictures. This makes it possible to date any such pot with some precision. Though technical innovation was negligible, artistic innovation, as in tragedy, was continuous. For this to have happened, there must have been appreciative consumers in the Kerameikos as well as in the theatre. The leading connoisseurs were no doubt rich men – rich enough to commission vases or sets of vases on special occasions. Such patrons' opinion of the potters and painters of their choice presumably lay somewhere between that of Plutarch and that of the potters and painters themselves.

Unlike the potters and the painters of pots, the sculptors and large-scale painters of, or at least resident in, Athens have left a mark on the literary record. Thus we know that the original bronze group of the Tyrant-killers, Harmodios and Aristogeiton, in the Agora was the work of an Athenian, Antenor. Xerxes removed Antenor's group to Persepolis and it was not returned to Athens until after Alexander's capture of Persepolis. It was then installed beside a replacement group that had been set up in 477, the work of two Athenians, Kritios and Nesiotes. With the aid of copies we can gain some idea of the replacement work. It showed the pair poised to strike with their swords, but it is not possible to be sure just how the two figures were related. Because of resemblances to the replacement Harmodios and Aristogeiton, a standing marble figure in the Akropolis Museum is known as the Kritian Boy. He had not stood on the Akropolis long before a Persian knocked him down. He is chiefly remarkable for not being, like most of his predecessors, an almost symmetrical personage to be confronted face-to-face but rather a work of art to be looked at.

Neither Antenor nor Kritios and Nesiotes attempted what we should call portraiture, and although late Archaic funeral monuments in marble sometimes gave the name of the deceased on the plinth (Kroisos, the larger-than-life *kouros* or young man found at Anavysos, or Aristion, the larger-than-life hoplite from Marathon, carved by Aristokles), their sculptors were more interested in the ideal and generic than in the specific. The aim was to realise an ideal form in an appropriate material. It is, however, possible that a Roman head in marble, bearing the name of Themistokles, is a copy of the head of a bronze original. (Classical Greeks did not sculpt busts without bodies.) The treatment of the hair and head resembles that of the replacement Aristogeiton. If it is a copy of an original, then Themistokles is the first Athenian, or indeed Greek, of whom we have a portrait. It is not very flattering, but it is credible.

It was now, in the early Classical Age, that bronze began to displace marble as the principal material of the sculptor. The sixth-century invention of hollow-casting had made it possible to produce figures as big as those of the marble-carvers, and the material was more tractable.

The sculptor Myron came from Eleutherai, the village on the Boiotian frontier from which the cult of Dionysos Eleuthereus had entered Athens. Eleutherai was not an Attic deme, but Myron may be counted an Athenian. We can gain some idea of his most famous piece, the bronze Diskobolos, from later marble copies. The athlete was represented as wound up to throw his discus. The emphasis fell on a pattern discernible in action rather than on facial expression mirroring thought.

Pheidias seems to have been somewhat junior to Myron and a contemporary of Polykeitos of Argos. How readily recognisable, among the Athenian heroes on the outside of the shield of the Parthenos, were the bald old man raising the stone in both hands and the man with his spear-hand in front of his face as the artist and Perikles is hard to say.

If we have a marble copy of the head of a bronze portrait-statue of Themistokles, it is possible that we have two, named, marble copies (one

of them in the British Museum) of the head of a bronze portrait-statue
of his political heir, Perikles. Kresilas of Kydonia in Crete, who seems
to have worked mainly in Athens, cast a famous bronze statue of
Perikles, and it is possible that our copies are copies of it. If so, Kresilas
represented the bearded statesman wearing his Corinthian helmet pushed
back, that is, as a general. The eyes are narrowed, the skull, as we should
expect from comedy, is high, the lips are full. That portraiture in marble
and bronze, so far as it existed, celebrated men of action, should not
surprise us, and eager though we may be for revealing personal details
about eminent Athenians other than Sokrates, extant art does not
provide them. Its central concern is with ideal human forms or divine
ones, like those in the east frieze of the Parthenon.

Greek painters were interested in landscape only in so far as it
provided a setting for human figures. Unfortunately, to trace in Athens
the painting by individuals of individuals in particular settings is even
more difficult than to trace the sculpting of individuals: if many bronze
originals have been melted down, all the wooden panels on which most
large-scale painting was done have perished. Hence our dependence on
painted pottery and literary accounts.

The black-figure technique of decorating pottery, invented in Corinth
in the first half of the seventh century and then adopted in the Kerameikos, represented stout figures in silhouette on a single base-line and
against a more or less empty background. Details were incised on the
silhouettes, and touches of purple or white might be added. It was also
in or near Corinth that free painting was invented. In Athens the tradition of figured vase-painting was so well established that painters were
slow to see the limitations of painting on pots. By about 550 Athenian
supremacy in figured vase-painting was virtually unchallenged anywhere.
Twenty years later came the invention, perhaps by the so-called Andokides Painter, of the red-figure technique, which reversed the black-figure
technique. Now the background was painted shiny black, and the figures,
still on a single base-line, were left in the orange colour of the clay, with
details supplied by painted lines. By 500 black-figure had virtually been
abandoned except for Panathenaic amphorae.

Red-figure painters were soon showing increasing interest in the
patterns discernible in action, and this led to an interest in the technique
of foreshortening. Two successors of the Andokides Painter, Euphronios
and Euthymides, achieved great mastery of anatomical drawing. On one
side of a mixing-bowl now in New York Euphronios featured the broken
body of Sarpedon, son of Zeus, being borne away by Sleep and Death.
It was on an amphora decorated with a picture of three very solid
revellers that Euthymides wrote: 'Drawn by Euthymides, son of Polias
– as Euphronios never did.' (Euthymides' father may have been the
sculptor who signed himself 'Pollias'.) Skilful though the anatomical

drawing is, there is no sense of the figures being in space and little use of shading or highlights.

Athenian red-figure painting reached its acme at the end of the Archaic Age – the opening decades of the fifth century – by which time developments in free painting, following on the loosening of Archaic conventions in sculpture, were beginning to reveal the limitations of painting on pots. These developments are chiefly associated with Polygnotos of Thasos and his circle. It is reasonable to suppose that it was the work of Polygnotos and his circle that was reflected in a striking innovation to be found in the painting of a number of pots of about 460: they abandon the single base-line. The most famous of these pots is the Niobid mixing-bowl, so-called because on one side was depicted the destruction of the children of Niobe by Apollo and Artemis. On the other side is an enigmatic picture of eleven figures – Athena and Herakles and nine others whose identity is not clear – scattered, it seems, on a steep hillside. That they are on a hillside is suggested by the painter's use of a few coloured lines.

Polygnotos and Aristophon were sons and pupils of Aglaophon. Polygnotos' most famous paintings – *Troy Taken* and *Odysseus in Hades* – were done at Delphi. In Athens he worked with an Athenian, Mikon, son of Panokhos. He was a friend of Kimon, who was the leading man in Athens until he was ostracised in 461 for his pro-Spartan policy. Most of the Athenian work of Polygnotos and Mikon was to be seen in three buildings more or less closely associated with Kimon – the Theseion, the Anakeion and the Painted Stoa. The first two buildings lay somewhere on the north side of the Akropolis. The Theseion housed the supposed bones of the hero Theseus, brought back from Skyros by Kimon in about 475. The Anakeion was the shrine of the Anakes or Dioskouroi – the heroes Kastor and Polydeukes, sons of Zeus and Leda and brothers of Helen, much worshipped in Sparta. The Painted Stoa, still unexcavated, lay on the north side of the Agora and originally bore the name of Kimon's brother-in-law, Peisianax, who was somehow responsible for its erection. These three buildings were not temples. Temples were designed to make their impression externally. As painting began to vie with sculpture for supremacy among the visual arts, it tended to be placed in buildings other than temples.

Relying chiefly on the traveller Pausanias, one may assign different paintings to different buildings. In the Theseion were exhibited Mikon's painting of the young Theseus proving, by having dived to the bottom of the sea, that he was the son of Poseidon, an unattributed painting of Athenians (including Theseus) fighting Amazons, an unattributed painting of Lapiths (assisted by Theseus) fighting Centaurs, and perhaps also an unattributed painting of Theseus being raised from Hades. If the building was rectangular, there may have been one painting on each wall. It is possible that Polygnotos painted one of the unattributed works. In the Anakeion were exhibited Mikon's painting of the Argonauts (no doubt including the Dioskouroi) and Polygnotos' painting of the wedding of the Dioskouroi to the daughters of Leukippos.

On the long wall of the Painted Stoa, which was perhaps so called from the bright colours in which it was painted, were exhibited Mikon's painting of Athenians (including Theseus) fighting Amazons, Polygnotos' earlier *Troy Taken*, and a painting of the battle of Marathon by Mikon or his junior Panainos, the brother or, more likely, nephew of Pheidias. On a short wall Pausanias saw an unattributed painting of the Athenians drawn up in battle against the Spartans at Oinoe in the territory of Argos. Nothing is known of such a battle, and such a picture can hardly have been put up in the heyday of Kimon. Mikon's painting of Theseus would have pleased the man who brought his bones home to Athens, and the painting of Marathon would have pleased the son of Miltiades. The uncertainty about the attribution of what was the most famous painting in Athens is strange. It showed first the Athenians and Plataians closing with the Persians, then the Persians fleeing, and finally the Greeks killing the Persians as they tried to board the Phoenician ships. Identifiable human figures on the Greek side were Kallimakhos (the Polemarch), Aiskhylos and his brother Kynaigeiros, and Miltiades, urging on his men. Identifiable on the Persian side were the commanders of the expedition, Datis and Artaphernes. We are told that Miltiades was not named, which may imply that the others were. If the poet was named, that part of the picture at least was perhaps not completed until after his death in 456. In his Athenian *Troy Taken* Polygnotos was said to have used as a model for the head of Laodike (fairest daughter of Priam, according to Homer's *Iliad*) that of Elpinike, sister of Kimon and perhaps his own mistress. Plutarch believed that Polygnotos did not adorn Athens for money, but he was rewarded with the rare honour of Athenian citizenship.

For forming an idea of Polygnotan painting we are chiefly dependent on literary descriptions. Aristotle (*Poetics* 6) tells us that Polygnotos knew how to convey character and that he idealised his figures. Pliny (*Natural History* 35.58), writing five centuries after the lifetime of Polygnotos, tells us that he was the first to explore variety in facial expression, even painting figures with open mouths, and that he was the first to represent women in transparent clothing. Pausanias describes in detail his two huge pictures in the club house of the Knidians at Delphi – *Troy Taken* and *Odysseus in Hades*. They each contained some seventy figures, arranged in small groups and unified only by their presence in a single pictorial space. From what Pausanias says, it is clear that Polygnotos strove not only to convey the minds of his figures in their faces but also to place them in pictorial space. For him painting had become something more than the decoration of surfaces: it had acquired another dimension. Figures in his *Troy Taken* were higher or lower in the composition, as they are in the picture of the Niobid Painter, though they were not seen from a single viewpoint.

What colours did Polygnotos use? A tomb of about 480, found near Paestum (Poseidonia) in AD 1968, provides the only surviving specimens of Classical Greek mural painting. On white plaster the painter uses black, blue, red, brown, maroon, green and grey-green. It is unlikely that Polygnotos' range of colours was much narrower than this.

A development in the colouring of painted pottery which brought it much closer to the Polygnotan range of colours than red-figure was the growing use of a white slip to give a white or creamy ground on which it was possible to draw outlines and then apply washes of colour – dull at first, brighter later. For an early example we may take the interior of a cup by the Pistoxenos Painter in the British Museum, showing Aphrodite riding on her bird (perhaps a goose). The goddess's name is written behind her head. The bird is lightly golden. Aphrodite's tunic has a purple border and her cloak is entirely purple. Unfortunately, the more concessions that were made to the Polygnotan revolution, the harder it was to celebrate the shape of the pots themselves. Painting that was essentially decoration of ceramic shapes could not for long keep up with developments in free painting.

Perhaps because of the instability of the medium, white-ground cups went out of fashion after the early Classical Age (about 480 to about 450), and the red-figure technique remained dominant in vase-painting. Thereafter the white-ground technique was largely confined to slender, one-handled *lekythoi* or oil-flasks, used in funeral rites. (When a corpse had been washed, it had to be anointed with oil.) The master of this kind of vase-painting is known, from a red-figure amphora in the Vatican, as the Achilles Painter. The developed technique consisted of outline drawing with colour-washes for clothing. One very common scene shows the deceased with one or more of the deities associated with death – Kharon, the ferryman of the river of Hades, the brothers Sleep and Death (as in the mixing-bowl of Euphronios), Hermes, the guide of the dead (Psykhopompos). Other very common scenes were the laying out of the dead and visiting the grave, in front of which the deceased seems often to be sitting.

To judge from these funeral *lekythoi*, the standard Attic grave-marker in the middle of the century was a slender *stele* or slab. From the time of Kleisthenes to about 435 it seems that gravestones with figures in relief were prohibited by sumptuary legislation. From about 435 begins the series of shorter and broader gravestones with figures in relief, commonly under a gable. Some of the pieces are fine enough to suggest that craftsmen who had been working on the Parthenon frieze, in a subordinate capacity, began carving grave-reliefs when it was finished. Such grave-reliefs might show a single standing figure, male or female, facing outwards. Standing males might be represented as athletes or warriors. Alternatively, single figures, especially women and older men, might sit. With just two figures three combinations of standing and sitting were possible. Two figures were often shown shaking hands. The manner of death was rarely even hinted at: the emphasis fell on characteristic activity in life.

In the British Museum is the gravestone of the cobbler Xanthippos. (Names ending in -*hippos* were not necessarily those of aristocrats, though Xanthippos was no pauper.) With his two small daughters cling-ing to him, he sits, holding his last and gazing at it. If his features are not very distinctive, the reason is more likely to be that there was still no tradition of individual portraiture and that even if there had been, his family had no photographs of him to show the sculptor, than that such a piece, cobbler with last and two small daughters, was already in stock.

In the Kerameikos Museum sits Ampharete, holding in her right hand a pet bird and in her left hand a baby, at whom she looks sadly. A couplet carved on the architrave explains that they are both dead: the baby is her daughter's child, whom she used to hold in the light of the sun and whom even in Hades she continues to hold. The famous *stele* of Hegeso shows the seated mistress, her feet on a footstool, taking jewellery (once painted in, but no longer visible) from a box held out to her by a short-haired slave-girl. In these three *stelai* it is clear enough who has died, but in some cases, though an atmosphere of subdued sorrow is easily felt, it is not clear which of the figures has died. Even if there is an inscription, it may not enable us to conclude that such-and-such a figure in the composition was called so-and-so and has died.

As white-ground *lekythoi* went out of fashion, towards the end of the fifth century, some figured tombstones were given the shape of ceramic *lekythoi* or, if the deceased had not married, *loutrophoroi* – tall vessels normally reserved for bringing water from the spring Kallirrhoe for ritual washing at a wedding. Most of these marble vessels were decorated on one side with a panel in low relief, depicting one of the scenes commonly found on other tombstones. On the large marble *lekythos* of Myrrhine, Hermes holds a young woman by the hand and leads her towards the river of Hades.

Polygnotos and his followers were not interested in exploring pictorial space for its own sake. Their main concern was to provide appropriate settings for their human groups, and for this purpose foreshortening and the use of different levels sufficed. Towards the end of the century additional techniques for the creation of pictorial space were introduced. Apollodoros of Athens became known as the Shadow Painter because he modelled with shadow, and his technique was developed by Zeuxis of Herakleia in southern Italy, who used highlights as well as shading. A painting of a flower-wreathed Eros, alluded to by Aristophanes in 425 (*Akharnians* 991f.), was probably his work. Plato (*Protagoras* 318b) implies that Zeuxis arrived in Athens as a young man in about 430. The new interest in pictorial illusion is conveyed in a famous story told by Pliny (*Natural History* 35.65). In competition with Parrhasios of Ephesos, Zeuxis painted, apparently as part of a stage-set, grapes so realistic that birds were deceived into flying to them, but when Zeuxis asked for the curtain covering Parrhasios' picture to be drawn back, he himself was deceived, since what had appeared to be the curtain was in fact the picture. Plato (*Republic* 602d) viewed the art of Apollodoros and Zeuxis, the art of appearance, with great hostility: such art could only distract from the search for knowledge of reality. Aristotle (*Poetics* 6,25) compared Zeuxis with Polygnotos and judged that Zeuxis sacrificed character to beauty. According to Lucian (*Zeuxis* 3), Zeuxis was attracted to unusual subjects, as in *The Centaur's Family*.

According to Quintilian (12.10.4), Parrhasios 'examined lines more subtly'. His curtain must have required some use of light and shade, but perhaps not much (Zeuxis was certainly not expecting a trompe l'oeil curtain), and it seems that he preferred to use contour lines to suggest volume. According to Pliny (35.68), his drawings on panels and parchment were preserved and valued by later artists. Xenophon (*Reminiscences* 3.10.1–5) has Sokrates call on Parrhasios and suggest to him that painting is the representation of what is seen, but he goes on to assert that it is possible and necessary to show character in facial expression and bodily posture. The prolific output of Parrhasios included, according to Pliny (35.69), *Demos* or *The People of Athens* in which Demos was somehow portrayed, as 'irascible, unfair and fickle and at the same time placable, merciful and compassionate; boastful . . . proud and humble, fierce and fearful'. One may compare Aristophanes' dramatic portrayal of Demos in *Knights* in 424.

The status and the self-esteem of the painter were rising. Under his *Athlete* Apollodoros had inscribed: 'Easier to criticise than copy.' Zeuxis and Parrhasios became rich, and they were modest neither in dress nor in utterance.

Another technique for the creation of pictorial space is perspective. According to Vitruvius (7, Preface 11), Agatharkhos of Samos wrote about a stage-set which he had painted for Aiskhylos, and this encouraged Demokritos and Anaxagoras to write about perspective. The production of Aiskhylos must have been a posthumous one – after 456. According to Aristotle (*Poetics* 4), scene-painting was introduced by Sophokles, but his career lasted more than half a century. Agatharkhos presumably used perspective to give some depth to a standard set – the façade of a palace or temple.

Some time before 415 Alkibiades lured Agatharkhos to his house and confined him there until he had decorated its walls, probably in a fashion similar to that of the stage-set. This is the earliest known instance of domestic wall-painting in Athens, and the story may serve to illustrate a new level of personal consumption. Not long after, Zeuxis performed the same task in the palace of Arkhelaos, King of Macedon. According to Athenaios (534d), on his triumphant return from Olympia in 416, Alkibiades dedicated two pictures in Athens, one showing Olympias and Pythias (nymphs personifying the Panhellenic sites of Olympia and Delphi) crowning him and the other showing him sitting on the lap of Nemea (a similar nymph). The pictures were perhaps the work of Aglaophon, the son or nephew of Polygnotos.

By the end of the fifth century big steps had been taken in the direction of realistic representation of figures and objects in pictorial space – steps big enough to alarm Plato; but the achievement of thorough-going perspective, with a single viewpoint and a single vanishing-point, belongs to the art of the Italian Renaissance.

· 8 ·

Science, Nature, Culture and the Sophists

Just as there was no Greek word precisely equivalent to our 'art', so there was no Greek word precisely equivalent to our 'science'. (The word 'tekhne' had a range of meanings overlapping the ranges of both English words, and so had 'sophia'.) Nevertheless various forms of scientific enquiry were being pursued in Athens during our period, though it is sometimes hard to say how widely or with what success.

As we have seen, Athenian boys who went to school for any length of time probably learnt enough elementary arithmetic to enable them to perform simple calculations. Few young Athenians proceeded to more advanced mathematics, but some did. We learn from Plato (*Parmenides* 127a) that Parmenides and Zenon of Elea, the founders of western metaphysics, visited Athens on the occasion of a Great Panathenaia, and, in a private house, Zenon read from his book, which was intended to disprove the possibility of plurality and of change. One of his celebrated paradoxes was that of the arrow: if a supposedly moving arrow is where it is at each instant, it must always be at rest.

A longer-staying visitor to Athens was Theodoros of Kyrene who worked on the problem of irrational numbers, like $\sqrt{2}$. In Plato's *Theaitetos* (143 de), Sokrates says to Theodoros:

> I am eager to know which of our young men seem likely to turn out well. I keep an eye on this myself, so far as I can, and I also ask those others with whom I see that the young like to associate. Now you have a sizeable following, and rightly: you deserve it for several reasons and especially for your geometry.

Theodoros then tells Sokrates that he has found a young Athenian of exceptional promise, Theaitetos of Sounion, later to become the first eminent Athenian mathematician. As well as being very able, he is also generous with his money. (Did Theodoros charge for his lessons?) From Theodoros Theaitetos learns all he can of geometry, astronomy, music and arithmetic. ('Astronomy' meant accounting geometrically for the apparent movement of the heavenly bodies, and 'music' meant the mathematics of intervals.) By 414 Aristophanes (*Birds* 1005), and presumably a good many of his audience, knew of the squaring of the circle as a current mathematical problem, but in the lifetime of Sokrates it is unlikely that there were in Athens more than a few teachers or learners of mathematics who even approached the level of Theodoros and Theaitetos.

Instruction in serious mathematics must largely have been given by foreigners like Zenon and Theodoros, who were drawn to the imperial city for longer or shorter periods. Whether he discovered the curve called quadratrix or not, Hippias of Elis had certainly taught at some time the four subjects later taught by Theodoros (Plato, *Protagoras* 318e) and perhaps done so in Athens.

The architects who designed Greek temples were greatly interested in mathematical proportion, and the subtle refinements of the Parthenon – the rising curve of the horizontal lines, and the inward inclination and the *entasis* of the columns – exhibit remarkable mathematical precision, but it is hard to say how mathematically precise were the instructions that the mason received from the architect.

An episode in Aristophanes' *Clouds* (144–148) might suggest that the importance of measurement was widely understood. A student at the Thinkery tells Strepsiades that Sokrates had asked Khairephon how many times the length of its own feet a flea could jump, and though he is only a rustic, Strepsiades at once asks: 'Well, how did he measure it?' On the other hand, Aristophanes thought Herodotos' claim to have measured the pyramids of Kheops and Khephren sufficiently remarkable to deserve parody (*Birds* 1130). Measurement of time by means of such a device as the water-clock used in court was not very precise. Perhaps the oldest scientific instrument was the *gnomon*, a vertical pointer on a flat base. By the length of the shadow it cast, it marked the solstices and also midday. Other times of day were commonly indicated by reference to human activities: 'when the Agora is full' (Xenophon, *Reminiscences* 1.1.10), or 'ox-unyoking time' (*Birds* 1500), or 'lamp-lighting time'. Under such conditions our minor virtue of punctuality could hardly exist.

By 432, if not earlier, observational astronomy had begun at Athens. Meton and Euktemon, both Athenians, discovered that the astronomical seasons – from solstice to equinox and from equinox to solstice – were, perhaps surprisingly, not equal. The same pair also travelled around the Aegean making meteorological observations, which they dated by risings and settings of fixed stars, which would be affected by variations of latitude. It therefore appears that they had accepted the Pythagorean doctrine of the sphericity of the earth and could deal with variations of latitude.

It is likely that what originally led Meton and Euktemon to investigate the astronomical seasons was a concern with problems of dating. The religious calendar at Athens, as elsewhere, was lunar: festivals fell on specified days of lunar months, twelve in number. These months were normally of twenty-nine or thirty days, the true lunar month being just over twenty-nine and a half days long, but the Arkhon was empowered to intercalate months or omit days. In *Clouds* (610ff.) Aristophanes has Selene, the moon, complain that the Athenians were not keeping their months in step with her phases, with the result that the gods were missing their feasts. Evidently months were not beginning with the first appearance of the crescent of the new moon.

Unfortunately, lunar month and solar year are incommensurable: 12 lunar months amount to 354 days and 13 to 384. The earliest known systematic solution of the problem of how often to intercalate months is called the Metonic cycle. In this cycle of 19 years there were 235 lunar months, of which 7 were intercalated, and 6,940 days. (110 months were of 29 days and 125 of 30.) Dividing 6,940 by 19 gives 365 5/19, which is only a little above the true value. According to Theophrastos (*Signs* 4), Meton got the idea of the nineteen-year cycle from a metic called Phaeinos, who had observed solstices from the top of Lykabettos, a hill 900 feet high to the north-east of the city.

The Metonic cycle was used only for scientific purposes. In about 422 we find the diviner Lampon moving a rider to a decree in the Assembly (ML 73). It instructs the next Arkhon to intercalate a second Hekatombaion, the first month of the year (rather than, as was usual, a second Posideion, the sixth month of the year). Meton's manual *On the Calendar* has not survived, but it is likely that he and Euktemon intended to provide a reliable basis for the dating of astronomical observations.

The adoption, for scientific reasons, of the spherical earth of the Pythagoreans (whose reasons for adopting it had been anything but scientific) was an important advance on the acceptance of a flat earth by Anaxagoras of Klazomenai, who had introduced Ionian natural philosophy to Athens. With the work of Meton and Euktemon an astronomy that was observational and mathematical had detached itself from the enormously suggestive but insufficiently controlled matrix of natural philosophy.

Since he is known to have spent some time in Athens, it is curious that Anaxagoras is not named in what survives of Old Comedy, but in Aristophanes' *Clouds* (227ff.) there is plain enough reference to the theories of his younger contemporary, Diogenes of Apollonia, to suggest that he too may have spent some time in Athens. Aristotle preserves his detailed account of the vascular system. Diogenes does not distinguish veins from arteries, but his account must rest on some observation, perhaps of animals. If true, Plutarch's story of how Anaxagoras had the skull of the one-horned ram split open would be an early example of animal dissection, and the possibility of such dissection is mentioned in the Hippokratic writing known as *The Sacred Disease* (14). For religious reasons there was little or no dissection of human corpses in the fifth century.

Although the earliest of the medical works traditionally attributed to Hippokrates of Kos are datable to the latter part of the fifth century, we can hardly say how deeply or widely Hippokratic medicine had penetrated Athens in the lifetime of Sokrates. According to Xenophon (*Reminiscences* 4.2.10), Sokrates told Euthydemos that medical treatises were abundant in Athens, and presumably they were mostly Hippokratic.

The last of the Hippokratic Aphorisms (7.87) outlines the range of treatment available: 'What medicine does not cure, the knife cures; what the knife does not cure, fire [cautery] cures; what fire does not cure must be regarded as incurable.' It is hard to be much more precise about the work of a private physician, like Eryximakhos, son of Akoumenos, or of the public physicians.

The speech of Eryximakhos in Plato's *Symposion* does not suggest that the philosopher had a high regard for this presumably eminent doctor. It has been taken for a parody of the lengthy Hippokratic treatise *Regimen*. As we might have expected, Eryximakhos' father Akoumenos had himself been a physician. (The art of medicine had supposedly been passed down from father to son since its invention by Asklepios, but Plato (*Protagoras* 311b) makes Sokrates say that anyone could pay Hippokrates for medical training.) Denounced for profaning the Mysteries, Akoumenos went into exile in 415, the year after the dramatic date of the *Symposion*. In *Phaidros* (268 a-c) Plato describes the medical *tekhne* of father and son as involving knowledge not only of treatments, such as raising and lowering the body's temperature and giving emetics and purges, but also of which patients to treat in which way and when and how much. Knowledge of the former kind could be gained from reading a book, but that would not suffice to make one a doctor. A few pages later, Hippokrates 'the Asklepiad' is said to have insisted that knowledge of the nature of the body involved knowledge of the body as a whole. Was it simple or complex? How and upon what did it, or its parts, act? How and to what did it, or its parts, react?

Centuries later Hippokrates was said to have been the first to distinguish medicine from philosophy. In the Hippokratic treatise *Ancient Medicine* (20) the writer argues that the general or philosophical question 'What is man?' is not the starting-point of medicine. Rather, the general question cannot be answered without the help of medicine. We have first to answer such questions as 'What is man in relation to eating, say, cheese?' And since different men react differently to cheese, we arrive at the particular and practical question 'How does this man react to eating cheese?'

Like Plato, the writer is using the fundamental notion bequeathed by the Ionian thinkers, that of nature (*physis*). It is part of the sun's nature to move, or appear to move, each day from east to west at a steady rate. Anything that all men do under certain circumstances – there will not be many such things – is part of human nature. Anything that this man always does under certain circumstances is part of his nature. The *physis* of a thing is its predictable tendency to behave in certain ways.

Thucydides, as we shall see, makes much use of the notion of human nature in the psychological sense. He was not just telling the story of a great war: he was also exhibiting political behaviour. And when he came to describe the Athenian plague, he was not solely concerned with its effect on Athenian manpower. Amongst other things, he shows us plainly enough the impotence of Athenian medicine in the face of epidemic disease. (He does not say whether the medical danger of overcrowding was appreciated by anyone.) In the spring of 430 a plague, probably typhus, reached Peiraieus and then struck Athens. Thucydides did not attempt to explain it, but he resolved to describe its symptoms and effects so precisely that if it struck again it could be recognised. From his use of medical terminology, it is clear that he was familiar with Hippokratic writings.

According to Thucydides (2.47.4), 'Treating it as they were for the first time, physicians in their ignorance could do little – indeed they themselves died the most since they came into most contact with it.' Later (2.51.2) he says: 'Some died in neglect, others amid every attention. No single cure established itself as a specific; for what did good to one did harm to another.'

Unique as it was in recorded experience, this disease could not be explained, nor could it be cured, but it had an observable *physis*. For example, most of its victims died on the seventh day or the ninth. Should such a disease strike again, anyone familiar with Thucydides' account would at least be ready for its physical, mental and social consequences. Without microscopes, the cause and cure of infectious diseases would remain elusive, but *prognosis*, foreknowledge of the course of events, was as valuable in medicine as it was in politics. A doctor who could recognise his patient's disease at an early stage would be much better able to sustain him and his family through the later stages. The more familiarity he showed with the disease, the more confidence they would have in him. It was their foresight that Thucydides admired above all in Themistokles and Perikles.

As well as describing the symptoms and effects of a disease, it might be possible to say something about the circumstances of its outbreak. *Airs, Waters and Places* deals first with the effect of climate, water supply and situation on health and then with the effects of climate on character. 'Soft countries tend to breed soft men', declared the Persian King Kyros at the end of Herodotos' *Histories* (9.122.3). The author of

Airs, Waters and Places (24) knows that culture can do something to modify nature: the inhabitants of hot valleys are not by nature (*physis*) brave or hardy, but the imposition of custom or law (*nomos*) can make them so.

It is perfectly possible to combine general acceptance of the notion of *physis* with talk of divine intervention in certain spheres. *Physis* is then what happens except when it seems preferable to talk of divine intervention. As far as we know, almost all Greeks continued to make some use of the idiom of divine intervention, sometimes as an alternative to natural explanation, but some abandoned it. The Ionian natural philosophers (*physiologoi*) abandoned it quietly. The Hippokratic doctors abandoned it a little less quietly. According to the author of *The Sacred Disease* (1), contrary to popular belief, there was nothing specially sacred about epilepsy. Thucydides too abandoned the idiom, which is perhaps what chiefly distinguishes him from Herodotos.

It is probable that Herodotos survived the Arkhidamian War (431–21) and that his *Histories* were not published in full in Athens until about 415. If so, his working life was more nearly contemporary with that of Thucydides than has commonly been supposed, and their two great, but at first sight very dissimilar works were products of much the same milieu. The thinking of Herodotos may be not so much naive as old-fashioned.

Some time after the conclusion of hostilities between Athens and Persia in 449, Herodotos, travelling in the steps of Hekataios of Miletos, visited Egypt and in the second book of his *Histories* we have the literary result – an account of the geography, people and history of that country. He composed similar accounts of Libya, Skythia, Babylonia and elsewhere. (It was not in the writing of such accounts that his originality lay, but in his conception of history on the grand scale. He made, as we have seen, an astonishingly successful attempt to reconstruct – on the basis of what he could see and what he was told, often by dragomans or interpreters – the growth of the Persian empire and its eventual repulse, a generation before he began his enquiries, by the disunited, but hardy and freedom-loving, communities of Old Greece.)

Even if we assume that Herodotos' *Histories* were not published in full in Athens until about 415, it is still possible that he had earlier given public readings from his ethnographies. Certainly the demand for such information was already there. Back in the Archaic Age the revival of maritime trade and the great colonial outpouring (*c.* 750–550) from many of the cities of Old Greece had put into circulation a mass of more or less reliable travellers' tales. Then in Ionian Miletos Anaximandros and Hekataios had invented cartography and descriptive geography. The Athenian appetite for hearing about 'faraway places with strange-sounding names' had been fed by Aiskhylos, who had perhaps read

Hekataios, in such plays as *Persians* and, if he wrote it, *Prometheus*. Imperial Athens or its port attracted visitors from most parts of the known world. Anaxagoras, for example, came from Klazomenai, which had been under Lydian and then Persian control. A Persian grandee, Zopyros, deserted to Athens at some point in the 430s (Herodotos 3.160.2). Embassies and expeditions set out and returned. Something was known of the Near East, but not enough to satisfy curiosity.

Such curiosity was perfectly compatible with much ignorance of places nearer home. According to Thucydides (6.1.1), most Athenians were ignorant of the size and population of Sicily, but geography was not a school subject.

As the diversity of customs (*nomoi*) becomes known, the immediate effect is likely to be that many people draw relativist conclusions. The neatest formulation of relativism, and one that does away with the notion of *physis*, was given by Protagoras of Abdera at the beginning of his book *On Truth*: 'A man is the measure of everything – of what is as to how it is, and of what is not as to how it is not.' Once it is known that communities with strikingly different customs have 'great and wonderful works' (Herodotos' opening sentence) to their credit, thoughtful people must cease to say 'Our customs are the best.' Instead, they may say 'Our customs are the best for us,' or even 'All customs are arbitrary.' The latter position will be likely to commend itself to any who have ceased to believe in divine government of the world. In the second half of the fifth century many thoughtful people were wondering about the status of culture, the web of attitudes, beliefs and practices that raises human life above the life of beasts.

One large question concerned the direction of human history. Was human life on the way up or the way down? Contrasting sharply with Hesiod's pessimistic conception of decline from Golden Age to Iron Age, there emerged a new conception, apparently shared by, among others, Aiskhylos, Sophokles, Euripides and Protagoras. Ionian thinkers like Anaximandros and Xenophanes had put forward evolutionary ideas in the sphere of biology, and now similar ideas were being put forward about culture. Whatever initial role might be ascribed to Zeus or Prometheus or anonymous deity, the essence of the new conception was that, under pressure from a hostile environment, man had had the wit to create, stage by stage, both technology and society. The prevailing attitude to life was no doubt still pessimistic, but in Euripides' *Suppliant Women* (196–199) Theseus ventures to voice an avowedly eccentric opinion: 'People say that men's misfortunes outnumber their blessings, but I disagree: men's blessings outnumber their misfortunes.' And in Sophokles' *Antigone* (360–364) the Chorus claims (rather surprisingly in view of the limitations of medicine) that man 'never meets the future without resource; from death alone shall he find no escape; but from baffling diseases he has devised escapes.'

In his *Protagoras* (320c-328d) Plato makes Protagoras tell a story that may well represent the Sophist's own views in mythological form. According to the story, through the incompetence of Epimetheus, man at first lacked the means of survival. Prometheus was able to give him technology, but Zeus had control of political wisdom, and until he sent Hermes to distribute respect (*aidos*) and justice to all men, humanity's chances of survival remained poor; men were unable to defend themselves against the wild beasts because they lacked the art of politics (*politike tekhne*), of which the art of warfare was a part. The moral of the story is that while only a few men possess this skill or that, all, or almost all, have some share in respect and justice; which is why political life is possible – provided that innate tendencies to respect and justice are properly fostered by education.

Arkhelaos, who was said to have taught Sokrates, summed up the evolutionary account of culture thus: 'Men were separated from the other animals, and then set up leaders [*hegemones*], customs [*nomoi*], arts [*tekhnai*], communities [*poleis*] and so on.'

Thoughtful people were no doubt inclined to agree that technology must have evolved stage by stage, and Thucydides (1.71.3) makes the Corinthians tell the Spartans: 'As in the case of a *tekhne*, the latest developments are always bound to prevail.' But the origin and justification of custom and morality seemed more problematical. Was it possible, some wondered, to identify a conventional and therefore, it might be supposed, merely arbitrary, layer of morality by subtracting from current morality patterns of behaviour that were shared by animals? Human parents differed from animal parents in expecting their offspring to tend them in old age (Xenophon, *Oikonomikos* 7.19). That expectation might reasonably be viewed as merely conventional. But Pheidippides' argument (Aristophanes, *Clouds* 1427ff.), that human sons could retaliate against their fathers because cocks and other animals retaliated against their fathers, and such creatures differed from human beings only in not moving decrees, was open to the obvious rejoinder of Strepsiades: 'Well, if you model yourself on the cock, why don't you eat dirt and roost on a perch?' It appeared that animal behaviour, which was not an object of systematic study, could not provide an adequate criterion of natural human behaviour.

A more promising line was to enquire whether there were any 'unwritten' customs, observed by the whole of humanity. According to Xenophon (*Reminiscences* 4.4.19ff.), Hippias told Sokrates that he thought that there were two such customs: that of revering the gods and honouring one's parents. He did not think that avoidance of incest between parents and children or the rendering of good for good counted.

Since it was impossible that all those who observed the two customs should have met, or have understood one another if they had met, Pheidippides' suggestion (*Clouds* 1421f.) that behind any such universally observed *nomos* lay a human legislator (*nomothetes*) who had once talked the ancients into accepting his *nomos* would not do: the two customs had to be ascribed to the gods. Sokrates thought that the list could be extended, but at least a start had been made.

In a famous passage (3.38), Herodotos pointed out that what counted as honouring fathers when they died depended on one's culture, but both Greeks and Indians did honour their dead fathers, albeit in different ways – the former by burning them, the latter by eating them.

Another line of enquiry was to search not for customs universally observed, but for an unchanging human nature, underlying the diversity of customs, that is, for a normal psychology. When the individual has shuffled off self-restraint (*aidos, sophrosyne*) and freed himself from all taboos, how does he behave? According to Wrong in Aristophanes' *Clouds* (1073), he enjoys boys, women, the party-game of *kottabos*, good food, drinking and laughter; and the man who yields to 'the compulsions of nature' typically commits adultery (1075f.).

In practice, of course, few people are able to defy society at all frequently, and we have to infer what human nature is like from our observation of how people behave in society. Thucydides believed that there was such a thing as human nature and that accurate history was useful because it showed just how human beings had once behaved in situations of various kinds and therefore how they would behave again when such situations recurred (1.22.4).

In his account of civil war (*stasis*) in Kerkyra and elsewhere, Thucydides wrote (3.82.2):

Civil war brought upon the communities many disasters. They occurred then and will occur, so long as human nature remains the same, though proving more or less severe and varying in character with each new combination of circumstances. In peace and prosperity both communities and individuals have better intentions, because they are not involved in necessities that leave them no choice; but war, which takes away easy livelihoods, is a teacher of violence and assimilates the emotions of most people to their circumstances.

Thucydides proceeds (3.82.8) to ascribe all these disasters to 'power pursued out of greed and ambition'. Elsewhere (1.75.3, 76.2), as we have seen, he makes the Athenians in Sparta on the eve of the Peloponnesian War ascribe the creation and preservation of their empire to fear as well as to gain and ambition. These three motives are said to be 'the most powerful'. His account (2.51.4–6) of the tending and visiting of the victims of the plague attributes much of the visiting to love of honour, but it also leaves some room for simple compassion. Thucydides does not suppose that all men always act out one or more of the three most powerful motives – only that most men do so most of the time. It is not obvious that he is wrong.

Nor is it obvious that his account of human behaviour is so very different from that of Herodotos or even Homer. The gods are very conspicuous in Homer and Herodotos, and very inconspicuous in Thucydides, but it does not follow that Homer and Herodotos believed that the gods might make men behave quite out of character (though all men make strange mistakes) or that Thucydides was an atheist.

In the course of a single speech in *Iliad* 9 Aias says of the still angry Achilles both that he had made savage the proud-hearted spirit within his chest (629) and also that the gods have made the spirit in his chest implacable and malignant (636f.). It is hard to doubt that the two accounts of what has happened to Achilles are equivalent, but they are not synonymous. The use of the psychological mode does not render the theological otiose. To use the psychological mode is to stress the agent's responsibility – *he* did it. To use the theological is to say something about the character of the world – unpredictable error is a force in human life. (As Euripides, who was a shrewd psychologist, well knew, the theological mode might be abused, either in order to withhold due praise (*Medeia* 526–531) or to evade due blame.)

If, to take a related example, 'Zeus sent Ate to take away his wits' is equivalent to 'He made a strange mistake,' then saying the former will not be proof of naivety, nor will saying the latter be proof of atheism. If theology's essential concern is with the character of the world and men's place in it, the theologies of Homer, the tragedians, Herodotos and Thucydides do not appear so very different. Herodotos, like Aiskhylos in *Persians*, wrote a tragedy of Persia, including in his version oblique references to the tragedy of Athens, which was to be the subject of Thucydides. Herodotos often used theological language, whereas Thucydides almost always used the neutral language of naturalistic psychology; but although Herodotos believed many things that Thucydides did not believe, the morals to be drawn from their two works are similar. Herodotos has much to say of the effect on men of arrogance (*hybris*) – itself the effect of satiety (*koros*), according to Solon and Theognis – and Xerxes is destroyed by a god-sent dream (7.12–18). In Thucydides (3.45.5) Diodotos voices views that the historian surely shared:

Everywhere are hope and desire, desire leading, hope following, desire thinking out the plan, hope suggesting that fortune will supply the means to its accomplishment. Both do infinite harm and, invisible as they are, they prevail over dangers that are manifest. And fortune too plays a part, contributing as much encouragement.

Does it matter whether we print 'hope', 'desire' and 'fortune' or 'Hope', 'Desire' and 'Fortune'?

Thucydides was concerned with more or less normal psychology; Hippokratic medicine paid some attention to mental disorder, and the author of *The Sacred Disease* (17) attributed it to abnormal brain states. Ordinary people might attribute it to brain disturbance or to excess of black bile (Aristophanes, *Clouds* 1275f., 833) and throw stones at its victims (*Wasps* 1491, *Birds* 524f.). A popular remedy was a purgative drink made from hellebore (*Wasps* 1489). The tragedians did not ignore myths in which insanity was prominent, and they represented it as god-sent. Aiskhylos had depicted the prophetic frenzy of Kassandra in *Agamemnon* and then the maddening of Orestes by the Eumenides or Furies, and Sophokles depicted the delusion of Aias in his play of the same name. Euripides knew most about these matters. In *Bakkhai* Kadmos, by skilful question and suggestion, revives in Agave the repressed memory of what she has done to her son Pentheus. The poet had perhaps witnessed in Macedon therapeutic procedures unknown to the Hippokratics. Antiphon of Rhamnous is said to have practised a kind of psychotherapy in Corinth for a while (Plutarch, *Moralia* 833c), but it may have been another bearer of the same name.

Very closely linked with the development of anthropology and psychology was that of rhetoric, the theory of oratory, the ancient equivalent of advertising and public relations. In part, the new subject merely analysed and systematised the best existing practice, but in part it exploited new knowledge.

The commonest Greek word for 'I know' originally meant 'I have seen.' The best way of knowing that the butler committed the murder is to have seen him committing it, but in forensic and political oratory the speaker is commonly concerned with matters that witnesses cannot settle, either because, though the event in question occurred, there was no reliable witness, or because the event in question has yet to occur. In default of reliable witnesses, speakers must appeal to probability, but appeals to probability must rest on an agreed understanding of normal human behaviour. Rhetoric was concerned not only with elegance of expression, but also with plausibility of reasoning, which involves much more than valid deduction.

Rhetoric had supposedly been invented in democratic Syracuse, and perhaps its first teacher in Athens was Protagoras, whose visits to Athens began in about 460. In 443 he was apparently sufficiently highly regarded to be invited to draft the constitution of Thourioi. The rhetorical contest (*agon*), unknown to Aiskhylos, is a feature of the earliest surviving plays of Sophokles and Euripides. Whether Protagoras or anyone else taught rhetoric to Perikles is not known, but, according to Plutarch (*Perikles* 36.3), the Sophist and the statesman once spent a whole day discussing whether the javelin, the javelin-thrower or the organisers of the event should in the strictest sense have been held responsible when an athlete had accidentally hit someone with his javelin and killed him. That such a question was eminently relevant to rhetoric we can see from the second of the three *Tetralogies*, sets of model speeches, ascribed to Antiphon of Rhamnous and datable to about 425. A young man, practising the javelin in a gymnasium, has accidentally killed a boy who ran in front of the target.

Each *Tetralogy* consists of two speeches for the prosecution and two for the defence in a case of homicide. Normally, of course, a professional speech-writer (*logographos*) would compose speeches only for the prosecution or for the defence and not for both. Although in each *Tetralogy* the final speech for the defence is supposed to be decisive, the exercise as a whole suggests the influence of Protagoras. He who claimed that a man was the measure of everything claimed also to be able 'to make the weaker argument the stronger', taught his pupils to praise and blame the same argument, wrote two books of *Contrary Arguments*, and said that on any subject there were two contrary arguments.

We find a typical appeal to probability in the third speech in the third of the *Tetralogies*. An older and a younger man had been drinking. A quarrel broke out, and according to witnesses (4.3), the older man attacked the younger. The younger man retaliated to such good effect that the older man, despite or because of medical attention, subsequently died. In their second speech, the prosecution, instead of calling witnesses to testify that the younger man was the aggressor, say that young men are more likely to be aggressors and to make drunken assaults than old (3.2). The reasonable reply of the defence is that many young men are self-controlled, and many old men commit drunken assaults (4.2); and anyhow there were witnesses.

The work of the professional speech-writers like Lysias and Antiphon, including their publication of model speeches like the *Tetralogies*, was closely related to that of the Sophists, who also published model speeches as well as manuals of rhetoric.

The case against the new subject of rhetoric was later put with force in Plato's *Phaidros*. Sicilian rhetoricians 'saw that probability was more to be esteemed than truth' (267a). In jury-courts no attention at all was paid to morality – only to plausibility.

Plausibility is a matter of probability, to which anyone who wants to speak with skill [*tekhne*] must attend. Sometimes prosecution or defence should withhold the actual facts, if they are improbable, in favour of what is probable. A speaker should always aim for probability and say good-bye to truth (272de).

Was there anything to be said on the other side?

One of Plato's Sicilian rhetoricians was Gorgias of Leontinoi, who in 427, at the age of about sixty came to Athens (not necessarily for the first time) to plead his city's case against Syracuse and astonished the Assembly by his elaborate style of oratory, with its antitheses and parallelisms. In another dialogue (*Philebos* 58ab) Plato mentions the Sophist's repeated claim that the art of persuasion far surpassed all other arts because it owed its supremacy to free choice rather than force. It might also have been urged that in default of knowledge of what happened, it is reasonable to believe that what most probably happened did in fact happen.

In so far as rhetoric aimed, in Protagoras' phrase, to make the weaker argument appear the stronger, it was eminently unscientific. But it did develop alongside anthropology and psychology, and it did promote interest in other more reputable subjects, such as logic. Both Protagoras and Prodikos devoted attention to Greek grammar and semantics. (Aristophanes mocks the study of grammatical gender in *Clouds* 658–694.) Hippias taught phonetics and metre. It is not possible to mark off sharply scientists and philosophers like Meton, Anaxagoras and Sokrates from Sophists like Protagoras, Gorgias, Prodikos and Hippias.

The word *sophistes* earlier meant an expert in an important subject and one likely to pass on his expertness (*sophia*) to others. In its later specialised and eventually pejorative sense it commonly meant an itinerant and professional lecturer and teacher of young men, who always professed rhetoric and usually other subjects too.

Too big for their own insignificant 'cities' – Abdera, Leontinoi, Ioulis in Keos, Elis – the original Sophists left their wives and children at home and visited the leading cities of Greece and also such festival centres as Olympia and Delphi. Often they went in the first instance as official representatives of their native cities. They were above all attracted to Athens, described by Hippias as 'the very headquarters of Greek *sophia*' (Plato, *Protagoras* 337d). Their disciples followed them from city to city. As influential but unaccountable foreigners, they might find that their presence was resented.

Doctors and sculptors charged fees for teaching their arts to others, as did Greek masters, music masters and trainers (Plato, *Protagoras* 311bc). Sophists too charged fees, often very high ones, for teaching young men how to speak (and also teaching young men how to teach other young men how to speak). According to Plato (*Menon* 91d), Protagoras earned more from his *sophia* than Pheidias and ten other sculptors put together. Whether the Sophists were as avaricious as Plato

suggests is hard to tell, but it would surely be wrong to think of the
Sophists are purely mercenary. Like other teachers, they hoped to see
their pupils succeed.

Sophists gave oratorical demonstrations (*epideixeis*) and in this they
were heirs of the rhapsodes. The display might take the form of declamation from a written text or of a one-man brains trust. As yet, very few
people read or consulted books at home. When Sophists declaimed at
the Olympic or Pythian games, they were competing for prizes. Usually,
they gave their displays in gymnasia, schools or private houses. Such
displays were the counterpart of doctors' cures or sculptors' statues:
evidence that they would be worth learning from.

As the authors of manuals (*tekhnai*, arts – of rhetoric), the Sophists,
though they wrote in prose, might be regarded as heirs of the didactic
poets; but as teachers of seminars, they filled a vacuum, since previously
there had been nothing corresponding to our sixth forms or universities.
Unfortunately, we know very little about their methods of instruction.
The Sophists' pupils were mostly young men, likely to be both impressionable and rebellious. Inevitably, they were rich, and often they were
highly ambitious. Though few in numbers, they would inherit influence.

Rhetoric, although not the invention of the Sophists, was the principal
subject offered by Protagoras and his successors. It was the most 'practical' or 'relevant' of all subjects. Whether anyone had taught rhetoric
to Perikles or not, there had clearly been good speakers before the
invention of rhetoric, but oratory was becoming increasingly important
in Athens. The introduction of radical democracy had meant that decisions affecting the community were taken much more publicly than
before. Matters that might once have been settled quietly between
influential friends were now debated publicly before thousands in the
Assembly and before hundreds in the Council or in jury-courts. Young
men knew that they could hardly hope to succeed, as the community
judged success, unless they could speak effectively, and that if they could
speak effectively, they might be able to trump the experience of their
elders. In Aristophanes' *Akharnians* (679f.), the Chorus-leader
reproaches the community for allowing old men to be prosecuted and
derided by the young.

The Sophists emerged to meet a growing demand for instruction in
effective speaking as a means to political success. In *Protagoras* (316bc)
Sokrates can assume that because his young friend wishes to learn from
Protagoras he wishes to make a name for himself in politics, and a little
later (318e–319a) Protagoras says that if a young man comes to him,
'he will learn only what he has come to learn – good sense [*euboulia*]
regarding private affairs and public: he will learn how best to manage
his own household and how to speak and act most effectively in politics.'
Protagoras readily agrees with Sokrates that he is talking about the art

of politics (*politike tekhne*) and is promising to make men into good citizens (*agathoi politai*).

It is noteworthy that nothing more is said about the management of one's own household and also that young men who sought instruction from Sophists were aiming higher than merely to become 'good citizens'. Athenian democracy called for more participation than does ours, but, even so, one could be a good citizen without paying large sums to Sophists. It was 'the best of the young men' that Protagoras claimed to attract (316c), and they were ambitious. In *Clouds* (432) Strepsiades is assured by the Chorus-leader that if he entrusts himself to 'Sokrates' no one will carry more resolutions in the Assembly than he.

Complementary to the prospectus of Protagoras is the account of what it is to be a good man given by Menon, a young Thessalian aristocrat and pupil of Gorgias, in the dialogue that Plato named after him (*Menon* 71e): 'to be capable of taking part in public life, in such a way as to help his friends and harm his enemies, while taking care to come to no harm himself.' Crudely formulated, this was the common account of *arete* or prowess. Thucydides (8.68.1) felt able to describe as 'second to none in *arete*' Antiphon of Rhamnous, who engineered the oligarchic revolution of the Four Hundred in 411 and subsequently entered into treasonable dealings with Sparta. Thucydides admired his practical intelligence, his ability to compose and, if necessary, deliver speeches, and perhaps also the loyalty to his friends and the courage that he displayed in not fleeing to Dekeleia when the Four Hundred were deposed.

It should not, however, be thought that Menon's Athenian counterparts were in general ambitious to succeed at the expense of the community. It was commonly assumed, though not by Sokrates or Plato, that reputation in the community was proportional to services rendered. It is clear therefore that Protagoras must have concerned himself with much more than rhetorical tricks. He must have considered individual morality, social psychology and political theory. If he was invited to draft the constitution of the 'Panhellenic' colony of Thourioi, that was a striking tribute to his standing as a political thinker. It is hard to speak effectively on how to treat a revolting ally if other speakers have thought about punishment and responsibility in general whereas you have not. The Sophists did more than transmit traditional techniques: they encouraged their pupils to question and to argue.

Selling a service was not highly regarded in Athens, though that is not to say that it was generally despised. The Sophists sold their services and were despised by some, such as Anytos, Sokrates and Plato. The reason can hardly have been merely that the service they sold was teaching. The Xenophontic Sokrates (*Reminiscences* 1.2.6, 6.5) felt that to charge fees restricted a teacher's choice of pupils and subjects. The Platonic Sokrates (*Theaitetos* 151a) was induced by his divine sign to turn certain former pupils away, but eminent Sophists like Protagoras and Hippias could choose their pupils and subjects (*Protagoras* 310de, 318de). It must be a question of what they taught. The one subject that they all taught was rhetoric, but that, as we have seen, involved more than the study of logico-linguistic tricks and figures of speech. In teaching rhetoric in the wide sense of the word they were teaching political advancement, and since politics was the most admired activity, they could claim, and apart from Gorgias did claim, to be teaching success in life or *arete*. Plato (*Protagoras* 349a) makes Sokrates say to Protagoras: 'You openly proclaimed yourself to the whole of Greece, gave yourself the name of Sophist, declared yourself a teacher of culture and *arete*, and were the first to ask a fee in return.'

The claim to teach *arete* brought the Sophists under attack from various directions. To conventional Athenians, not necessarily of the upper class, the notion that clever, sceptical foreigners should be telling some of the most gifted of their young men how to live was abhorrent: that task had always, and properly, fallen to fathers and uncles and others accounted 'brave and fair'. We can imagine the impact on rebellious young men and on their conservative elders of the revelation that there were two sides to every question. It was intolerable that the formal instruction of foreigners should supersede the informal instruction of responsible and respected citizens. It was feared, not without reason, that the new instruction would be both more efficient and less attentive to the claims of the community on the individual. The Sophists certainly helped to detach the gifted individual from his community and from his household.

To Sokrates, who had no high regard for the traditional, informal, instruction, the notion of selling instruction in *arete* (or *sophia*) was abhorrent. And it is an inadequate rejoinder to this point to say that teachers have to live. If *arete* is understood as success in life or the proper way to live, there is something abhorrent about selling instruction in it – certainly for large sums. We may compare modern distaste for affluent new religious cults. That Protagoras felt something of the force of this objection is suggested by Plato's making him say (*Protagoras* 328bc): 'Whenever anyone has completed his course with me, he pays me my fee, if he is willing; if not, he goes to a temple, states on oath how much he thinks the course is worth, and pays down that sum.' The point is a simple one: the nearer Protagoras came to making good men of his pupils, the less need he had to worry about charging fees, since all agreed that it was characteristic of the good man to render good for good.

There was a further objection from the Platonic Sokrates, which was that, though the Sophists claimed to be making men better and so to be teaching *arete*, they were not in fact doing so. Success in life could not be measured by the number of one's resolutions carried in the Assembly or by the number of verdicts given in one's favour in jury-courts.

Rhetoric-cum-*arete* was the only subject that all Sophists professed, but between them they covered a very wide range of subjects, some like grammar and semantics, closely related to rhetoric, and others, like mathematics and astronomy, seemingly unrelated – although Plato does make Sokrates claim that Perikles was a better speaker for his association with Anaxagoras (*Phaidros* 270a). While some of them made genuine contributions to knowledge or thought, Sophists must often have gone into subjects no further than was necessary to enable them to talk plausibly about them. Hippias aspired to encyclopaedic knowledge, a difficult achievement even then.

The Sophists were acquainted with the writings of the natural philosophers, and might be regarded as their heirs, at least to the extent that they accepted the notion of *physis* and did not, normally, use the language of divine intervention, but they were not primarily interested in cosmological questions. If they felt able to neglect such questions, it was partly because the answers returned by the natural philosophers were so diverse and so repugnant to common sense. In his *Praise of Helen* (13) Gorgias said: 'When Persuasion is added to speech, she can impress the soul as she wishes: witness first the natural philosophers who, by removing one opinion and implanting another, cause what is incredible and invisible to appear before the eyes of the mind.' In the same spirit, Thucydides, who was willing to make cautious conjectures about the early history of Greece (1.20.1, 21.1), where there was some evidence, declined to speculate on the probable origin of the plague or the causes of the violent changes it produced (2.48.3).

All Sophists made some use of the antithesis, perhaps introduced by Arkhelaos, between *physis* and *nomos*. That which happened by nature (*physis*), without personal choice or decision, might sometimes be contrasted with the misleading way men had chosen to describe it. Misleading though it was, such a choice might harden into a powerful custom (*nomos*). According to Hippias in *Protagoras* (337c), all men, or at any rate all Greeks, were akin by nature, but their kinship was obscured by convention. By convention Greeks were split into Athenians, Corinthians and so on, but naturally or really all Greeks were akin. The antithesis was mostly used to devalue *nomos*, often in the interests of selfishness, as by Wrong in *Clouds*, but it could be used to throw doubt on the institution of slavery. Though the earlier Sophists made less destructive use of it than their successors, any use of it implied a recognition of the mutability of morals.

The Sophists did not form a school, but they did share many beliefs and doubts. Their influence – in style of expression and thought – is apparent in the works of Euripides, Antiphon and Thucydides, and it is reasonable to speak of a Sophistic movement, which produced Europe's first Enlightenment. The philosophy of Sokrates and Plato was in part a reaction to that movement, and especially to its relativism. Aristophanes may not have been the only *laudator temporis acti* in late fifth-century Athens, but we cannot regard the heyday of the Sophists as a period of decline, and we must regret that so little of what the Sophists (and Demokritos of Abdera) wrote has survived. There are several reasons for this. First, like Herodotos and unlike Thucydides, they spoke and wrote to influence their contemporaries. Second, it is the fate of the textbook to be superseded by later textbooks. Third, the triumph of the hostile Plato and the more sympathetic Aristotle consigned even the Sophists' most ambitious works to oblivion. Consequently, in the case of Protagoras, for example, we are heavily dependent on the dialogues of Plato (especially *Protagoras* and *Theaitetos*) for our information, and though we may believe, we can hardly claim to know, that Plato's account is reliable.

There can be no doubt of the influence of the Sophists on literature – both that published in the theatre and that published in books – and consequently on educated thought and expression in Athens. It remains to consider their influence on public life during the thirty years from the death of Perikles to the death of Sokrates.

Apart from the men who came to power in the two brief periods of oligarchy in 411/10 and 404/3, the only prominent politician associated with the Sophists is Alkibiades, and he can hardly be called a democrat. Neither Plato nor Xenophon nor Aristophanes (except for one joke at the expense of Hyperbolos in *Clouds* 876) suggests that any democratic politician ever took lessons from a Sophist. Since Aristophanes repeatedly attacked both democratic politicians and Sophists, his failure to exploit more systematically any link between them suggests that there was no link to exploit. (As an example of what he might have said, we may take the malicious suggestions made in the Aristotelian *Constitution of Athens* (27.4) that Perikles, unable to think of the idea of pay for public service for himself, got it from his music master.) There is no evidence that Kleon, to whose powers of persuasion Thucydides testifies (3.36.6), had taken lessons from a Sophist, and it is exceedingly unlikely that Nikias had. In Plato's *Menon* (92b), Anytos is represented as knowing almost nothing about Sophists. By contrast, Theramenes, son of Hagnon, one of the ablest lieutenants of Antiphon in 411, had studied under Prodikos (Athenaios 220b).

Full-time politicians as gifted as Perikles or Kleon had little to learn from Sophists, though they might glance at their textbooks or note rhetorical novelties tried out on the Assembly by their pupils. It is likely that most of those pupils were young aristocrats, conscious that the political lore handed down to them by their fathers, uncles and grand-

fathers would not suffice to enable them either to compete under democracy with men like Kleon or, alternatively, to subvert the constitution
– no light enterprise (Thucydides 8.68.4).

In *Republic* (492ff.) Plato argued that the influence of a number of
individual Sophists on a number of young men was negligible by comparison with the pressures exerted on the individual by democracy itself
in such large gatherings as Assembly, jury-court, theatre or camp, and
reinforced by the sanctions of disfranchisement, fining or execution. The
Sophists' vaunted *sophia* amounted to no more than the opinions of the
assembled majority.

Even if one does not share Plato's low estimate of democracy, it must
be allowed that what he here says about the Sophists squares with our
other evidence. Athenian democracy antedated the Sophists and gave
them their scope. The Sophists were not on the whole original thinkers.
They had little to teach men of the rhetorical power and political acumen
of Perikles or Kleon. Their direct political influence seems to have been
largely confined to aristocratic, if not oligarchic, circles.

On the other hand, they gave articulate expression to the ideas of the
time. Furthermore, as the pupils they had taught and the textbooks they
had written began to influence other speakers and the professional
speech-writers, standards of speaking rose and so did critical standards.
Just as there had always been some good speakers, so good speaking
had always been enjoyed; but now performance and response in the
Assembly and in the theatre came to resemble each other more closely.
For an admittedly rhetorical account of the effect of rhetoric in the
Assembly we may turn to the speech given by Thucydides (3.37f.) to
Kleon in the second debate on what to do about the crushed rebel state
of Mytilene:

> Most alarming of all is the possibility that no decision of ours is
> going to be final, and that we shall forget that a community which
> enjoys laws that are bad but respected is better off than one which
> enjoys laws that are good but disregarded; that uneducated restraint
> is of more value than brilliant indiscipline; and that ordinary men
> generally administer their communities better than their more
> talented fellows. The latter want to appear wiser than the laws and
> to win every public debate . . . and thus they generally ruin their
> communities; whereas the others, mistrusting their own abilities, do
> not claim to be wiser than the laws or better able than the clever
> speaker to criticise a speech; and being impartial judges rather than
> contestants, generally get things right. We should do likewise, and
> not be so carried away by our own brilliance in a contest of wits
> as to give you advice that we do not ourselves believe in. . . .

In contests like this the community awards the prizes to others and takes the risks itself. The blame is yours – you stage these damaging contests. Your regularly watch speech-making, but only hear about deeds. You judge the feasibility of a project from the skill of its advocates, and the facts of history from the eloquence of denunciations, instead of placing more trust in action observed than in words heard. Easily deceived by novelty of expression, you are reluctant to endorse accepted opinions. Enthralled by every paradox, you despise what is familiar. Each of you wants if possible to be a speaker himself, but, failing that, you compete with the speakers by seeming to keep up with their ideas and applauding points even before they have been made. You are as eager to antici- pate the pattern of a speech as you are slow to foresee its conse- quences. You are, one may say, in search of a different world from ours, but without having an adequate idea of this one. Overcome in fact by the pleasure of listening to words, you are more like spectators sitting at the feet of Sophists than men deliberating about affairs of state.

It was later that summer that the Assembly listened with astonishment to the elderly Gorgias. Accustomed as they were to the fruits of rhetoric, this was something new in its elaboration. Gorgias was one of a delega- tion from his native Leontinoi and her allies. They wanted protection from Dorian Syracuse. The delegation appealed to an ancient treaty and to the Ionian connection with Athens. The Assembly voted to send a fleet, apparently swayed by the appeal to the Ionian connection, but in fact, says Thucydides (3.86.4), they wanted to stop the export of Sicilian corn to Peloponnese and to find out if they could conquer Sicily. The enjoyment of rhetoric was not incompatible with political realism.

· 9 ·

Philosophy, from Anaxagoras to Sokrates

By the mid-sixth century Athens was the second strongest power in Old Greece, but, except in pottery, her artistic preeminence and her intellectual preeminence hardly antedated the mid-fifth century. As the alliance of 477 turned into the empire, so ideas and thinkers from outlying parts of the Greek world were drawn to the centre of that empire. Plato (*Parmenides* 127) describes a visit paid to Athens in about 450, on the occasion of a Great Panathenaia, by the Eleatic philosopher Parmenides, the first man to produce a sustained deductive argument, and his follower Zenon. If the youthful Sokrates heard Zenon on that occasion, he will have experienced the power of the new-forged logical weapon of *reductio ad absurdum* – rendering a thesis absurd by showing that it involves an admitted absurdity.

Anaxagoras of Klazomenai, in northern Ionia, made known a revised version of Ionian natural philosophy in Athens. His dates are uncertain, but he may have lived from about 500 to 428. For some years he was resident in Athens, whence he was perhaps driven by religious intolerance. He had been a friend of Perikles, and may have suffered partly for that reason. He died, a revered figure, in Lampsakos, a colony of Miletos on the Hellespont. He probably wrote just one short prose work, of which about a thousand words are preserved. It may have been the first prose treatise seen in Athens.

Anaxagoras seems to have concerned himself chiefly with the problem of how to account for the apparent fact of change without violating the Eleatic principle that what *really* exists neither starts nor ceases to exist. A form of change that particularly interested him was assimilation. How does the bread that we eat turn into flesh and bone, as it apparently does? Anaxagoras' answer was that bread must contain portions or shares of flesh and bone (and indeed of every other natural substance and quality). These portions or shares the body assimilated, like attracting like, while eliminating the rest. Of course, no one sees flesh and bone when he cuts open a loaf, but the presence of these portions was inferred rather than observed. 'Appearances', said Anaxagoras, 'are a glimpse of the unobserved.'

Like his predecessors, Anaxagoras offered a cosmogony. In the beginning was an almost featureless, static mixture of infinitely small quantities of the infinitely many substances and qualities that were sooner or later to emerge. Alone exhibiting rudimentary order were minute 'seeds' or lumps predominantly of one substance. The denser, wetter, colder and darker seeds formed mist (aër), the rarer, drier, hotter and brighter seeds formed the aither. Both aër and aither were infinite in extent, and at first they were intermingled.

Apart from this largely undifferentiated mass, there was only Mind (nous). Though Mind too was material, it was much finer than the mass, and, unlike the mass and its constitutents, quite pure. It was also omniscient and supremely powerful. It was Mind that had originally set part of the mass spinning. Anaxagoras was thus a materialist, a dualist, and also a kind of deist: once rotation had got under way, purely mechanical principles began to operate. As the area affected by spin widened, differentiation within the mass increased, and aër and aither began to separate. Like attracted like, heavier seeds moving inwards to form the earth and lighter ones outwards. As the speed of rotation increased, masses of rock were torn from the earth. Heated to incandescence by the aither, they became the sun, moon and stars. The meteorite that fell at Aigospotamoi and probably gave Anaxagoras his idea of the composition of the heavenly bodies, had somehow defeated this centrifugal tendency, conforming instead to the earlier tendency of heavy things to move to the centre.

Anaxagoras believed that the earth was flat, floating on a cushion of aër. He knew that the moon shone by reflecting the light of the sun, and he knew the cause of eclipses, solar and lunar. He attributed the flooding of the Nile to the melting of southern snows, an opinion that Aiskhylos (Suppliant Women 559) may have taken over from him. Perhaps his most interesting biological opinion was that men were cleverer than animals because they had hands.

Like Alkmaion of Kroton before him and Diogenes of Apollonia and the author of The Sacred Disease after him, Anaxagoras located consciousness in the brain. (Tradition had long located it in the heart or liver or midriff.) He seems to have thought that both human and animal minds were fragments of Mind, but how he explained the prevalence of error is not clear. Understandably, in view of the novel and sublime role that he assigned to Mind, his answer to the question why a man should choose to be born rather than not to be born was: to contemplate the heavens and the order of the universe.

At the heart of Anaxagoras' physical theory was the difficult notion of there being in every visible piece of stuff – gold, say, or wood – an invisible portion or proportion of every other stuff. Mind was pure, but everything visible, however small, was impure. All the same, the system of Anaxagoras was bold and comprehensive, mainly literal and mainly intelligible. It would be hard to imagine thinking further removed from that of a barely literate Athenian peasant. Nor should the story of Anaxagoras' clash with Lampon surprise us: there was no room in the philosopher's system for an omen supplied by a personal god.

Anaxagoras was resident in Athens for a long time, perhaps for thirty years, all told. Apart from all the reflection and observation that lay behind his one short book, how did this illustrious metic pass the time, and how did he pay his bills? According to Plato (*Greater Hippias* 283a), he had inherited great riches but lost them. He is unlikely to have made much out of the sales of his book, and he probably did not teach for fees. Was he dependent in part at least on Perikles as patron (Plutarch, *Perikles* 16.7)? No doubt much time passed in discussions of the kind that Plutarch records as having taken place between Perikles and Protagoras, and we know of at least one Athenian disciple of his, Arkhelaos. He is not, however, named in what survives of Old Comedy, and it does not seem that he ever met Sokrates.

Arkhelaos was the first native Athenian philosopher, and is said to have been a teacher of Sokrates. In physical theory he modified without improving the teaching of his master, but, if, as seems possible, he was the first to advance the antithesis between *physis* and *nomos*, he precipitated an enormously fruitful controversy. He is said to have said that right and wrong existed by convention and not by nature, but without the context it is impossible to be sure precisely what he meant.

Diogenes of Apollonia (probably the colony of Miletos on the Black Sea) was a younger contemporary of Anaxagoras. There is no certainty that he was ever in Athens, but his views were familiar to Euripides and Aristophanes. In *Clouds* (227ff., for example) it is the views of Diogenes that Aristophanes is ascribing, albeit in garbled form, to Sokrates. (It does not follow that his audience recognised anything more than typical highbrow talk.) He wrote one book *On Nature* and perhaps others. He was an eclectic, borrowing from Anaximenes of Miletos, Herakleitos of Ephesos, Anaxagoras and from the atomist Leukippos, whose birthplace is uncertain. (Though they did not impinge on Athens so directly, Leukippos, Melissos of Samos, and Demokritos of Abdera were all contemporary with Diogenes and Sokrates, and active in the 430s.) Unlike Anaxagoras, Diogenes was a monist, and his one basic substance was that of Anaximenes – air. He did not see how different substances could interact to produce, for example, growth. The warmer and drier the air, the more intelligent and divine. Human intelligence was air warmer than the atmosphere, but much colder than that nearer the sun. Divine intelligence, omnipresent and omniscient, ordered all for the best. As we have seen, Diogenes was particularly interested in anatomy and physiology. He gave a detailed account of the veins and speculated about the physiology of perception.

The term 'Presokratics' is not always reserved, as one might expect it to be, for those Greek philosophers who flourished before Sokrates. Sometimes it excludes Sophists who advanced views that were certainly philosophical, and sometimes it includes contemporaries, and even successors, of Sokrates. Commonly, the line of Presokratics is thought of as coming to an end with Diogenes and Demokritos, both of them contemporaries of Sokrates. Demokritos was one of the widest-ranging thinkers of antiquity, but he may be passed over here, because, though he may well have come to Athens, part of the attraction of Athens for him appears to have been the fact that nobody there knew him. It is remarkable and regrettable that Plato never mentions him by name, the explanation perhaps being that Sokrates never met or never mentioned him.

Like his master Arkhelaos, Sokrates was an Athenian – better known to us than any other Athenian or indeed any other ancient Greek. The son of Sophroniskos, he was born in about 469. He was a member of the Urban deme (and *trittys*) of Alopeke, to the south-east of the city. His father, who is said by late writers to have been a sculptor or stonemason, seems to have been a man of some standing in the deme, and Sokrates served his country as a hoplite and not as an oarsman. By upper-class standards, at least, he was not handsome – thick-lipped, snub-nosed, pop-eyed. His way of life verged on the ascetic. He went barefoot even in the Poteidaian winter, but he would put on sandals for social occasions. More remarkable, he claimed (*Apology* 31d; references to *Apology* or *Symposion* are to the works of that name by Plato, unless Xenophon is mentioned as well) that even as a boy he had heard an inner voice, his 'divine sign', which always prohibited and never enjoined (though to prohibit A is to enjoin not-A) and he was capable of losing himself in thought for hours on end.

Sokrates left no philosophical or other writings; so we depend for our knowledge of the development of his thinking on the evidence of others – chiefly Aristophanes, Plato, Xenophon and Aristotle. The inconsistencies between these witnesses and within Plato constitute the Sokratic Problem, of which something will be said below.

In *Phaidon* (96a–99c) Plato gives us material of great value for reconstructing the intellectual scene in Athens in about 450 and, we may hope, for reconstructing the intellectual progress of Sokrates. (There is, however, some difficulty in reconciling what is there said with *Apology* 19d, where Sokrates is confident that none of the many jurors who have heard him talking has ever heard him say a word about astronomy.) Sokrates is made to describe his youthful passionate interest in natural philosophy. He longed to know why things came into and passed out of existence, and what they were for. He longed to know whether the first animals lived on a slime produced by the interaction of hot and cold. (This was the teaching of Arkhelaos, though Arkhelaos is not named.) Did men think with their blood, or with air, or with fire? (Such were the conflicting theories of Empedokles of Akragas, of Anaximenes followed by Diogenes, and of Herakleitos.) Was the brain the seat of perception, memory, opinion and knowledge? (This was the teaching of Alkmaion of Kroton, followed by Anaxagoras and Diogenes.) Was Anaxagoras right about nutrition? Was the earth flat or spherical, and was it at the centre of the universe? How could one become two both by having one added to it and also by being divided by two? (These uncertainties about arithmetical operations may have been the result of the visit to Athens of Parmenides and Zenon.) Plato thus gives us a vivid picture of the intellectual ferment in Athens in the middle of the century – zoology, psychology, astronomy and arithmetic were all being discussed with vigour. This ferment left the young Sokrates bewildered and feeling that he understood nothing.

Then he heard someone, presumably Arkhelaos, reading Anaxagoras' book aloud, wherein Mind was declared to be the disposer and cause of everything. This opinion conformed to Sokrates' own presuppositions, and from it Sokrates thought that it followed that everything was for the best. A truly scientific astronomy would thus proceed by stages: it would show first, for example, that the earth was flat or spherical, and then why it was best, for it and for everything else, that it should be so. In a state of great excitement Sokrates read on for himself. But his high hopes were dashed. The role of Mind was restricted to imparting the initial momentum, the first spin; thereafter mechanical causation reigned. One might as well hope, thought Sokrates, to explain human behaviour in terms simply of anatomy and physiology. Bones and muscles are necessary, but not sufficient, conditions of the performance of a bodily action; that is to say, you cannot have a bodily action without bones and muscles, but you can have bones and muscles without the bodily action.

At this point, Sokrates lost interest in natural philosophy and confined himself to ethics and linguistic philosophy, with momentous consequences for western thought.

Now this account of the mature Sokrates fits well enough with the evidence of Xenophon and Aristotle, but it appears to clash violently with the evidence of Aristophanes, the first edition of whose *Clouds* was produced in 423 and placed third. What we have is a partially revised second edition, intended for reading in the study and not for performance in the theatre, but the portrait of Sokrates was not significantly redrawn, it seems. Sokrates is represented as an impious natural philosopher and also as a grasping teacher of rhetoric. It is barely credible that Sokrates' preoccupation with ethics did not begin until he was forty-five, and, even if it were credible, there would remain the picture of the grasping teacher of rhetoric, which is at variance with everything else that we are told about Sokrates' attitude both to money and to rhetoric. We are in fact driven to conclude that, apart from allusions to Sokrates' gait (*Clouds* 362, *Symposion* 221b), to his austerity of life, and perhaps to his interest in grammar, Aristophanes' portrait of Sokrates bore little resemblance to the real Sokrates of 423.

Two questions arise:

(i) Could Aristophanes have believed that his portrait was accurate enough, allowing for comic exaggeration?
(ii) If not, what was his motive?

The answer to the first question must, for reasons given in chapter 7, be that he could not have. He must have known something about the interminable conversations that Sokrates was holding in gymnasium, *palaistra*, stoa and *symposion*, and known that they differed greatly from the conversations held in the Thinkery. By 423 Sokrates, who, unlike the itinerant Sophists, hardly ever left Athens, was the most prominent intellectual in the city, with the largest following. In the opinion of Aristophanes the comic poet, if not of Aristophanes the private person, all intellectuals, whether they studied astronomy or grammar, whether they charged high fees or lived ascetically, were both ludicrous and dangerous. What made them ludicrous was their remoteness from the work and play of ordinary decent people. What made them dangerous was that they asked awkward questions about the city's traditional beliefs and practices, and, what was worse, encouraged the young to do likewise. (In the AD 1960s, if there was one thing more distasteful to respectable people than a revolting student, it was a junior, or not so junior, member of the academic staff giving the student ideas that he would never have thought of for himself, or at least not until he was too old to do much with them.)

If Aristophanes wanted to write a play mocking contemporary teachers of young men and drawing attention to what he took to be the ill effects of their activities, he would have wanted an Athenian victim (Aristophanic comedy was primarily critical of Athenians – individually or collectively) and one who was well enough known to his audience. He was almost bound to choose Sokrates. If, further, he wanted to make Sokrates more ludicrous than he actually appeared and also to bring in other kinds of teaching, which, though different in subject matter and method, he judged to be similar in effect, it was likely enough that he would ascribe to Sokrates the medley of traits and practices that he did. It was his concern to write an amusing, and partly serious, play rather than to be fair to Sokrates.

It is unfortunate that we cannot give much chronological structure to the life of Sokrates. We cannot say when he despaired of natural philosophy, or when Khairephon made his remarkable enquiry of the Delphic oracle (*Apology* 20eff.). At an early age Khairephon had become a companion (*hetairos*) of Sokrates, some time before the Peloponnesian War (*Kharmides* 153b), and on one occasion, with characteristic impulsiveness, he went to Delphi to ask if anyone were wiser (more *sophos*) than Sokrates. Apollo's priestess obligingly replied that no one was. According to Xenophon (*Apology* 14), she replied that no one was freer, juster or more prudent.

Sokrates, like his companion Plato, appears to have taken the institution of the Delphic oracle entirely seriously, and he thought hard about the meaning of the reply that Khairephon had brought back. He was conscious of having no specialised knowledge of anything, and yet at the same time he could not doubt the truth of the oracle – his post-Homeric Apollo was not allowed to lie. Feeling obliged to disprove the obvious meaning of the oracle in the hope of discovering its hidden meaning, he reluctantly set about doing so by the laborious method of interrogating all those reputed wise in Athens – politicians, poets, artists and artisans. The politicians proved to be unjustifiably pleased with themselves, the most eminent with the least reason. The poets (including presumably Sophokles) were inarticulate about their poetry, which was the product not of art but of nature or inspiration, on a par with the deliverances of diviners and oracle-chanters, and they fancied that such expertness as they had qualified them to pronounce on other matters.

To both classes Sokrates felt himself superior, if only in virtue of his lack of pretension to knowledge. In this context the Delphic maxim 'Know yourself' could be interpreted as 'Know how little you know'. The artists and artisans knew much that was worth knowing, but, like the poets, they fancied that their artistic or technical expertness qualified them to pronounce on other, graver matters. (Sokrates seems to have approached them without prior knowledge of their ways; so perhaps Sophroniskos was not a stonemason.) Understandably, Sokrates' exposure of the pretensions of the leading men of Athens did not endear him to them, but his young followers enjoyed themselves, and tried to copy his technique (*Apology* 23c).

The hidden meaning of the oracle was revealed: human wisdom was worth little or nothing. Hearing the god's reply brought back by Khairephon seems to have marked the start of what may be called the 'mission' of Sokrates. He felt he had a duty to examine not merely himself but anyone in Athens, whether citizen or foreigner (*Apology* 23b), with a reputation for wisdom. Supported by his 'divine sign' and by Apollo's oracle, he had the strength to ignore the strongest force in the lives of most Athenians – public opinion. Come what might, he would probe reputations for such underlying worth as he could find. Athens contained some 40,000 citizens, of whom at least some hundreds must have enjoyed a reputation for *sophia* of some kind. (Three of his companions, Plato, Xenophon (*Symposion* 2.9) and Aiskhines of Sphettos (*Aspasia*), testify that Sokrates was no male chauvinist, and he may well have had a healthy respect for the intellect of Aspasia, and of Diotima, if she ever existed. But he can elsewhere describe (Plato, *Theaitetos* 150b) his collocutors as men, as opposed to women, because, apart from Aspasia, no free woman in Athens had any reputation for wisdom. (Nor, of course, had any slave.) This enterprise, worthy of Herakles himself, left him little time for conventional politics or for family affairs. (Just how Sokrates met the simple needs of his family and himself is not at all clear.) Since we can date neither Sokrates' rejection of natural philosophy nor the return of Khairephon from Delphi to Athens, we can say nothing about the relation between the two events.

We can do more about dating some much less important events – the military campaigns on which Sokrates served. It is probable, though not certain, that he served with Arkhelaos at the siege of Samos in 440 (Diogenes Laertios 2.23). If he did, he served against a force commanded by Melissos. He certainly served at the siege of Poteidaia in 432, saving the life of Alkibiades, and at Delion in 424 (*Symposion* 219e, 221ab). He also served at Amphipolis, probably when the 'Panhellenic' colony was established there in 436. His military record was thus a distinguished one, and it is curious that he should have been ridiculed in the theatre by Aristophanes and also, it seems, by Ameipsias (in *Konnos*, named after Sokrates' music-teacher (*Euthydemos* 272c)) in the year after Delion. Unfortunately, we know nothing of Sokrates' views of the rights and wrongs of these campaigns, but he did not question his country's right to call men up for military service (*Kriton* 51b). The evidence of Plato suggests that he combined general loyalty to the city and its laws, with criticism of its preoccupation with the sources of power – ships, dockyards, walls. These campaigns were almost the only occasions on which he left Athens. In *Kriton* (52b) Plato makes the customs and laws of Athens say to Sokrates:

> You would never have stayed at home more than all other Athenians, had you not been exceptionally happy there. You never left the city to see other sights, except for one visit to the Isthmos. You never went anywhere else except on military campaigns. . . .

It is not easy to reconstruct the mature philosophy of Sokrates. Setting aside Aristophanes, we have to consider the evidence of Plato, Xenophon and Aristotle. Aristotle's evidence, though slight in amount, is very valuable: he was near enough but not too near in time to Sokrates to be objective, and he was himself both a philosopher and something of a historian. Xenophon's evidence, which is that of a straightforward, practical man, is useful if it is consistent with what Aristotle says and is not based simply on his reading of published dialogues of Plato. Plato's evidence presents great difficulties. The one thing we can be sure of is that not everything he tells us in different dialogues can be relied on, because he tells us incompatible things. It is possible, mainly on stylistic grounds, to arrange the dialogues in approximate order of composition, and so the problem becomes one of saying where in the fairly well-established sequence of dialogues Sokrates ends and Plato begins. It will rarely if ever be the case that a given dialogue is wholly Sokratic in doctrine or wholly Platonic, but in general it is reasonable to assume that the earlier a dialogue is the more Sokratic it is. This principle justifies attaching especial weight to the evidence of the *Apology* (which is not strictly a dialogue) and *Kriton*. The *Apology*, written not long after 399, was a reconstruction of speeches that had been heard not only by Plato himself but also hundreds of jurors and many members of the general public. It is therefore hard to believe that Plato did not at least adhere to 'the general intent of what was actually said' (Thucydides 1.22.1). (In later dialogues Plato was not perpetrating fraud in fathering on Sokrates doctrines that he never advanced. Rather he was paying his master the conventional compliment of attributing to him doctrines that he had himself arrived at – from Sokratic starting-points.)

A preliminary difficulty arises when we consider the repeated protestations of ignorance made by the Platonic Sokrates. If we took them literally, we might have to conclude that Sokrates was a sceptic who held no positive views. But such a conclusion would be at variance with the evidence of Aristotle and indeed with other features of the Platonic dialogues. The protestations of ignorance are in part ironical, and serve the pedagogical purpose of encouraging his collocutors to think for themselves. In *Theaitetos* (148c–151d) Sokrates is made to describe himself as a midwife unable to conceive ideas, but ministering to men who can. Sokratic midwifery was indeed a drawing out of the opinions of others, but this midwife was not without opinions of his own. In *Apology* 29b, for example, Sokrates says: 'I do know that it is bad and shameful to do harm and to disobey one's superior, whether god or man.' The same fact is apparent from the systematic character of Sokratic interrogation. (It is necessary to say ' in part ironical', because Sokrates was not a dogmatist – most of his opinions were hypotheses, entertained provisionally.)

At first sight, Sokrates appears to have been almost exclusively concerned with ethics and, to a lesser extent, politics, the two subjects being virtually indistinguishable, since the community of citizens was more like a family than a modern nation state (an analogy was often drawn between fatherland and parents); but behind the ethical and political enquiries lay strong theological convictions.

The early Platonic dialogue that is most theological in character is

Euthyphron. In it (5a) Sokrates says to Euthyphron: 'In the past I thought it of great importance to know about religion.' We can hardly suppose that he did not talk about it often. Passages in Xenophon, which are not likely to be Xenophon's own invention and which it is unnecessary to regard as interpolations, make it probable that Sokrates, developing ideas of Anaxagoras and Diogenes, believed in an omniscient and omnibenevolent Designer (*Reminiscences* 1.4.18). Consequently, he held that no object or phenomenon in the universe had been fully explained until its role in the grand Design had been shown (*Phaidon* 97c–e). In the case of astronomical phenomena, it might be useless or worse for men to try to do this.

If Sokrates was the inventor of the teleological argument for the existence of God, it remains uncertain how he reconciled such advanced theology with traditional piety. In *Euthydemos* (302c) Sokrates claims to have all the religious resources of other Athenians, including altars and shrines, domestic and ancestral. Asked in *Phaidros* (229c–e) whether he believes the story of Boreas, the north wind, carrying off Oreithyia from beside the Ilisos, he makes a number of preliminary points. First, a rationalising interpretation is possible. Second, there is more than one version of the story. Third, it would be a very long and arduous business to provide rationalising interpretations of all the strange creatures known to mythology. But in any case, since he acts on the Delphic maxim 'Know yourself', Sokrates has no time for such enquiries, and is content to accept the traditional view of such creatures. This does not, of course, mean that he is content to accept the traditional view of the gods. When Euthyphron relates his own behaviour to the stories of the unfilial behaviour of Zeus and Kronos, Sokrates asks, ironically (6a):

Can this be the reason why I am being prosecuted, Euthyphron, that whenever someone tells such stories about the gods, I cannot bring myself to accept them?

Xenophanes and Pindar had not been able to accept them either, but they had come to no harm in consequence.

The implications for ethics are clear. Man has his part in the Design. The end of life is to discover and then and therefore to play the part intended for him by the Designer (though right actions are not right merely because desired by the Designer, as Sokrates was perhaps the first to realise (*Euthyphron* 10a)). The good man is no longer a latter-day Homeric hero concerned for his honour; he is a man concerned for his *psykhe*, that is, as Sokrates used '*psykhe*', a man who preserves and makes proper use of his own rationality – the best and most godlike part of himself. Indeed, man and *psykhe* are identical, the body being but the possession of the *psykhe* (*First Alkibiades* 130c). The rational self should stand to the body as the Designer to the material world. So

to live is to achieve success in life (*arete*) and to be truly happy ✳
(*eudaimon*). 'No harm can befall a good man either in life or in death,
and the gods do not neglect his fortunes' (*Apology* 41cd; compare
Matthew 10²⁸). Like Jesus, Sokrates can recommend his friends and
followers to behave in a way that most of his contemporaries would
regard as oppressively austere, not because, if they do, they will be
rewarded in the end (though he may think they will), but because such
behaviour is natural and in accordance with the Design. What is right
for man must be good for man, and what is good for man is advantageous for man and conducive to his happiness. (This at least was a
conventional opinion.) Once we know, in the fullest sense, what our
part or function is, we shall not fail to perform it; for no one deliberately
harms himself – knowledge (of function) is (sufficient, and necessary
too, for) virtue or success in life.

No kind of success – in athletics, politics or any other sphere – is
achieved without effort. Success in life is, paradoxically, trying to
discover what success in life consists of, that is, trying to discover our
function. The method of discovering our function is the laborious one of
searching for analytical definitions of the words for the various particular
virtues or parts of virtue, and also searching for an analytical definition
of 'virtue' itself:

The greatest good for man is each day to discuss virtue and the
other matters about which you hear me arguing ... (*Apology* 38a).

Sokrates made the plausible assumption that whenever a general word,
such as 'just' or 'justice', 'courage' or 'courageous', was applied correctly,
it was bound to indicate the presence of a factor common to all the things
or phenomena to which the general word could be applied correctly. (In
Latin, this is the doctrine of *unum nomen, unum nominatum*.) It was
the business of an analytical definition to specify what the common
factor was. Many of Plato's early dialogues show Sokrates first eliciting
definitions of the required form from his collocutors and then testing
them to destruction. This destructive process is called in Greek *elenkhos*. ✳
It commonly takes the form of showing that a proposed definition D
must be rejected because it, or some statement deducible from it, is
incompatible with some statement Q, which is deducible from another
statement P, which is more certain than D.

Perhaps because he thought that, even at its best, the method of
Sokrates could never bring about the moral revolution that he sought,
Plato may have exaggerated the negative character of the *elenkhos* by
failing to show it being used to refine successive definitions. At all events,
the difficulty of finding acceptable analytical definitions of general words
in ethics is apparent from the repeated failures recounted in the dialogues, and also perhaps from the fact that Sokrates entertained the

hope that, after death, he would have the pleasure of testing the shades of the illustrious dead for wisdom (*Apology* 41b). This suggests that, in the absence of any revelation of the good for man, the search might be very lengthy, but a lifetime devoted to an unsuccessful search would be a lifetime well spent, since 'the unexamined life is no life for a man' (*Apology* 38a). Presumably, however, Sokrates did not exclude the possibility of a successful conclusion to the search. The search was the means to the most desirable end rather than an end in itself. Arriving would be even better than travelling.

The existence of the Designer ensures that, though the moral notions from which we have to start may be confused, they are not wholly mistaken. In a certain situation, A and B may differ over which possible course of action would be just, and they may both be wrong; but they are not wrong in believing that *some* course of action would *really* be just. (Protagorean relativism, ruling out as it did the possibility of error and argument, was incredible.) Because we are distracted by such false goods as honour, gain and pleasure, we allow our moral notions to remain confused, and so our actions go awry and our happiness is impaired.

The implications for politics too are clear. Given the rule of law (as opposed to the arbitrary rule of a tyrant or oriental potentate) and the possibility of changing the laws by peaceful means (*Kriton* 51bc), and given therefore the possibility of leading a virtuous life, what matters is not the choice between constitutional monarchy, oligarchy and democracy, but the quality of the lives of the individual citizens, which is a matter of their concern for virtue. Sokrates tried to quicken the concern of his fellow-citizens for virtue by his innumerable encounters with individuals. His divine sign deterred him from trying to convert the Assembly; had he tried to do so, his life would have been shorter (*Apology* 31c–e). Unlike Plato and Aristotle, Sokrates does not seem to have thought that it was the business of the state to try to instil a concern for virtue in the young. Though he described himself as a probably unique gift of Apollo to Athens, asking the jurors in effect 'When comes there such another?', he warned them that, after his execution, others more numerous and more troublesome (because more youthful) than he would arise to agitate their consciences (*Apology* 39cd). He does not seem to have shared Plato's pessimistic assessment of the city's moral and political prospects.

If this reconstruction of the positive thinking of Sokrates is anywhere near the truth, that thinking is open to at least four objections. First, in the light of vastly increased knowledge of historical astronomy, geology and biology, the argument from design looks less plausible than it did, and even Plato, well aware of the general scepticism of his day, sought in *Republic* to recommend justice more on psychological than on theological grounds. Second, the identification of man and *psykhe* creates more problems than it solves. Third, unless 'know' is given a specially 'high' redefinition, it seems clear that men of weaker will than Sokrates can know that a possible course of action is right for them and still not adopt it. Fourth, closer attention to the nature of language shows that *unum nomen, unum nominatum*, though plausible, is false.

In considering the life of Sokrates, we must distinguish between Sokrates as teacher and Sokrates as researcher. We have seen that Sokrates feigned ignorance in order to draw out his collocutors, but that in fact he held positive doctrines of his own. How did he arrive at them? In most of the early dialogues Plato represents him as arguing with his intellectual inferiors. Protagoras was a tougher nut to crack than his usual adolescent collocutors, but even he was worsted. In such encounters the question-and-answer method was eminently appropriate, but it is hard to believe that Sokrates learned much from the answers. His positive philosophy must have been arrived at partly through encounters with his intellectual equals, partly through reading (Xenophon, *Reminiscences* 1.6.14), and partly by private thinking of the kind twice mentioned by Plato in *Symposion* (174d–175c, 220cd).

Even if Sokrates began his mission genuinely expecting to be enlightened by his interrogations of the eminent Athenians of his day, the time must surely have come when he realised the extreme unlikelihood of there being more than a handful of people in Athens with anything to teach him about ethics. Presumably it was when he realised this that he decided to start teaching others. Of course, his was teaching of a very special kind. He was both reluctant to obtrude his own views and willing to discuss them. He did not think of education as instruction in a subject (*mathema*) but rather as converse between friends. His collocutors had to observe two main rules: they had to answer in accordance with their own opinions, and at the same time they had to avoid contradicting themselves. Sokrates' part was to elicit their opinions and then, by means of examples and analogies, to examine their implications.

In *Apology* (33a) Plato makes Sokrates claim never to have been anyone's teacher (*didaskalos*), partly, no doubt, because he is anxious to suggest that ergo he was never the teacher of Alkibiades or Kritias, who had been one of the Thirty, the oligarchs brought to power by the Spartans in 404. The claim is true only if '*didaskalos*' is taken to mean 'paid instructor', and indeed Sokrates stresses that he did not take payment for teaching (*Apology* 19d). According to Xenophon (*Reminiscences* 1.2.60), his popular sympathies made him share his wisdom with all alike (compare Plato's *Apology* 33b), whereas he regarded the sale of wisdom as no better than prostitution (*Reminiscences* 1.6.13). Moreover, the salesmen of wisdom had to take such pupils as presented themselves, however unpromising, and that was an infringement of independence (*Reminiscences* 1.6.5).

Even if he did not take fee-paying pupils (*mathetai*), Sokrates certainly had a band of devoted companions (*hetairoi*), and they tended to be the sons of the rich, partly because their labour was not required at home (*Apology* 23c). Despite what Xenophon says about Sokrates' popular sympathies, this tendency will not altogether have displeased him, but not because he was a snob. It was a fact of political life that the leaders of the community, and especially the generals, mostly came from the upper classes, and, if Sokrates was to influence the life of Athens otherwise than by addressing the Assembly, his best chance lay in influencing the future leaders of the community while they were still malleable. In *Kharmides* we find Sokrates, just back from Poteidaia, making for the *palaistra* of Taureas. When he has given his news, he enquires about the current state of philosophy and about the young men (153d; compare *Theaitetos* 143d).

In *Gorgias* (521d) Plato makes Sokrates claim to be almost the only political theorist in Athens and certainly the only one to translate theory into practice, because he speaks not to win favour but to tell people what is truly to their advantage. In the light of his thinking about what is really good for the *psykhe*, he tries to improve the *psykhai* of others.

It seems that it was normally the young men who sought out Sokrates, whereas Sokrates sought out those of their elders who interested him; but the reverse processes did occur. In the case of the young men the result of interrogation by Sokrates was helplessness and in the case of their elders resentment of criticism. The inducement of helplessness by the use of *elenkhos* is well illustrated in *Menon*, where both the young Thessalian aristocrat and his slave are disabused of their pretensions to knowledge but are then quite unable to proceed.

The effect of *elenkhos*, which is described in *Sophist* (230d) as the 'most potent of purifications', on those who did not share Sokrates' theological assumptions was likely to be utter scepticism (compare Matthew 12[45]). It is in *Menon* that Anytos, the most influential of the three accusers of Sokrates, warns him against being too ready to run down the heroes of Athenian democracy, among whom he probably reckons himself.

Unlike some modern philosophers, Sokrates was not afraid to make moral judgments, some of them very striking – for example, the judgment that we should never render evil for evil (*Kriton* 49c). Kallikles was quite right in saying (*Gorgias* 481c) to Sokrates: 'If you are serious and what you say is really true, human life would be upside down; we appear to be doing quite the opposite of what we should be doing.' In *Symposion* (215e–216b) Plato makes Alkibiades describe how the private words of Sokrates affected him as the public words of his guardian Perikles never had, making him enraged at his own slavish condition; alone of men, Sokrates had made him feel ashamed of his neglect of himself; only when he had escaped from the presence of Sokrates, did he yield to the temptations of popularity.

Though Sokrates may have had unattractive traits, it can hardly be doubted that he was an unusually good man. Furthermore, Athenian citizens prided themselves on their *parrhesia*, their right to speak their minds fully and freely. How then did it come about that Sokrates was put to death for speaking his mind?

Like *isegoria* or equality of speech, *parrhesia* was exercised primarily in the courts, the Council and the Assembly, and also on the comic stage. It was essentially a matter of being able to say what you liked about any other citizen, however eminent, in those public settings. Even on the comic stage, there was no licence to mock certain deities or their worship or to attack religion in general or democracy in general. Anti-democratic writing, such as the Old Oligarch's pamphlet, and anti-democratic talk at home would have been unlikely to arouse public displeasure. Sokrates mainly talked in semi-public – to small groups in public places. That some of Sokrates' semi-public talk was anti-democratic might not have aroused public displeasure, but some of his former companions had translated anti-democratic talk into anti-democratic action. Though he broke with Kritias (Xenophon, *Reminiscences* 1.2.29f.), Sokrates, as far as we know, remained friendly with Alkibiades until he sailed for Syracuse in 415.

Sokrates was prosecuted for irreverence in the jury-court presided over by the Basileus. (What had happened at the preliminary stage of *anakrisis* we are not told, but Meletos must have convinced the Basileus that there was a case to answer.) The irreverence alleged was that of not recognising the gods of the city and of introducing a strange religion. It was alleged also that he corrupted the young men, a rider of which the Basileus can have taken cognizance only on the assumption (made in *Apology* 26b) that the way in which Sokrates corrupted them was by infecting them with his own heresies. Of the first part of the main charge, Sokrates was apparently innocent. Although he cites no evidence for the fact in *Apology*, so far as is known, he performed every public act of worship that convention demanded. He was also convinced that Apollo spoke to him through oracles and dreams (*Apology* 33c). He was not the Sokrates of *Clouds*. Nor was the second part of the main charge much better founded. New cults, such as those of Asklepios and the Thracian Bendis, were not infrequently introduced into Athenian public worship. It was true that Sokrates claimed that his private inhibitor was the voice of a god, but, in a society in which oracle-chanters flourished, such a claim was hardly remarkable.

More serious was the rider about corrupting the young men. Whether it should have been accepted as irreverence or not, corruption of the young men was something with which Sokrates could be charged with some plausibility, on the following grounds:

1   Sokrates showed young men that the moral and religious notions that they had inherited were incoherent, but he was unable to persuade at least some of them to accept his theologically based reconstruction.

2   Like the Sophists, Sokrates usurped the traditional educational role of fathers, uncles and *erastai*.

3   Sokrates exposed the baseless pretensions of the leading men of the day – politicians, poets, craftsmen – bringing them into ridicule and at the same time casting doubt on the worth of their occupations. This habit was copied by his followers, who doubtless tended to be more interested in knocking down than building up.

4   Sokrates criticised the heroes of Athenian democracy – Miltiades, Themistokles, Aristeides, Kimon, Perikles, Thoukydides – either for having had wrong objectives in politics or for having been unsuccessful fathers or on both grounds.

5   Sokrates criticised at least one democratic institution – the selection of magistrates by sortition. He argued in a characteristically analogical way that in no other sphere of human activity were tasks calling for expertness so assigned, and presumably a magistracy called for some sort of expertness.

6   Whether he accepted the right of all citizens to speak in the Assembly (*isegoria*) or not, Sokrates criticised the willingness of the Assembly to listen to unqualified people speaking about the running of the community's affairs. The Assembly would not listen to unqualified people speaking about technical matters:

> but whenever some matter affecting the running of the community has to be decided, anyone can get up and give advice – carpenter, smith, cobbler, merchant and shipowner, rich and poor, high and low – and no one reproves him . . . for trying to give advice without having learnt and without being taught (*Protagoras* 319c).

7   Sokrates criticised the working of democracy, particularly the way it had worked on one occasion in 406, when he had been a member of the standing committee of the Council and, alone of those fifty men, had, at the risk of his life, opposed the putting of an illegal motion to an hysterical Assembly (*Apology* 32b).

8 Fortified by his divine sign, Sokrates ignored public opinion as he ignored the opinions of absent worthies. When Kriton expresses the fear that his friends will be thought to have been too mean to rescue him from prison, Sokrates asks (*Kriton* 44c): 'What is public opinion to us?' When Euthyphron tells him that he is laughed at when he speaks on religious matters in the Assembly, Sokrates suggests (*Euthyphron* 3c) that the derision of the Assembly may be a matter of no importance.

9 Sokrates was, at least superficially, apolitical. Apart from serving on the Council in 406/5 (unfortunately we do not know why he let his name go forward), he held no political office (*Apology* 32a). In the Funeral Speech Perikles claims that the Athenians are unique in regarding the man who takes no part in politics as useless (Thucydides 2.40.2). But what if such a man has among his companions some of the most promising young men in the community? What view should the community take of his urging those young men to ignore as externals practically everything that the Assembly concerned itself with and care for their own *psykhai* instead? In *Symposion* (216a) Alkibiades describes how Sokrates 'compels me to admit that, though I am still deficient in many ways, I nevertheless neglect myself in favour of the business of the community.'

10 Sokrates had remained in Athens during the régime of the Thirty, and his opposition to it had gone no further than his refusal to go to Salamis with four others to arrest Leon (*Apology* 32c). His only concern was to avoid doing wrong himself.

11 Some of Sokrates' former companions had shown themselves – Alkibiades for a time, Kritias and Kharmides more consistently – hostile to democracy. Development in court of this point, and indeed most of the others, must have been inhibited by the magnanimous decree of 403 (Aristotelian *Constitution of Athens* 39.6) which declared an amnesty for all past political offences except those committed by the Thirty and some twenty or thirty others, but the fourth-century orator Aiskhines, addressing an Athenian jury, says (1.173):

> You put to death Sokrates the Sophist, because it was apparent that he had been the teacher of Kritias, one of the Thirty who suppressed democracy.

Despite his disclaimer, it was assumed that Sokrates had been a teacher, and that a teacher did not stimulate independent thought but imparted information and opinions, and so could be held responsible for the opinions of his pupils. The fact that another of Sokrates' companions, Khairephon, had been driven from Athens by the Thirty and had returned with the democrats (*Apology* 21a) was accorded less significance.

We are unlikely ever to discover either why it was Meletos, Anytos and Lykon who prosecuted Sokrates or why it was in 399 that they did so. Anytos is well known to history as one of the architects of the restored democracy of 403 and therewith of the amnesty. He must have been the most influential of the prosecutors (*Apology* 18b), but it was Meletos who laid the charge before the Basileus. Unfortunately, 'Meletos' was a common name at the time, and it is not possible to be sure whether the Meletos who prosecuted Sokrates on behalf of the poets (*Apology* 23e) and on behalf of traditional religion (*Euthyphron* 3b) was the same as the Meletos who had taken part in the unsuccessful prosecution of Andokides in 400/399 for attending the Mysteries when legally debarred. If he was the Meletos who prosecuted Andokides, he may have delivered a speech against him, Lysias 6, which exhibits a primitive level of religious thought, appropriate, it may be felt, alike in the mouth of a Eumolpid (Lysias 6.54) and of a prosecutor of Sokrates for irreverence. Of the third prosecutor, Lykon, said (*Apology* 23e) to be representing the speakers or politicians, nothing more is known.

Sokrates was found guilty by 60 votes (*Apology* 36a) out of perhaps 500. We may be inclined to think that the prosecution was unable to prove any part of its case. Even if the charge made in the rider had some plausibility, it was nevertheless false in substance: the defects in the dispositions of Alkibiades and Kritias had not been implanted by Sokrates. But, as we have seen, in public cases Athenian juries tended to convict or acquit on the basis of whether the defendant appeared to have harmed or benefited the community. We may be inclined to think that the seventy-year-old philosopher constituted no serious threat to the restored democracy and that to criticise various aspects of democracy is not enough to make one an oligarch. But the cumulative weight of the grounds listed above, hardly any of which could be mentioned in court, but many of which must have occurred to many of the jurors, is considerable, and the jurors, all of whom had lived through the Sicilian disaster, the revolution of 411, the surrender to Sparta and the régime of the Thirty, may perhaps be forgiven for having erred on the side of caution. It may also be felt that the *Apology* is more defiant than defensive.

It is unlikely that Anytos and his colleagues wished to do more than silence Sokrates. Their concern was not to harm him but to put an end to what they took to be a public nuisance if not danger – the oral publication of Sokrates' opinions. They would have been satisfied with a decision to go into exile or with an undertaking to keep quiet. In

Menon (92b), Plato makes Anytos criticise to Sokrates the communities that admit Sophists or do not expel them, foreigners or citizens. In *Apology* (29c–30c) Sokrates considers the possibility of his renouncing philosophy and rejects it as incompatible with the divine inspiration of his mission. If he were acquitted on the current charge, he would resume his mission and so face the prospect of a fresh prosecution. As for going into exile, Sokrates did not oblige by doing so before his trial came on, nor would he propose exile as his alternative to the death-sentence, proposed by Meletos after his conviction (*Apology* 37cd), nor was he interested in escaping from prison after he had been sentenced to death. 'I have lived long enough,' said Caesar shortly before his death, and Xenophon ascribes Sokrates' refusal to consider the possibility of escaping from prison to a similar sentiment. Perhaps it was an element in his thinking, like his recognition that there was no obvious place of exile for him to go to (*Kriton* 53b–e), but more important were surely his firm beliefs that the *worst* that death could hold was oblivion, and that it was wrong to harm others. And he was quite right to think that if *he* were to try to escape from prison, the community would be harmed. Had it not been 'agreed that Sokrates was somehow distinguished from the majority of men' (*Apology* 34e)? That distinction lay partly in his admission of his own ignorance, but chiefly in his determination to discover the right and do it.

We know enough about the values and way of life of ordinary Athenians to be able to say with some precision how extraordinary Sokrates was. The central institutions of human life were marriage, sacrifice and agriculture. Every self-respecting Athenian aimed to perpetuate, if not strengthen, his household and benefit his community: in so far as he achieved those aims he would win honour, the reward and proof of virtue.

Sokrates was the child of a no doubt fully conventional marriage (betrothal, handing over with dowry, lasting cohabitation). He was himself both husband and father, and we cannot be sure that he discharged those roles worse than did many other Athenians. According to Xenophon (*Reminiscences* 1.1.2), he was constantly sacrificing, both at home and at the public altars. According to Plato (*Phaidon* 118), his very last words enjoined Kriton to be sure to offer a cock to Asklepios – a thank-offering to the god of healing from one cured of 'life's fitful fever'. Plato would hardly have made those the last words of his Sokrates if the historical Sokrates had abstained from blood sacrifice, as some sectarians did. Sokrates was the most urban of men, but Athens had become the largest Greek city, and many Athenians – craftsmen and sailors – knew as little as Sokrates did about agriculture, even if it had originally been an Athenian gift to the world. It was not in relation to marriage, sacrifice or agriculture that Sokrates was extraordinary.

Marrying late in life, it seems, Sokrates begot three sons, but he neglected the estate that they would inherit in order to benefit the community in a novel way. The community could not, however, admire such neglect, since it depended on the preservation of more or less prosperous households.

Although he was unusually respectful of law, as opposed to custom, Sokrates' political service to his communtiy was unimpressive; his military service, unless it has been magnified by Plato, was more impressive. He was in no position to perform liturgies. Nevertheless, unchecked by false modesty, he apparently claimed to be Athens' greatest benefactor.

We might describe that benefaction as the invention of moral philosophy. Traditional thinking had already been refined by the expository, persuasive and critical techniques of public debating, variously practised in various settings in the city – Assembly and Council, law-courts and theatre. Public debating was itself being refined by the techniques of prose writing. Moral problems, faced by the private person in the conduct of his own life, had hitherto been illuminated by the lively symbols of myth. Sokrates now tried to solve them with a verbal precision far exceeding that of oratory or dramatic poetry. All the help he sought in this enterprise was that the ablest men in the city should give him their honest opinions.

His advanced religious belief – in divine power without moral blemish – assured him that what he was looking for could, with difficulty, be found: a clearly defined set of moral terms, yielding a consistent, complete and self-evident set of moral principles, from which the right course of action in any situation could be deduced. As soon as it had been so deduced, it would be taken. To one determined to discover the right and do it public opinion, confused as it was, could be of no help. Rejecting honour among men as the measure of success in life, Sokrates gave a new content to 'good citizen' and 'good man'. His good man might well be unpopular with his fellow citizens.

Sokrates' enterprise, highly original as it was, clashed with the pronouncements of no church, Bible or revered guru. Myth, though still vivid enough to inspire poets and sculptors, did not supply answers to such general questions as Sokrates was raising, and there was no religious orthodoxy to feel itself threatened by his activity. Nevertheless, how it struck, or could be made to strike, ordinary people as early as 423, may be seen in *Clouds*. That a man so gifted and so well-intentioned should in the end have fallen out with so many of those he had been trying to benefit is at first sight surprising but not in fact inexplicable or unparalleled.

It is proper to consider the work of Sokrates – or Sophokles or Pheidias or Thucydides – in relation to the Athens of his day and to posterity, including ourselves. Whatever we may feel about the feasibility of Sokrates' enterprise, we can hardly fail to admire its intentions or its consequences, from Plato onwards. His blend of the rational and the nonrational has appealed to very diverse people over the centuries.

Whether he is the most remarkable son of Classical Athens may be disputable, but he is in many ways central. He had at some time conversed with most, if not all, of the leading men of Athens (not to mention Aspasia) and with most, if not all, of the foreign intellectuals who visited the city; he conversed with most of the young men of promise; he examined most of the religious, moral, social and political norms of the city; he was aware of the intellectual and artistic innovations taking place.

In his lifetime Athens rose to the zenith of her power, overreached herself and suffered the bitterness of defeat. Tragedy died with Euripides and Sophokles, and the spell of Sokrates' conversation may have hastened its death, but other arts and sciences – some introduced into Athens or invented there in his lifetime – continued to develop under the restored democracy of the fourth century. Much had been lost, but much remained to thrive.

Appendix 1

Athenian Money

$$6 \text{ obols} = 1 \text{ } drakhme$$
$$100 \text{ } drakhmai = 1 \text{ } mna$$
$$60 \text{ } mnai = 1 \text{ talent}$$

Mnai and talents were not coins but weights of silver. Fractions and multiples of the *drakhme* were coined, up to 10-*drakhmai* pieces. The commonest coins were 2- and 4-*drakhmai* pieces. In considering Athenian public expenditure the most useful equation is: 6,000 *drakhmai* = 1 talent. Because the conditions of life have changed so much, it might be thought that no useful equivalence with modern money could be established. It may, however, be helpful to think of a *drakhme* as very roughly what a moderately skilled man can earn in a day now.

Appendix 2

Chronological Table

594 Arkhonship of Solon.
546 Peisistratos tyrant for third time. Kroisos of Lydia defeated by Kyros of Persia.
527 Death of Peisistratos. Succession of Hippias.
514 Assassination of Hipparkhos.
510 Expulsion of Hippias. Invasion of Kleomenes of Sparta.
508 Legislation of Kleisthenes.
490 Battle of Marathon.
480 Battle of Salamis.
479 Battle of Plataiai.
478 Capture of Sestos.
477 Foundation of Athenian alliance.
476 Capture of Eion-on-Strymon.
472 Aiskhylos' *Persians*.
469 Birth of Sokrates.
468 Destruction of Mycenae by Argos.
467 Fall of meteorite at Aigospotamoi.
462 Legislation of Ephialtes.
461 Ostracism of Kimon. Assassination of Ephialtes.
458 Admission of Zeugitai to Arkhonship.
457 Spartan force in Boiotia.
456 Death of Aiskhylos.
454 Egyptian disaster.
451 Perikles' law of citizenship.
449 Peace with Persia.
447 Parthenon begun.
446 Revolt of Euboia. Thirty Years' Peace with Peloponnesians.
443 Foundation of Thourioi.
440 Revolt of Samos.
438 Dedication of Parthenon.
436 Foundation of Amphipolis.
433 Defensive alliance with Kerkyra. Megarian Decree.
432 Revolt and siege of Poteidaia.
431 Outbreak of Peloponnesian War. Arkhidamos invades Attike.
430 Outbreak of plague.
429 Festival of Bendis introduced. Death of Perikles.
428 Revolt of Mytilene.
427 Civil war in Kerkyra. Gorgias in Athens.
426 Purification of Delos.

425 Aristophanes' *Akharnians*. Occupation of Pylos and capture of Spartans on Sphakteria. Tribute trebled.

424 *Knights*. Battle of Delion. Loss of Amphipolis. Thucydides into exile.

423 *Clouds*.

422 *Wasps*. Brasidas and Kleon killed.

421 Peace of Nikias.

420 Cult of Asklepios introduced.

416 Siege of Melos. Alkibiades' victory at Olympia.

415 Mutilation of Hermai. Sicilian expedition. Recall and flight of Alkibiades.

414 *Birds*.

413 Spartan occupation of Dekeleia. Destruction of Sicilian expedition.

411 Oligarchic coup. Régime of the Four Hundred.

410 Restoration of democracy.

407 Alkibiades back in Athens.

406 Deposition of Alkibiades. Battle of Arginousai.

405 *Frogs*. Battle of Aigospotamoi.

404 Fall of Athens. Régime of the Thirty.

403 Fall of the Thirty. Restoration of democracy.

399 Trial and death of Sokrates.

Further Reading

It is hard to select from the huge number of books about Athens, but any of the following may be recommended for further reading. None of them requires a knowledge of Greek.

The people

V. Ehrenberg, *The People of Aristophanes*, Schocken, New York.
W. K. Lacey, *The Family in Classical Greece*, Thames & Hudson, London.
C. Mossé, *The Ancient World at Work*, Chatto & Windus, London.

The city

R. E. Wycherley, *The Stones of Athens*, Princeton University Press.
The Athenian Agora, American School of Classical Studies at Athens (3rd edn).

Politics and law

A. H. M. Jones, *Athenian Democracy* (Chs 1, 3, 5), Blackwell, Oxford.
M. I. Finley, *Democracy Ancient and Modern*, Chatto & Windus, London.
D. M. MacDowell, *The Law in Classical Athens*, Thames & Hudson, London.

Empire

R. Meiggs, *The Athenian Empire*, Oxford University Press.

Education and books

H. I. Marrou, *A History of Education in Antiquity* (Part 1, Chs 4, 5), Mentor, London.
F. G. Kenyon, *Books and Readers in Ancient Greece and Rome* (2nd edn), Oxford University Press.

Religion

H. W. Parke, *Festivals of the Athenians*, Thames & Hudson, London.
E. R. Dodds, *The Greeks and the Irrational*, Berkeley, London.

H. Lloyd-Jones, *The Justice of Zeus*, Berkeley, London.

Morality

A. W. H. Adkins, *Moral Values and Political Behaviour in Ancient Greece*,
   Chatto & Windus, London.
K. J. Dover, *Greek Popular Morality*, Blackwell, Oxford.

Drama

H. C. Baldry, *The Greek Tragic Theatre*, Chatto & Windus, London.
O. Taplin, *Greek Tragedy in Action*, Methuen, London.
K. J. Dover, *Aristophanic Comedy*, Batsford, London.

Visual art

J. Boardman, *Greek Art*, Thames & Hudson, London.
G. M. A Richter, *A Handbook of Greek Art*, Phaidon, London.

Thought

G. B. Kerferd, *The Sophistic Movement*, Cambridge University Press.
W. K. C. Guthrie, *Socrates*, Cambridge University Press.

Index

Nominative singular and plural forms of most transliterated Greek nouns and adjectives are given.